# THE ISO 14001 IMPLEMENTATION GUIDE

WILEY SERIES IN ENVIRONMENTAL QUALITY MANAGEMENT

John T. Willig, Series Editor

AUDITING FOR ENVIRONMENTAL QUALITY LEADERSHIP: BEYOND COMPLIANCE TO ENVIRONMENTAL EXCELLENCE

John T. Willig, Editor

STRATEGIC ENVIRONMENTAL MANAGEMENT: USING TQEM AND ISO 14000 FOR COMPETITIVE ADVANTAGE

Grace Wever, Ph.D.

THE ISO 14001 IMPLEMENTATION GUIDE: CREATING AN INTEGRATED MANAGEMENT SYSTEM

Suzan L. Jackson

# THE ISO 14001 IMPLEMENTATION GUIDE

## Creating an Integrated Management System

Suzan L. Jackson

John Wiley & Sons, Inc.

NEW YORK ■ CHICHESTER ■ BRISBANE ■ TORONTO ■ SINGAPORE ■ WEINHEIM

This material is reprinted from ISO 14001:1996 with permission of the American National Standards Institute (ANSI) on behalf of the International Organization for Standardization. Not for resale. No part of ISO 14001:1996 may be copied or reproduced in any form, electronic retrieval system or otherwise or made available on the Internet, a public network, by satellite or otherwise without the prior written consent of the American National Standards Institute, 11 West 42nd Street, New York, NY 10036.

This text is printed on acid-free paper.

Copyright © 1997 by John Wiley & Sons, Inc.

All rights reserved. Published simultaneously in Canada.

Reproduction or translation of any part of this work beyond that permitted by Section 107 or 108 of the 1976 United States Copyright Act without the permission of the copyright owner is unlawful. Requests for permission or further information should be addressed to the Permissions Department, John Wiley & Sons, Inc., 605 Third Avenue, New York, NY 10158-0012.

This publication is designed to provide accurate and authoritative information in regard to the subject matter covered. It is sold with the understanding that the publisher is not engaged in rendering legal, accounting, or other professional services. If legal advice or other expert assistance is required, the services of a competent professional person should be sought.

*Library of Congress Cataloging-in-Publication Data*:

Jackson, Suzan L. (Suzan Linn), 1965-
    The ISO 14001 implementation guide : creating an integrated management system / Suzan L. Jackson.
       p.   cm. -- (Wiley series in environmental quality management)
    Includes bibliographical references and index.
    ISBN 0-471-15360-5 (cloth : alk. paper)
    1. ISO 14000 Series Standards.   I. Title.  II. Series.
TS155.7.J33    1996
658.4'08--dc20                                            96-31999

Printed in the United States of America

10 9 8 7 6 5 4 3 2 1

*To my husband Ken and my son Jamie,
for the love and joy they bring to my life*

# CONTENTS

**FOREWORD** *xi*

**PREFACE** *xiii*

**ACKNOWLEDGMENTS** *xvii*

## PART 1 ■ INTRODUCTION AND BACKGROUND

CHAPTER 1 ■ INTRODUCTION TO INTEGRATED MANAGEMENT SYSTEMS    3

CHAPTER 2 ■ ISO 14000 AND ENVIRONMENTAL MANAGEMENT SYSTEMS    11

CHAPTER 3 ■ THIRD-PARTY REGISTRATION    27

CHAPTER 4 ■ INTRODUCING ISO 14001    39

## PART 2 ■ POLICY AND PLANNING

CHAPTER 5 ■ ENVIRONMENTAL POLICY    47

CHAPTER 6 ■ ENVIRONMENTAL ASPECTS    53

CHAPTER 7 ■ LEGAL AND OTHER REQUIREMENTS    65

CHAPTER 8 ■ OBJECTIVES AND TARGETS   69

CHAPTER 9 ■ ENVIRONMENTAL MANAGEMENT PROGRAM   77

## PART 3 ■ IMPLEMENTATION AND OPERATION

CHAPTER 10 ■ STRUCTURE AND RESPONSIBILITY   85

CHAPTER 11 ■ TRAINING, AWARENESS, AND COMPETENCE   95

CHAPTER 12 ■ COMMUNICATION   105

CHAPTER 13 ■ ENVIRONMENTAL MANAGEMENT SYSTEM DOCUMENTATION   111

CHAPTER 14 ■ DOCUMENT CONTROL   125

CHAPTER 15 ■ OPERATIONAL CONTROL   143

CHAPTER 16 ■ EMERGENCY PREPAREDNESS AND RESPONSE   151

## PART 4 ■ CHECKING AND CORRECTIVE ACTION

CHAPTER 17 ■ MONITORING AND MEASUREMENT   159

CHAPTER 18 ■ NONCONFORMANCE AND CORRECTIVE AND PREVENTIVE ACTION   173

CHAPTER 19 ■ RECORDS   187

CHAPTER 20 ■ ENVIRONMENTAL MANAGEMENT SYSTEM AUDIT   197

CHAPTER 21 ■ MANAGEMENT REVIEW   215

## PART 5 ■ GETTING STARTED

CHAPTER 22 ■ STRATEGIC PLANNING   225

CHAPTER 23 ■ CHOOSING A REGISTRAR   239

CHAPTER 24 ■ IMPLEMENTING INTEGRATED MANAGEMENT SYSTEMS   249

**ADDITIONAL INFORMATION**  261

**REFERENCES**  265

**APPENDIX: SAMPLE ENVIRONMENTAL POLICIES**  269

**INDEX**  275

# FOREWORD

As our world becomes increasingly more complex and technology based, governments, the public, and the private business sector are all recognizing the necessity for comprehensive management of environmental responsibility. Responses to this have already taken many forms: Agenda 21; laws and regulations; public pressures expressed through environmental interest groups; and industry inititatives such as the chemical industry's Responsible Care® initiative and the Charter for Sustainable Development by the International Chamber of Commerce.

What has been lacking up until now has been a common and recognizable management system to assure that good intentions are carried through. ISO 14001 provides a simple understandable system to assure that an organization is able to achieve its commitments to environmental responsibility. ISO 14001 is a flexible global standard intended to apply to any size, type, or location of organization. As such, its application within a given organization may lead to a series of questions on interpretation and practicality.

Suzan Jackson's book provides vital guidance and answers to these questions in the form of international negotiations history and consensus, interpretation in the light of the U.S.A. infrastructure, and practical examples of how some companies are addressing implementation of ISO 14001. Her book can be quite helpful to those who are considering establishing a new environmental management system or those who just want a better understanding of ISO 14001.

*John Master*
*Chemical Manufacturer's Association, EHS Management Systems; Chairman of sub-TAG 4 to TC 207 on Environmental Performance Evaluation; Former Director of Environmental, Health, & Safety, Arco Chemical Co.*

# PREFACE

When I first graduated from college with my engineering degree, I didn't even know that the field of quality management existed! As I began to learn about quality in my first job at DuPont's Pontchartrain Works plant, I was instantly attracted to the field. I was just as fascinated and interested when I later became involved with environmental management. I was, and still am, highly motivated by the concept of helping businesses to improve and thereby helping to improve the world we live in.

I firmly believe that improved environmental performance and improved business performance are compatible goals. Many businesses and many professionals have come to see these two goals as mutually exclusive. They see environmental improvement as an idealistic goal supported by fanatical environmentalists who don't understand the business world.

I've worked with all kinds of manufacturing plants, with service companies, with many different industries, and I've managed a business myself. I understand the difficult and delicate balance involved in doing what's right for the environment *and* having a successful and profitable business. Companies that implement all the requirements of ISO 14001 will almost certainly show some environmental improvement. They can also experience business improvement but only with the right implementation approach.

Over the last eight years, I've seen many, many examples of quality and environmental management systems. In far too many cases, companies or sites have implemented overly complex, bureaucratic systems that have given them little value in return (other than registration). At times I've found it frustrating when the drive for registration has overcome good common sense and I've been unable to convince an organization of the potential benefits that are being missed.

This book represents that collective experience and describes some time-tested approaches for implementing management systems in a way that enhances and benefits the business. These approaches will also lead to successful third-party registration, if that's one of your goals. The key to success is to focus first on your own business needs. If you do this and implement an effective system that works well for your own organization, then the registration will take care of itself.

One element of the approach that leads to business improvement is the integration of management systems. Environmental management, quality management, and other areas need to be an integral part of an overall business management system. If these systems are implemented as separate entities, the result is more paperwork, more bureaucracy, and less efficiency. In order to achieve real business results, system integration must be part of the overall approach to ISO 14001.

This book is divided into five main parts. Part 1 (Chapters 1–4) provides some background information on integrated management systems, the development of the ISO 14000 standards, third-party registration, and an introduction to the ISO 14001 standard. This information is helpful in understanding how the standards and the registration system can benefit your own company. Chapter 3, on registration, includes detailed information and examples of the emerging drivers for ISO 14001 registration, particularly for U.S. companies.

Parts 2, 3, and 4 (Chapters 5–21) present each of the 17 sections of the ISO 14001 standard as a model for an effective environmental management system (EMS). Besides providing an insider's look at interpretation of the standard's requirements, these chapters use examples from real companies to explain how to establish an effective, business-focused EMS. Each chapter also includes specific information on how to integrate that EMS element with existing management systems. Look for the Tips, Warnings, and Keys to Success that appear throughout the text, as well as flowcharts that will guide you through the steps necessary to implement your own system. These features are indicated by the following icons:

✓ Tips

 Warnings

 Key to Success

Part 5 pulls all of this information together to help your company get started on the road to implementing or improving its EMS. Chapter 22 provides step-by-step guidance on how to develop a strategic plan for EMS implementation, and Chapter 23 covers detailed information on how to choose the third-party registrar that's best for your own business. Finally, Chapter 24 describes some important concepts and Keys to Success in using an integrated approach to management systems. All of the information in the book is based on real-life experiences—what works best and what doesn't.

My hope is that this book will help managers and professionals involved with environmental management to recognize and achieve business benefits such as reduced costs, improved efficiencies, and greater profits from their use of the ISO 14001 standard. The intent of this book is to make businesses aware of the potential improvements possible and to provide guidance on how to achieve those improvements. In this way, ISO 14001 can be a tool which leads to both environmental improvement and business success.

I hope that the readers of this book find it helpful on their path to environmental and business improvement.

*Sue Jackson*

# ACKNOWLEDGMENTS

I've learned so much over the years from my colleagues and clients that it would be impossible to name everyone who has had an indirect input into this book. I'm grateful for the opportunities I've had to work with and learn from so many experienced and insightful professionals.

I would also like to recognize those people who've had a direct impact on this book. First, I'd like to thank my editor, John Willig, for his support and encouragement in helping me to develop the concept and proposal for the book and for his help in the editing process. I also greatly appreciate the assistance and feedback of the many friends and colleagues who reviewed parts of the book and provided their honest opinions and suggestions to ensure that the book was accurate and understandable. These indispensable reviewers included Barbara McGuinness of DuPont, Joel Charm of Allied Signal, and Nick Lister, one of my colleagues at Excel Partnership.

My husband Ken also provided valuable feedback and suggestions as well as creating many of the drawings that appear in the book. Even more important, he provided the necessary support for me to complete this project by helping me through the long days, nights, and weekends of writing and editing.

Finally, I'd like to thank my parents for their continuous support, love, and encouragement over the years. They taught me that if I worked hard and did my best, I could achieve anything I wanted. Those lessons helped me to reach my long-held dream of writing and publishing a book.

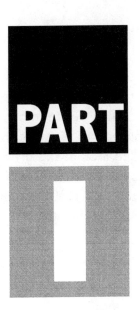

# PART I

# INTRODUCTION AND BACKGROUND

> Toyota and Sony plan to register all of their sites worldwide to ISO 14001 within the next two years. Ford is applying the ISO 14001 standard in all of its 150 manufacturing locations worldwide. Akzo Nobel, a multinational company that manufactures chemicals, pharmaceuticals, coatings, and fibers is using ISO 14001 at four plants in the Netherlands and the United States, and plans to implement the standard in all of its 250 sites. Organizations as diverse as Nike, Inc., and the U.S. Postal Service are evaluating ISO 14001 as part of their overall environmental efforts. Numerous small and medium-sized companies are also implementing ISO 14001.
>
> Why are these diverse companies from all over the world interested in ISO 14001? Why has this 20-page international standard attracted so much attention even before it was officially published? The answers lie in the environmental management concepts embodied by the standard, as well as the widely divergent drivers for third-party registration. Part 1 of this book will answer these questions and provide the information necessary for your company to capitalize on this emerging environmental management trend.
>
> Chapter 1 takes a look at the concepts and principles of integrated management systems, to help you better understand what

the companies mentioned previously have figured out—that effective management systems can result in business improvements. Chapter 2 describes the ISO 14000 standards, including where they came from and how they relate to other environmental management initiatives. Third-party registration is examined in Chapter 3, including a detailed look at the drivers that are compelling so many companies to consider ISO 14001 registration. Finally, Chapter 4 introduces the ISO 14001 standard itself and provides an inside view of the international debates and compromises that shaped it.

# INTRODUCTION TO INTEGRATED MANAGEMENT SYSTEMS

*Nothing astonishes men so much as common sense and plain dealing.* Ralph Waldo Emerson

Management systems are based on common sense, but many companies do not approach the use of the ISO management system standards in that way. They assume that a great deal of complexity and bureaucracy are necessary to meet these standards; in truth, the simplest systems work best. Let's take a closer look at what a management system really is and how it can benefit companies.

## WHAT IS A MANAGEMENT SYSTEM?

The term *management system* has become a common one in businesses worldwide over the last few years, but it is not necessarily a concept that is well understood. At the end of a half-day training class on environmental management systems and ISO 14001 several participants said, "Yes, but what is an environmental management system, really?" The term is used often but is rarely defined.

A management system can be partially defined by a set of common elements. All management systems, whether focused on quality, safety, or the environment, have certain core elements. These include the following:

- Policy
- Defined organization and responsibilities
- Control of critical operations, including standard practices
- Document control (ensuring that up-to-date documents are available where needed)
- Training
- Records system
- Internal audits
- Corrective action system
- Management review for continual improvement

In addition to these core elements, a management system may also have some elements that are unique to its particular focus area. A quality system will include evaluation of suppliers and review of customer contracts. An environmental system will include methods of evaluating environmental impacts and systems for responding to emergencies.

An effective management system, however, is not merely a collection of these different components. It is a planned and well-defined system in which all of the pieces work in conjunction with one another. The policies set the framework for the whole system. Plans and objectives are determined based on the overall policies. The system is implemented and operated according to the plans and objectives. Measurement and auditing programs ensure that the system is working and is effective, and a management review ensures that the overall system is meeting the stated objectives and fulfilling the policy. Based on the audits and review, the system may be revised to improve its effectiveness. In this way, the components of the system flow naturally from one to the next in a cycle of improvement (see Figure 1-1). In addition, documenting and maintaining inefficient processes will not improve your bottom line. Understanding your own business needs, improving your work processes, and sustaining them through a well-defined management system are the only ways in which you will achieve real, long-lasting business results.

A cohesive and effective system can only be achieved if business processes are well-defined, documented, and fully implemented. This is another critical characteristic of a management system. ISO 9000 (a series of standards for quality management systems) has often been summed up by the phrase "say what you do and do what you say." This is an oversimplification, but the basic tenet is valid. None of the critical elements of a system can be sustained over time unless they are defined and documented. This helps to ensure consistency in practice. The second part of

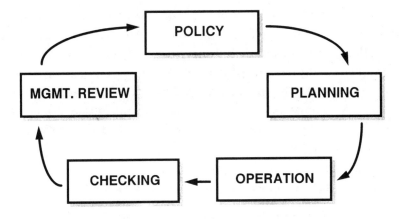

■ **FIGURE 1-1.** Cycle of Business Improvement

the phrase is at least as important: defined systems must be fully implemented. A well-documented system that is not followed consistently results in a lot of extra paperwork without any real business benefit.

Although documentation is an important element of a management system, it is often given too much significance. Many early ISO 9000 systems were so excessively documented that the documentation got in the way of doing business. The management system must always remain focused on the needs of the business first, with documentation adding to its effectiveness, not detracting from it. One client company with which I worked came to understand this concept through its own experience. I was helping this company to evaluate its existing environmental management systems against the ISO 14001 standard. We began by simply trying to identify all of the elements that play a role in environmental management within this large, diverse corporation. We found many parts of a management system, among many different departments. Some of these pieces were completely independent of others, with little connection or understanding between different departments of the role that each played in the overall system. The individual components were there, but the organized approach was missing. Many of the businesses that I have talked to agree that this situation is common.

When approaching a new standard for a management system, such as ISO 14001 for environmental management systems, many companies mistakenly believe they are starting from scratch and implementing a new system. In reality, most businesses already have some—or many—of the elements of the system in place. What's usually missing is the cohesive approach to link those elements together into a single system. This is especially true of larger companies where the system components may be spread out over multiple sites and functions within the company. In addition, many companies find that some of the existing elements are not as well defined as they thought or are poorly documented. Thus the best approach to implementing a "new" system is to begin with a look at existing systems. During this initial "gap analysis," keep in mind the key attributes of a management system—an organized approach that includes well-defined and documented processes for a set of core elements that are fully implemented.

## WHY INTEGRATE MANAGEMENT SYSTEMS?

### Growing Management System Requirements

Internal and external management system requirements come from many sources and have been expanding over the last five years. When considering management system requirements, many companies think only of the increasing pressures to become registered to the ISO 9000 quality system standards and the emerging ISO 14001 environmental management system standard, but other system requirements exist and continue to grow in number.

In addition to international standards, many industry-specific guidelines or standards for various management systems (most often quality, environmental, or health and safety systems) have been developed. Examples include the chemical industry's Responsible Care® program, the petroleum industry's STEP (Strategies for Today's Environmental Partnership) program, and the automotive industry's QS-9000 quality system requirements for suppliers. In addition, some government bodies require certain management systems. In the United States, the Occupational Safety and Health Agency (OSHA) requires a management system for process safety, per CFR 1910.119. The Department of Defense, NASA, and others have had quality system requirements since long before ISO 9000 was conceived. Finally, many companies must meet management system requirements imposed by their corporate headquarters, parent company, or customers.

All of the system requirements from different sources add up to a confusing situation for companies wishing to remain competitive, and a series of mad rushes to implement the latest set of requirements often results. This "program of the month" approach has become common among U.S. companies. Besides creating disenchanted employees, this approach reduces the effectiveness of the business and dilutes its overall mission. Management can easily lose sight of the ultimate goals of the company in the pressure to achieve each individual system recognition.

The only way to meet these increasing system requirements and stay competitive is to create a single integrated management system that is based firmly in the needs and values of the business itself. Then each new requirement that emerges can be carefully considered and integrated into the existing system framework. Rather than implementing separate systems for managing quality, environmental, and safety requirements, the company has a single business management system that encompasses all of these areas. The overall goals and processes do not change with each new initiative.

### Improved Effectiveness

Besides simply providing a mechanism to cope with all of the different system requirements, an integrated management system approach focuses on business needs and provides added value to the business. A key tenet of an effective management system is to do only what makes sense for the business. If the company feels it is doing something "just because the standard says so," it needs to reevaluate that requirement. Often, the standards are interpreted too narrowly. There is almost always a way to meet the standards' requirements while also meeting the needs of the business. This focus on adding value to the business results in improved effectiveness.

Most important, a single management system allows management to establish an overall mission and goals for the business. When this mission is communicated throughout all levels of the organization and continually reinforced, it becomes a unifying element against which all initiatives and activities are measured. With this framework in place, the focus does not swing from quality to safety to environmental to financial considerations; rather, it remains on the organization's central goals, which encompass all of these areas.

With a well-designed and thoroughly implemented management system in place, any new set of system requirements can be integrated into the company in a way that makes sense for the business. Contrast this with the panicked approach that many companies took in the 1980s, when ISO 9000 emerged. Too many companies were pressured into achieving ISO 9000 registration in the shortest time possible. The focus shifted to getting that certificate rather than upgrading existing quality systems. As a result, many companies implemented whole new systems based entirely on the seven pages of generic requirements in ISO 9001 or ISO 9002. These systems were often paper-heavy and bureaucratic. Some third-party registrars encouraged these standardized approaches and even added specific documentation requirements of their own. A few disenchanted companies blamed ISO 9000 itself for the extra documentation which produced no business benefit.

Fortunately, not all companies took this approach. Some businesses used ISO 9000 as a tool for improving their existing systems. Other businesses, which started out with a paper-intensive, "anything to get registered" approach, have gradually improved their systems as they have learned more about their own processes. When used appropriately, ISO 9000 and other management system standards can improve the effectiveness of a business and help to strengthen its mission.

### Reduced Costs

Improved effectiveness translates into reduced costs. Besides providing internal improvements, an integrated approach to management systems will be much less costly than implementing numerous systems for different requirements. The cost savings is based on two factors: initial implementation and ongoing effectiveness.

Many companies, large and small, spent a great deal of money implementing an ISO 9000 quality system. Typically, only 10 to 20 percent of this cost is for out-of-pocket expenses, such as registration and training. The remainder is due to reallocation of resources—people taking time out from their primary responsibilities to define, document, and implement the system. If this type of effort were duplicated each time a new management system initiative was implemented, the cost would be enormous.

Using a single business management system as the focal point, each new set of system requirements can be compared to the existing system. Any missing components can be implemented as appropriate, using the core system as a framework. Many of the "new" requirements can be satisfied by simply expanding the scope of an existing system element. These core elements are already familiar and are viewed simply as the way the organization does business. While there may still be a large organizational effort required (depending on the status of existing systems), the effort is certainly less than that required to start from scratch. In addition, the work that is done should be of value to the organization because of the focus on overall business mission and goals.

The other, perhaps greater, potential for reduced costs lies in the ongoing use and improvement of the system. When employees have to consider multiple systems in accomplishing their tasks, inefficiencies result. As an example, consider the job of an operator in a manufacturing plant. When a variable in the process goes outside of prescribed limits, action must be taken to bring the process back under control. With separate systems, that operator has to stop and consider whether the variable is critical to quality, safety, or environmental aspects of the operation. Once that is determined, he or she may be led to take different, possibly even conflicting, actions based on differing operating practices. In recording the incident, different forms may be required, depending on the variable's impact on quality, safety, or the environment. In contrast, a single management system, which reflects optimal operation for all of these different needs, would provide for a single, straightforward set of actions.

While an integrated approach that establishes a framework for the entire business is valuable for any organization, the ideal degree of integration may vary from company to company. Certain organizations may operate more efficiently with completely integrated systems, while others may thrive on systems that use the same core system elements but allow differences in implementation.

## ENVIRONMENTAL MANAGEMENT SYSTEMS

In 1991, McKinsey & Company conducted a worldwide survey of several hundred executives. According to the resulting report, *The Corporate Response to the Environmental Challenge*, 92 percent of the CEOs and board members surveyed stated that the environment should be one of their three top management priorities. Despite this stated priority, only 37 percent believed that they had successfully integrated the environment into daily operations. In response to these survey results, an article entitled, "It's Not Easy Being Green," published in the May-June 1994 issue of the *Harvard Business Review*, stated, "Clearly, today's managers lack a framework that will allow them to turn their good intentions into reality." An integrated approach to ISO 14001 can provide that framework.

Besides providing the same kinds of organizational benefits as any management system (e.g., streamlined work processes, clearly defined responsibilities, greater efficiency), an environmental management system can also contribute to the bottom line by facilitating environmental improvements. Although some companies still consider environmental and economic improvement as mutually exclusive, more companies are learning that improving the environment can contribute to business success.

Baxter International, a medical products company, saved $21.7 million, or 16 cents per share, in 1994 as a result of its efforts to prevent pollution and to minimize wastes. Reduced energy costs, raw material usage, and waster disposal costs all translate easily into positive economic impacts. Even so, when I cite examples such as these, skeptical managers frequently reply, "Well, sure, any company can save some money at the beginning, but we already have some environmental systems in place. We've picked the low-hanging fruit—there are no major savings left to be gained."

The experience of companies that have worked on environmental improvements over many years contradicts this pessimistic view. For example, 3M began its "Pollution Prevention Pays" program, which is based on employee suggestions, in 1975. The company has saved more than $500 million since then and says that its annual savings now are just as high as when the program started 20 years ago. With this kind of ongoing improvement possible, it's clear that an environmental management system can have a positive impact on business success.

# ISO 14000 AND ENVIRONMENTAL MANAGEMENT SYSTEMS

**WHERE IT ALL BEGAN**

Over 100,000 businesses worldwide have been registered to the ISO 9000 quality system standards. This fast-growing trend of quality system registration has laid the foundation for the development of the ISO 14000 standards and associated ISO 14001 registration systems, but the real spark that ignited the environmental management standards effort was the United Nations Conference on Environment and Development (UNCED) that took place in Rio de Janeiro in 1992. In preparation for this meeting, the International Organization for Standardization (ISO) and the International Electrotechnical Committee (IEC) formed the Strategic Advisory Group for the Environment (SAGE) in 1991 to make recommendations regarding international standards for the environment. Over 100 environmental experts from all over the world, representing 20 countries and nine international organizations, participated in SAGE.

SAGE concluded that an environmental management system (EMS) was a critical element in achieving environmental excellence and in meeting future environmental needs worldwide. An EMS provides a way to achieve a company's environmental performance goals, using the company's own environmental policies and principles as a base. An effective EMS is a part of sustainable development, defined by SAGE as "operating activities [that] meet the needs of present stakeholders (shareholders, employees, customers, and communities) without impairing the ability of future generations to meet their needs."

SAGE recommended that ISO establish a Technical Committee to develop international environmental management standards. Like all international system standards, it should be generic so that it could be used by any company in any industry in the world. In addition, SAGE recommended that the new environmental management standard should

- Fit with existing management system standards (i.e., ISO 9000)
- Describe best practices in environmental management
- Provide consistency worldwide
- Provide a model for elements of an effective environmental management system
- Not include performance criteria (these should be left to regulatory bodies)
- Include requirements for leadership commitment
- Be voluntary
- Add value to an organization when applied
- Be challenging yet be available to and within the capability of any business worldwide
- Include requirements for communication to stakeholders
- Be flexible
- Link to ISO 9000 and other management systems standards through the use of common language to enable a single cohesive management system (see Figure 2-1)

You can see from this list that the approach of integrating management systems was one of the key considerations in the original concept of an international environmental management systems standard. Figure 2-1 illustrates SAGE's view of integrated management systems.

Based on SAGE's recommendations, ISO formed a new Technical Committee (TC 207) in 1993. TC 207's scope of work is "standardization in the field of environmental management tools and systems." Participation in the committee was high from its beginning, with more than 46 member countries now actively involved. The Canadian Standards Association is the Secretariat of the committee. TC 207 has been given a series of numbers from 14000 to 14100 to identify these new ISO standards for environmental management tools and systems.

## THE ISO PROCESS

All ISO standards are developed within Technical Committees (TCs), which are made up of experts from the various countries that participate

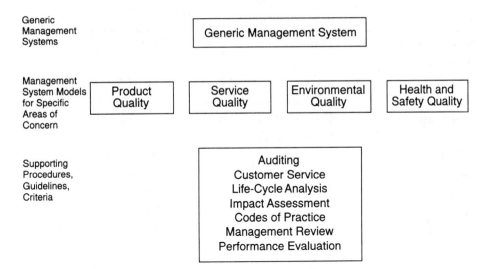

■ **FIGURE 2-1.** SAGE Diagram of Integrated Management Systems.
*Source:* SAGE, 1992.

in ISO. There are more than 100 member countries in ISO, including the United States (see Table 2-1). Each country participates through its national standards body. ANSI (American National Standards Institute) officially represents the United States, although other U.S. standards groups also get involved in various ISO standards activities.

Within each TC, work is divided among Subcommittees and Work Groups. Each nation participating in a particular TC typically sets up a process to generate a consensus position for the nation. In the United States, this is done by a Technical Advisory Group (TAG), with individual sub-TAGs that correspond to the various Subcommittees. This organizational system makes possible very broad participation from many individuals within countries all over the world. The United States has a very open and democratic approach to its participation in ISO Technical Committees. TAG and sub-TAG participation is open to all interested parties, with a goal of including input from all major stakeholder groups.

ISO standards all evolve through a well-defined process, as illustrated in Figure 2-2. The TC Secretariat circulates a New Work Item Proposal (NWIP) to all participating member countries for review and vote. Once a proposal is approved, Subcommittees begin by creating working drafts using any pertinent existing national standards. Much of the writing and editing actually occurs at the national level, in sub-TAGs and work groups. Differing versions and suggestions are brought to the Subcommittee level, where representatives from each participating country present their own national perspective.

## TABLE 2-1  Nations Participating in ISO

| Member Bodies | | |
|---|---|---|
| Albania | Japan | Turkey |
| Algeria | Kenya | Ukraine |
| Argentina | Korea, Democratic People's Republic of | United Kingdom |
| Australia | Korea, Republic of | Uruguay |
| Austria | Libyan Arab Jamahiriva | United States of America |
| Bangladesh | Malaysia | Uzbekistan |
| Belarus | Mauritius | Venezuela |
| Belgium | Mexico | Vietnam |
| Brazil | Mongolia | Yugoslavia |
| Bulgaria | Morocco | Zimbabwe |
| Canada | Netherlands | |
| Chile | New Zealand | **Subscriber Members** |
| China | Nigeria | Armenia |
| Colombia | Norway | Bahrain |
| Costa Rica | Pakistan | Barbados |
| Croatia | Panama | Brunei Darussalam |
| Cuba | Philippines | Estonia |
| Cyprus | Poland | Hong Kong |
| Czech Republic | Portugal | Jordan |
| Denmark | Romania | Kuwait |
| Ecuador | Russian Federation | Kyrgyzstan |
| Egypt | Saudi Arabia | Latvia |
| Ethiopia | Singapore | Lebanon |
| Finland | Slovakia | Lithuania |
| France | Slovenia | Malawi |
| Germany | South Africa | Malta |
| Greece | Spain | Mozambique |
| Hungary | Sri Lanka | Nepal |
| Iceland | Sweden | Oman |
| India | Switzerland | Papua New Guinea |
| Indonesia | Syrian Arab Republic | Peru |
| Iran, Islamic Republic of | Tanzania | Qatar |
| | Thailand | Turkmenistan |
| Ireland | The Former Yugoslav Republic of Macedonia | Uganda |
| Israel | | United Arab Emirates |
| Italy | Trinidad and Tobago | Yemen |
| Jamaica | Tunisia | |

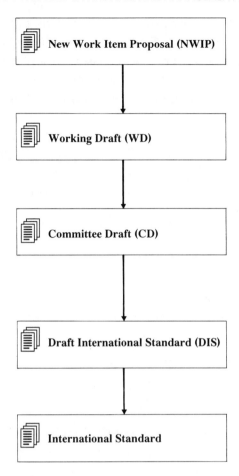

■ **FIGURE 2-2.** ISO Standards Process

When the Subcommittee arrives at the point of having a well-defined consensus draft that meets the needs of all represented countries (no small task!), it submits a resolution making it a Committee Draft (CD). The CD goes to each country's review committee (TAG in the United States) for review and balloting to advance the standard to the next stage of the process. During a three-month balloting process, committee members in each country can either vote "yes," "yes with comment" or "no" (with reasons). The votes are compiled to determine the country's vote. A CD must be approved (with or without comment) by a majority of the member countries in order to advance.

Once approved, the CD moves to the next stage, the Draft International Standard (DIS). At this point in the process, no substantial content changes may be made, although editorial changes may occur. During the six-month public balloting process for the DIS, it is distributed through each country's national standards body and anyone may submit comments. The voting process at the national and international levels is then repeated. Two-thirds approval is required for the DIS to become an ISO standard.

Once the DIS is approved, any final editorial changes are made, and it is translated into ISO's three official languages: English, French, and Russian. The standard is then published by ISO and made available to the public. Each country has the option of adopting any ISO standard as its own national standard. If this occurs, the country may then publish the standard through its national standards bodies in its own language.

## THE ISO 14000 SERIES

### Scope of Work

TC 207 is divided into six Subcommittees (SC) and one Working Group (WG), as follows:

- SC 1    Environmental Management Systems (EMS)
- SC 2    Environmental Auditing (EA)
- SC 3    Environmental Labeling (EL)
- SC 4    Environmental Performance Evaluation (EPE)
- SC 5    Life Cycle Assessment (LCA)
- SC 6    Terms and Definitions
- WG 1    Environmental Aspects of Product Standards

Figure 2-3 shows all the standards being developed by these groups.

Another way to look at these various sets of ISO 14000 standards is to consider their intended use. Figure 2-3 shows a "Road Map" created by TC 207 to describe how the standards in the ISO 14000 series can work together. The EMS standards are the central focus of the group and define a basic framework for a comprehensive management system. Auditing and EPE describe methods of assessing the EMS and environmental performance, respectively. Labeling and Life Cycle Assessment are more closely related to the products and/or services associated with a business than to the management system. Environmental Aspects of Product Standards is actually a standard written for other standard writers—to provide guidance in considering environmental aspects when specific product standards are written.

Although the management systems standards are the focus of this book, the other standards being developed by TC 207 will be helpful to a

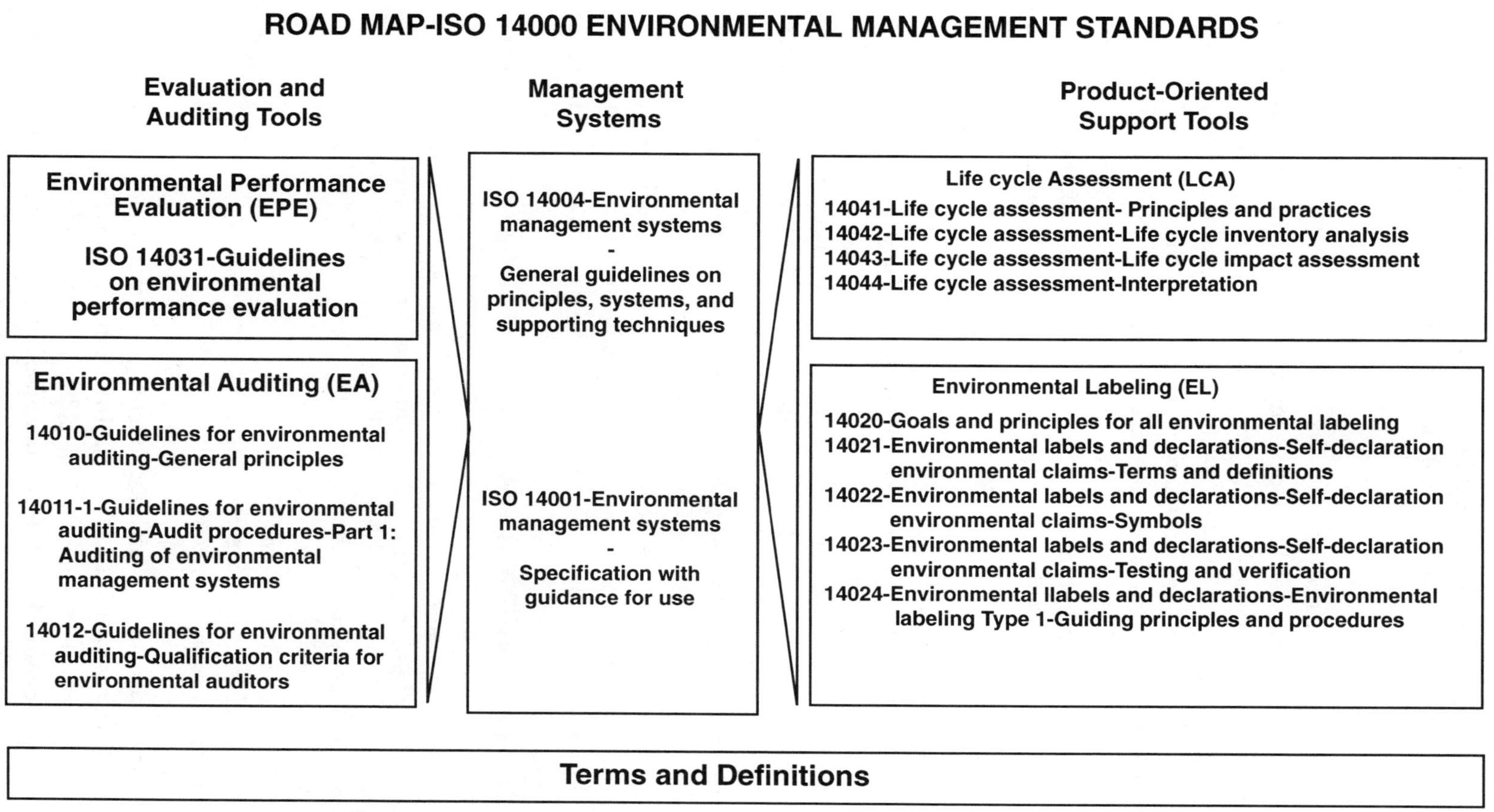

# ROAD MAP-ISO 14000 ENVIRONMENTAL MANAGEMENT STANDARDS

## Evaluation and Auditing Tools

**Environmental Performance Evaluation (EPE)**

ISO 14031-Guidelines on environmental performance evaluation

**Environmental Auditing (EA)**

- 14010-Guidelines for environmental auditing-General principles
- 14011-1-Guidelines for environmental auditing-Audit procedures-Part 1: Auditing of environmental management systems
- 14012-Guidelines for environmental auditing-Qualification criteria for environmental auditors

## Management Systems

ISO 14004-Environmental management systems - General guidelines on principles, systems, and supporting techniques

ISO 14001-Environmental management systems - Specification with guidance for use

## Product-Oriented Support Tools

**Life cycle Assessment (LCA)**

- 14041-Life cycle assessment- Principles and practices
- 14042-Life cycle assessment-Life cycle inventory analysis
- 14043-Life cycle assessment-Life cycle impact assessment
- 14044-Life cycle assessment-Interpretation

**Environmental Labeling (EL)**

- 14020-Goals and principles for all environmental labeling
- 14021-Environmental labels and declarations-Self-declaration environmental claims-Terms and definitions
- 14022-Environmental labels and declarations-Self-declaration environmental claims-Symbols
- 14023-Environmental labels and declarations-Self-declaration environmental claims-Testing and verification
- 14024-Environmental labels and declarations-Environmental labeling Type 1-Guiding principles and procedures

## Terms and Definitions

■ **FIGURE 2-3.** ISO 14000 Standards Road Map

wide range of industries. A brief overview of these standards follows. Additional details can be obtained through TC 207 or the U.S. TAG (see References at end of book).

### EMS Standards

The EMS standards being developed by Subcommittee 1 are the focus of this book. There are actually two standards on EMS: ISO 14001, a specification standard, and ISO 14004, a guidance standard. Both these standards have been finalized and are being published in 1996.

ISO 14004, the guidance standard, is designed to be used internally by businesses that wish to implement or upgrade an EMS. It contains guidelines and helpful hints on all aspects of an EMS and even provides advice for small or medium-size businesses. Meant to be used for internal improvement, it cannot be used as the basis for third-party registration. If you're implementing or improving an EMS, this is a good reference document to have.

ISO 14001 is referred to as a specification standard because it contains requirements that organizations can be measured against. It can be used for the purpose of third-party registration, which will be discussed in depth in Chapter 3, or to implement an EMS without registration. The nature of a specification standard is to contain very generic requirements, without prescribing specific methods, tools, or implementation approaches. ISO 14001 describes the critical elements a business must have in place in order to have a comprehensive and effective environmental management system. It also includes an interpretative annex, the contents of which are not meant to be used as requirements for registration.

ISO 14001 describes the requirements of an effective EMS. It is organized to follow the Plan-Do-Check-Act cycle that is common to quality management systems and that represents a sound, commonsense approach to any business issue. ISO 14001 has five basic sections:

- Environmental Policy
- Planning
- Implementation and Operation
- Checking and Corrective Action
- Management Review

The process begins with establishing an environmental policy and follows through each of these parts. Information from the Management Review is then used to reassess the policy and make changes to the system as appropriate. This type of business cycle promotes continual improvement of the management system (refer again to Figure 1-1).

## Auditing Standards

Subcommittee 2 is writing Environmental Auditing standards that provide guidance on performing environmental audits of all types. Three auditing standards have been developed to date: general principles of environmental audits, EMS audit procedures, and qualification criteria for environmental auditors. These standards will be guidance standards and are due to be published at about the same time as the EMS standards.

## Labeling Standards

The Environmental Labeling standards being developed by SC 3 include a series of multiple guidance standards to address various labeling issues. The focus of this work is on organizations that would like to make public claims about their products' environmental impacts and degree of "greenness." Planned and drafted standards cover basic principles, self-declaration, guidance for third-party certification programs, and Type III labeling. It's likely that some of these guidance standards will be published beginning in 1997.

Third-party certification (also called Type I labeling) refers to the growing number of multiple criteria programs. These third-parties measure a product against defined criteria to determine if it meets their definition of "environmentally friendly." If a product meets a program's criteria, permission is granted to use that program's symbol on product packages. Many such programs, including Blue Angel and Green Seal, are emerging worldwide. Many of the nations involved in the development of international standards in this area feel a sense of urgency to bring consistency to these programs and to clarify the meaning of the various symbols for consumers. A Draft International Standard (DIS) on this topic is expected by the end of 1996.

Self-declaration (Type II) labeling refers to various environmental claims that companies make about their own products or services. For instance, a company may include a statement on its packaging that its product is "biodegradable," "recyclable," or "made from 10% post-consumer recycled materials." All kinds of environmentally related claims are showing up on products around the world. The ISO standards being developed in this area, covering terms and definitions, symbols, and testing methods, would provide consistent guidelines worldwide so that environmental assertions would be more meaningful to consumers.

Type III labels, which have been compared to the standard U.S. nutrition labels introduced in 1995, would provide a voluntary summary of a product's various environmental attributes. Once again, the idea behind international standards is to encourage a level of consistency so that these labels would be meaningful to consumers. Type III labeling is the least well defined of the current labeling standards and is not likely to be published until 1999 or after.

### EPE Standards

Another evaluation tool is Environmental Performance Evaluation (EPE). SC 4 is developing this guidance standard, which will focus on methodologies and tools to help an organization evaluate its environmental performance with respect to its policies, objectives, and relevant regulations. It includes specific guidance on developing indicators to help measure an organization's environmental performance. This subcommittee has agreed to a general framework and has written a draft document. A final guidance standard is expected to be published by late 1998.

### LCA Standards

Subcommittee 5 is working on guidance standards for Life Cycle Assessment (LCA). LCA is a tool used for evaluating the environmental impacts of a product or service throughout its entire life, including raw materials, production, use, and disposal. Standards are being developed for LCA general principles, inventory analysis, impact assessment, and interpretation. Inventory analysis is the first phase of LCA, which compiles and quantifies all of the inputs and outputs associated with the product or service throughout its life cycle. Impact Assessment builds on the inventory analysis to evaluate the magnitude and significance of the environmental impacts. Interpretation of the LCA can involve comparison of various products or services or identification of methods for minimizing environmental impacts.

Some of the better-known LCAs conducted in recent years include assessments of cloth and disposable diapers, washing machines, and recycled paper. It is widely thought that the methodologies for impact assessment and LCA interpretation are still in their infancy and are therefore not yet an appropriate topic for international standards. Because of this belief, only the first two standards from this subcommittee—on general principles and inventory analysis—are likely to be published in 1997–1998; the remaining two standards are still at an early stage of development.

Finally, a Working Group within TC 207 is writing a document for use by other standards writers. Environmental Aspects of Product Standards will provide guidance for writers of product-related standards in considering environmental impacts as they create or revise standards. This document will be published as an ISO Guide rather than as a standard. Additionally, a Terms and Definitions standard is also being developed, which will include terms used by all other subcommittees, with consensus definitions.

Notice that all standards, with the exception of ISO 14001, are guidance standards. This means that they will be available for organizations to use for internal guidance and will not be required as part of any type of registration program. In addition, only EMS and auditing standards are being published as actual ISO standards in 1996. All other standards are at earlier stages of drafting.

## OTHER ENVIRONMENTAL MANAGEMENT SYSTEM STANDARDS

To understand the impact and potential use of ISO 14001 fully, it's important to look at other EMS standards, guidance, and requirements that exist worldwide and to examine their relationship to ISO 14001.

### European Union: Eco-Management and Audit Scheme (EMAS) Regulation

In March 1992, the European Union (EU) proposed a regulation to encourage businesses to review and improve their environmental performance continuously. This Eco-Management and Audit Scheme (EMAS) was adopted in 1993 and officially went into effect on April 10, 1995. Because it is an EU regulation, all member nations were required to adopt it. EMAS applies to companies operating sites in Europe where industrial activity is performed. Although the concept of a nonmandatory regulation is hard for Americans to accept, participation in EMAS by particular sites or companies is entirely voluntary. In fact, the EU is using EMAS as a test case to see if environmental improvement can be achieved from market forces alone, without the kind of complex regulatory and enforcement system that we have here in the United States. If enough European companies do not choose to participate in EMAS voluntarily, the EU could make it mandatory.

To be registered to EMAS, a site has to meet the following criteria:

- Adopt an environmental policy that includes a commitment to continuous improvement of environmental performance;
- Conduct an environmental review of the site;
- Implement a program and an environmental management system to address the results of the review and to achieve the environmental policy;
- Conduct environmental audits at the site;
- Set specific objectives, based on audit results, and update the environmental program to meet those objectives;
- Prepare an environmental statement specific to the site;
- Have the environmental policy, program, management system, review/audit procedure, and environmental statement(s) exam-

ined by an independent, accredited environmental verifier to confirm that they meet the requirements of the regulation;
- Forward the validated environmental statement to the appropriate body of the member state in which the site is located for communication to the public, as appropriate (after registration).

A number of these EMAS requirements—those regarding environmental policy, environmental management system, conducting internal EMS audits, and having specific environmental objectives and a plan to meet them—are similar or identical to ISO 14001 requirements. Despite these similarities, however, there are several critical differences between EMAS and ISO 14001. In fact, the origin and purpose of the two documents are quite different. EMAS is part of a regulation for the European Union and has the clearly stated purpose of improving the environmental performance of European industry. ISO 14001 is an international standard, developed to describe the core elements of an environmental management system for any business in the world. Because of its unique focus, EMAS registration can be attained only by industrial sites operating with the EU. ISO 14001 is a broad-based standard which can be applied to any type of business organization anywhere in the world.

While EMAS is focused on the end result of improved environmental performance, ISO 14001 focuses on establishing an effective management system that should result in improved performance. This different focus explains why EMAS includes requirements for a policy that includes a commitment to performance improvement and a public environmental performance statement. The required public statement reports data to describe and quantify the company's environmental performance and must be validated by an independent verifier (see Chapter 3). Despite these differences, ISO 14001 and EMAS are not necessarily in conflict with one another, since each has a unique purpose. CEN, the Committee for European Standardization, has reviewed the details of ISO 14001 and determined that it (along with some additional requirements that are described in a bridging document) is acceptable in fulfilling the EMS requirement of EMAS.

### BS 7750: British EMS Standard

Based on the expected emergence of EMAS and the enormous popularity and spread of ISO 9000, the British Standards Institute (BSI) developed a standard for environmental management, BS 7750. This EMS standard was first published in March 1992 and was piloted with more than 200 U.K. companies in 1993. Based on the extensive piloting, BS 7750 was revised in January 1994. This standard was used for several years throughout the United Kingdom and in many other countries as a basis for implementing an EMS. In fact, the British Ministry of Defense suggested that all of its contractors use BS 7750 to establish an EMS.

BS 7750 and ISO 14001 are quite similar in content, with the same basic requirements for an EMS, although there are differences in the way each standard approaches those requirements. These differences are not significant, and the United Kingdom will adopt ISO 14001 as its national EMS standard when it is published. Although BS 7750 is being replaced by ISO 14001, it is important in the field of environmental management systems because it was the first EMS standard to be published and widely used. The extensive British experience with EMSs, due in part to the BS 7750 pilot program, is a great source of information and guidance for companies around the world now implementing or improving their own EMSs for ISO 14001.

### Responsible Care®

The U.S. Chemical Manufacturers Association (CMA) and many other chemical industry organizations worldwide encourage their members to take part in the industry's voluntary Responsible Care® program. The U.S. version of Responsible Care® includes six Codes of Management Practice that together encompass a commitment to effective management of health, safety, and environmental responsibilities in chemical manufacturing, transportation, handling, and disposal. These six codes are

- Community Awareness and Emergency Response
- Pollution Prevention
- Distribution
- Process Safety
- Employee Health and Safety
- Product Stewardship

In the United States, CMA leads and administers member companies' self-assessments based on the six Codes of Management Practice and encourages companies to use the codes to measure progress and to strive for full implementation. CMA is also working to implement a verification program for Responsible Care®.

Although Responsible Care® and ISO 14001 have different scopes, they do not conflict with one another in any way. The scope of Responsible Care® is much broader than ISO 14001, since it encompasses health and safety as well as environmental aspects. Of the six codes, the Pollution Prevention and Community Awareness and Emergency Response Codes have the most overlap with ISO 14001 requirements, and there is additional crossover in all areas except Employee Health and Safety (see Table 2-2).

**TABLE 2-2** Comparison of ISO 14001 and Responsible Care®

| ISO 14001 | Responsible Care® Codes of Management Practice ||||||
|---|---|---|---|---|---|---|
| | CAER | Pollution Prevention | Distribution | Process Safety | Employee Health/ Safety | Product Stewardship |
| Policy | | **X** | | x | | x |
| Environmental Aspects | | **X** | x | x | | x |
| Legal Requirements | | **X** | x | | | |
| Objectives/Targets | | **X** | | x | | x |
| EM Program | | **X** | x | x | | x |
| Responsibility | | | | x | | x |
| Training | **X** | x | x | x | | x |
| Communication | **X** | x | x | | | |
| Documentation | | | | x | | |
| Document Control | | | | | | |
| Operational Control | | **X** | x | x | | x |
| Emergency Response | **X** | | | x | | |
| Monitoring/ Measurement | | **X** | x | x | | |
| Corrective Action | | x | x | x | | |
| Records | | | | | | |
| EMS Audit | | x | | | | |
| Management Review | x | x | | | | x |

Note: A bold **X** indicates complete overlap; a lowercase x indicates that there is some degree of overlap.

Within the area of environmental management, ISO 14001 contains a greater depth of requirements than does Responsible Care®. The EMS requirements of ISO 14001 are quite detailed, whereas Responsible Care® outlines more general concepts of effective management. Both standards can coexist and even strengthen each other when implemented in an effective and integrated way (see Chapter 5, "Environmental Policy").

## International Chamber of Commerce (ICC) Business Charter for Sustainable Development

In April 1991, the International Chamber of Commerce (ICC) formally launched its Business Charter for Sustainable Development to encourage environmental improvement. The charter consists of sixteen principles for environmental management created by a task force of business representatives. The principles describe critical elements for environmental management:

- Corporate priority
- Integrated management
- Process of improvement
- Employee education
- Prior assessment
- Products and services
- Customer advice
- Facilities and operations
- Research
- Precautionary approach
- Contractors and suppliers
- Emergency preparedness
- Transfer of technology
- Contributing to the common effort
- Openness to concerns
- Compliance and reporting

Many of these elements are similar to those found in ISO 14001. Note that the second principle, integrated management, specifically addresses the need to integrate environmental management fully into the business. As of 1995, more than 1,200 companies around the world had signed on as supporters of the ICC Charter.

# THIRD-PARTY REGISTRATION

*This is not the end. It is not even the beginning of the end. But it is, perhaps, the end of the beginning.* Sir Winston S. Churchill

Although management system registration was not even conceived of when Winston Churchill made this statement, it reflects perfectly the meaning of registration in the context of overall business improvement. Despite all of the publicity to the contrary, registration is only a milestone along the way. Registration is achieved when a third party audits your management system against a standard and determines that your system addresses all of the requirements of that standard. Once an organization has been registered, the auditors will return periodically to ensure that the system is being maintained and improved over time. Obviously, it is very important that these third-party auditing organizations be properly qualified—that's the purpose of accreditation systems.

## ISO 9000: A REGISTRATION SYSTEM MODEL

Many of the nations that have adopted the ISO 9000 standards have set up systems for third-party registration. Although there may be some differences with ISO 14001, it is helpful to consider these ISO 9001[*] sys-

---

[*] Note: I will refer to ISO 9001 throughout the text of this book. Since there are three quality system standards, ISO 9001, 9002, and 9003, available for registration at the time of this writing, any reference to ISO 9001 also applies to 9002 or 9003.

tems as a model in understanding the basic structure of most registration and accreditation systems.

The terms *registration* and *certification* are often used interchangeably. The U.S. convention is to use "registration" when referring to systems and "certification" when referring to products. Thus, companies can register their quality systems to ISO 9001 and may also choose to certify their products against whatever product standards exist for their industries. This book will abide by U.S. convention and use the term "registration" when referring to ISO 9001 and ISO 14001 systems.

There are three levels in a typical national third-party registration structure. These levels are depicted in Figure 3-1. The supplier companies are those companies which seek to register their management system. "Registrar" is the term used in the U.S. to designate the third-party auditing organizations which register supplier companies (some countries use the term "certifying body"). Accrediting bodies evaluate the registrars, and national governments frequently provide some sort of official recognition to the whole process.

When a company chooses to register its quality management system, it hires a registrar to conduct a thorough audit. The registrar should be chosen very carefully, as the company would choose any critical supplier, because this will be a long-term relationship (see Chapter 23, "Choosing a Registrar"). Once the registrar is chosen, the supplier company and registrar will agree on an audit date and on the scope of the assessment. The length of the audit depends on the size and complexity of the busi-

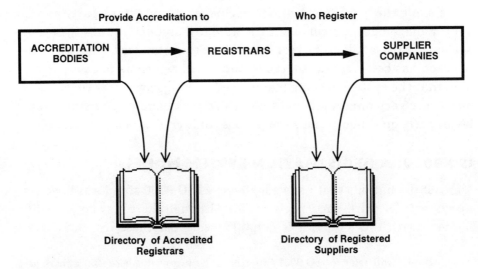

■ **FIGURE 3-1.** ISO 9000 Registration and Accreditation Structure

ness being audited. The auditors will do some pre-audit work, reviewing the business's quality manual and learning about its systems.

During the actual assessment, the audit team will interview people throughout the business, read procedures and other documentation, and observe how the management system works. The team will assess whether the documented system meets the basic requirements of ISO 9001 and also whether the company is following its own documented procedures and practices. At the assessment's end, the team will write a report and tell the company whether it has passed the audit. If minor nonconformances were found, the auditors may recommend registration once the minor problems are resolved. If any major nonconformance is discovered, the company will not become registered at that time and will be required to undergo partial or full reassessment after correcting the nonconformances. Most registrars define a major nonconformance as a critical system element that is either missing or not implemented effectively. Objective evidence must back up any nonconformances cited.

As noted earlier, registration is only a starting point, not a final goal. After a company is successfully registered to ISO 9001, it will continue to be audited to ensure that the system is being maintained and improved over time. Most registrars conduct shorter surveillance audits every six months, and many conduct complete reassessments every three years. The relationship formed with a registrar is truly long-term.

Most companies want to be able to trust that their chosen registrar is properly qualified and free of any potential conflicts of interest. Accreditation can help to ensure this. Many countries have established national accreditation programs. Registrars are evaluated by the accrediting body to ensure that their auditors are qualified, that the registrar organization has a management system of its own with procedures in place to ensure consistency, and that the organization is an independent third party, with no potential for conflict of interest. When a company chooses an accredited registrar, it has some level of confidence that the registrar has met certain criteria. Some national accreditation programs will only accredit registrars with offices in their own country; other programs are open to registrars operating anywhere in the world.

Many countries have an additional level within their accreditation system—recognition by a government body. Some systems combine the accreditation and recognition levels by establishing an accreditation body within the government itself. Some sort of government recognition helps to assure other countries of the credibility of the accreditation.

In the United States, the American National Standards Institute (ANSI) and the Registrar Accreditation Board (RAB) have established the American National Accreditation Program for Registrars of Quality

Systems. ANSI provides oversight for the program and a degree of international recognition since ANSI is the official U.S. standards body participating in ISO. The RAB, which is a subsidiary of the American Society for Quality Control (ASQC), handles the actual operation of the program and has also established programs for certifying quality system auditors and for accrediting auditor training courses. All of these components work together to ensure a basic level of confidence in ISO 9001 registration services. A company can choose an accredited registrar whose auditors have been trained through accredited courses and certified.

Because of the growth of so many national accreditation programs, choosing an ISO 9001 registrar has been somewhat confusing. A registrar operating in the United States might be accredited by the RAB or by some other national accreditation program in another country. The registrar might even have multiple accreditations from bodies in several countries. In addition, many registrars have established memorandums of understanding (MOUs) with other registrars to recognize one another's ISO 9001 registrations.

Recently, progress has been made in establishing global recognition of accreditations and reducing the need for individual MOUs and multiple accreditations. In 1995, ISO and IEC created the Quality System Assessment Recognition (QSAR) program, which is intended to provide global acceptance of ISO 9001 registrations. This program relies in part on peer reviews among the participating accreditation bodies. Because mutual recognition is provided at the accrediting level, the need for multiple MOUs between registrars is eliminated, and companies seeking registration can have confidence in the acceptance of their certificate worldwide.

## ISO 14001 REGISTRATION SYSTEMS

While registration systems are becoming better established for ISO 9001, they are still in the process of being defined for ISO 14001 registration. Most countries (and supplier companies) agree that the two registration/accreditation systems must at least be compatible, if not actually joined in a single system. Redundancies in the systems would only end up costing more for all parties—registrars, individual auditors, course providers, and supplier companies.

The United Kingdom was the first country to establish a national accreditation program for environmental management systems, initially focused on its national EMS standard, BS 7750 (a precursor to ISO 14001), and on EMAS. The British program was established within the same organization that handles accreditation of ISO 9001 certification bodies, the United Kingdom Accreditation Service (UKAS), formerly known as NACCB. Although the environmental program operates out of the same organization, it does differ from the ISO 9001 accreditation system in order to take the unique needs of auditing environmental systems into account.

For example, EMS audit teams are required to include four different areas of competence:

- EMS standard (BS 7750, EMAS, and/or ISO 14001)
- Environmental effects/impacts
- Technical knowledge of activity to be assessed
- Management systems assessment

The U.K. accreditation system must meet the needs of companies applying for BS 7750, ISO 14001, and EMAS registrations. Validation of an environmental performance statement for EMAS (see Chapter 2) verifies that the data arise from a certified EMS and that it is compatible with the previous year's statement. Ideally, the same accredited organizations could verify the public statement, audit the EMS, and possibly also register the quality system against ISO 9001. Obviously, any organization accredited to do all of these activities would have to have a wide range of experience and expertise.

In the United States, the U.S. TAG to TC 207 established an advisory group called the Standards Conformity Registration Assessment Group (SCRAG). SCRAG was asked to do the following:

- Identify the criteria and process for meeting stakeholder needs in establishing an institutional framework empowered to provide the services listed above (accreditation of registrars, certification of environmental auditors, accreditation of course providers);
- Provide for the notification of candidates for these services;
- Educate the U.S. TAG on what is important to consider and weigh;
- Help to develop consensus within the U.S. TAG on one or the other of the available options.

The group provided some recommended criteria for accreditation programs and identified some preliminary candidates to fulfill the roles described. The major candidates were an ANSI/RAB partnership (similar to ISO 9001), ANSI alone, RAB alone, and the Environmental Auditing Roundtable (EAR).

Since SCRAG made its recommendations, things have become a bit more complicated. Initially, ANSI and RAB were unable to agree on terms for a joint program for EMS accreditation, and each was developing its own separate accreditation system with plans to offer registrar accreditation, auditor certification, and training course accreditation. Many key stakeholders, including the U.S. TAG to TC 207 and the Independent Association of Accredited Registrars (IAAR), objected strongly to the concept of competing accreditation programs in the United States. Dual accreditation systems would likely result in higher costs for registrars, course providers, auditors, and companies seeking registration.

Fortunately, the threat of competing systems seems to be behind us. On July 1, 1996, ANSI and RAB announced that they will work together to provide a single American accreditation system for EMS registration, as they have for quality system registration. The joint program will accredit EMS registrars and EMS auditor training courses. RAB will provide EMS auditor certification independent of ANSI. EAR has provided extensive technical expertise to both ANSI and RAB throughout their development efforts. As of this writing, EAR is still considering whether to provide EMS auditor certification, either alone or in partnership with another organization.

## WHY PURSUE REGISTRATION?

> Rumor travels faster, but it don't stay put as long as truth. *Will Rogers*

Nowhere are rumors more evident than in the area of registration drivers. Stories are constantly circulating about companies requiring their suppliers to get registered to ISO 14001 or government agencies planning to make registration mandatory for contractors. Most of these stories fade significantly when you try to verify them. In reality, the reasons a company may need to consider registration of its management systems are seldom so clear-cut.

What value does management system registration bring to a business? This is a critical question for companies considering implementing an EMS. Obviously, registration adds cost to a business—an ongoing cost that will continue for as long as the company wishes to maintain its registration. What internal benefits may be gained from this added cost?

Implementing an EMS and registering it are two separate acts requiring two very separate decisions for any business involved with ISO 14001. For maximum business value, these must be considered separately. The registration process itself may have both external and internal benefits for some companies, but it's not necessary or desirable for all companies.

## External Registration Drivers

Supporters of third-party registration most often point to its external benefits. Depending on a business's industry and stakeholders, registration may be seen as a competitive advantage or may even be required (although this is rare). As environmental performance becomes more important to both society and industry, registration of an EMS can provide a degree of confidence that a particular company or facility is managing its environmental affairs effectively.

***Customer Requirements*** Once again, considering the history of ISO 9001 can provide some insight into the future of ISO 14001. ISO 9001 registration was strongly driven by the marketplace. Throughout many different industries, customers requested or demanded that their suppliers become registered to ISO 9001. Those suppliers without such customer demands saw their competitors getting registered and using ISO 9001 as a marketing tool. In this way, ISO 9001 was quickly pushed through various industries.

The ISO 9000 standards were first published in 1987. By January 1993, 28,000 ISO 9001, 9002, and 9003 certificates had been achieved worldwide. By October 1995 that total had increased to nearly 100,000, about 6,000 of which were issued in the United States. These numbers continue to grow rapidly as requirements or requests for registration move through industry supply chains.

The customer pressure for ISO 9001 registration is easy to understand. Customers have a great interest in the quality of goods and services they purchase, and ISO 9001 registration ensures that a quality system is in place. Many people have argued that there will be no similar pressure for ISO 14001 because customers are not interested in their suppliers' environmental systems. This may have been true in the past, but attitudes are quickly changing.

Many customers have already begun to show an interest in the environmental impacts associated with their suppliers' products and services. The British Ministry of Defense announced in 1994 that it would give preference to contractors certified to BS 7750. Cathay Pacific Airways, Ltd., a large airline based in Hong Kong, plans to achieve registration of its own EMS and then to require its suppliers to do the same. In the United States, the Department of Energy (DOE) is encouraging all DOE facilities and contractors to implement an EMS such as that defined by ISO 14001. Many other companies and government agencies around the world are interested in ISO 14001 but are taking a wait-and-see approach.

***Environmental Stakeholders*** Although there may be some customer-driven need to register an EMS, there is a significant difference between ISO 9001 and ISO 14001. Quality directly impacts only one set of external stakeholders—the customers—but environmental issues are important to a wide variety of stakeholders, including regulatory agencies, customers, shareholders, local communities, and environmental interest groups. This creates the potential for many more and more varied drivers for registration than has been experienced with ISO 9001. A company may not have any customers requiring ISO 14001 registration but may feel pressure from environmental activists, regulatory bodies, and local communities to prove that its environmental systems meet a certain standard.

This more complex arena means that an individual business has to consider many inputs in making its decision whether to register its EMS. Moreover, many of these inputs are still evolving. Although local communities and the general public may not be demanding registration right now, they will likely become increasingly interested in the concept as they learn more about it.

***Competitive Pressures*** For many companies, competitive pressures will create a strong incentive for seeking registration to ISO 14001. Although some customers request or require their suppliers to get registered to one of the ISO 9000 standards, most companies pursue the quality system registration in order either to get ahead of or to catch up to their competitors. ISO 9000 registration has been a primary marketing approach for these companies. The same sequence of events is already beginning to unfold with ISO 14001 registration.

AT&T, IBM, Ford, Motorola, Texas Instruments, and Akzo Nobel are just a few of the major international companies that have already begun to publicize their use of the ISO 14001 standard. Other companies, including Toyota, Sony, and Lucent Technologies, have already made public commitments to companywide registration goals. As news of these industry giants' environmental efforts is reported, competing companies will move forward with their own ISO 14001 plans in order to keep from being viewed as environmentally insensitive.

Besides individual corporate programs, entire regions are making plans for ISO 14001 and gearing up to compete internationally. European and Asia-Pacific countries have been especially zealous in embracing the ISO 14001 standard. Take a look at a sample of what countries around the world are doing in preparation for ISO 14001:

- The Japanese Ministry of International Trade and Industry (MITI) is encouraging Japanese companies to implement environmental management systems, conforming with the ISO 14001 standard.

By June 1996, six Japanese sites (in Toyota, Sony, Ricoh, Canon, Fujitsu, and Nippon Petroleum) were already registered to the draft ISO 14001 standard.

The Japanese electronics industry has stated its goal to register 8,000 sites in the next two years.

- The Korean electronics industry also has been aggressive in its pursuit of EMS registration. Samsung was registered to the BS 7750 standard in 1994, and other large Korean electronics firms are following suit.
- France is conducting a pilot for ISO 14001 and EMAS implementation. As of June 1996, three French sites—Omya, Lexmark, and Canon—were registered to ISO 14001, with five more registrations pending.
- In the United Kingdom, over 120 sites have been registered to BS 7750.
- Poland, Slovenia, and other Eastern European nations have begun to train EMS auditors and to provide information to industries on the ISO 14001 standard. At least six sites in Poland have already committed to seeking ISO 14001 registration.

With this kind of activity evident before the standard is officially published, competitive pressures to seek registration are likely to be a powerful driver for many companies.

***U.S. Regulatory Drivers*** A potentially strong driver for registration in the United States is the Environmental Protection Agency (EPA) itself. Until the emergence of environmental management systems, most companies' environmental programs were based solely on compliance with stringent EPA regulations. The strong base of compliance is due mainly to the very real threat of enforcement actions, including heavy fines and/or criminal penalties.

Many U.S. industries have begun to focus on a more proactive approach in order to manage this huge compliance effort more effectively and, in some cases, to move beyond the "compliance only" mentality. Some companies have discovered that good environmental management is simply a part of good business management. These companies have been working with the EPA to try to shift the focus from enforcement to prevention. Several voluntary programs within EPA include the use of an EMS to improve environmental performance. The Environmental Leadership Program (ELP), Common Sense Initiative (CSI), and Project XL all allow and encourage the use of management systems to aid in environmental improvements. In fact, Lucent Technologies (formerly AT&T Microelectronics) is participating in Project XL, with a program based strongly on ISO 14001. Under the program, Lucent Technologies will register all of its ten manufacturing facilities to ISO 14001 as a way to drive environmental performance improvements.

Another significant use of EMS concepts comes from EPA's Region 1 (New England), which proposed and set up a new project as a part of the Environmental Leadership Program. Called StarTrack, the project was launched in late 1995 through a pilot with the Gillette Company and was expanded in 1996. The project offers enforcement amnesty for certain violations, reduced inspections, and regulatory flexibilities such as expedited permitting for companies that have had a third-party review their environmental performance, EMS, and compliance audit program. StarTrack does not actually require use of ISO 14001 but does assume that each participating organization has an EMS in place based on the model described in the standard. In fact, the third-party audit guidelines are based in part on ISO 14001.

Eight company sites, representing a wide range of industries, have been selected to participate in StarTrack:

- Chesebrough-Ponds, Clinton, CT
- EG&G Electro-Optics, Salem, MA
- International Paper, Jay, ME
- Petroleum Heat and Power Co., Canton and East Hartford, CT
- Sanders (a Lockheed Martin Company), Nashua, NH
- Spalding Sports Worldwide, Chicopee, MA
- Texas Instruments Materials and Controls Group, Attleboro, MA
- Whyco Chromium Co., Thomaston, CT

This New England initiative could be used by other EPA regions in the future.

At the same time, many state regulatory bodies are beginning to recognize the benefits of an EMS. Several states are working closely with industry to define regulatory relief programs that use an EMS approach. Pennsylvania was, until recently, the only state agency represented in the U.S. TAG to TC 207 and has been especially active in proposing ways to use ISO 14001 to improve environmental performance in industry and to reduce the burden of regulatory approaches that add no value. James Seif, secretary of the Pennsylvania Department of Environmental Protection, testified before the State Senate Environmental Resources & Energy Committee in March 1996 as to the value of ISO 14001 in replacing certain regulatory requirements. Seif voiced his strong belief that ISO 14001 represents the next generation of tools in environmental protection and said that "a company with ISO 14001 [registration] and a superior environmental compliance record may never have to see another regulator again." Many other states, including Texas, California, North Carolina, Minnesota, Illinois, Colorado, and Wisconsin, are considering similar ways to use ISO 14001 to benefit both industry and the environment.

EPA has stated that it will not require ISO 14001 registration as a regulatory requirement. The voluntary programs and initiatives discussed here will recognize implementation of an EMS only when backed up by third-party registration. As long as the EPA and state regulatory bodies continue to recognize and reward use of a registered EMS, there will be another strong external driver for U.S. businesses to consider third-party registration.

### Internal Benefits of Registration

In any discussion of third-party registration, the focus is usually on the external drivers that might require a company or business to register its management systems. Potential internal benefits are frequently overlooked in the initial analysis and only recognized after registration is achieved.

Many companies that achieved ISO 9001 registration later stated that it was the first quality program or system that lasted. "Program of the Month" syndrome was (and still is) a common complaint. In the early 1980s, many companies embraced various quality programs that promised to cure all of their problems and result in delighted customers. For some of these companies, the unexpected result was a great expenditure of resources with few sustained benefits. In case after case, the quality program that had been "implemented" gradually faded away until the next one emerged to take its place. Employees became jaded and distrustful of any newly introduced program.

ISO 9001 looked much the same to many of these disgruntled employees: another new program, a lot of work, a big celebration when registration was achieved, and then a letdown. The difference emerged after the initial registration audit. The third-party auditors returned every six months to assess the maintenance and improvement of the quality system. This system had to be maintained or the registration, which became a key marketing tool, would be in jeopardy.

The registration itself contributed an external pressure to maintain and improve the system. Companies were reluctant to admit it, but many of them found they needed that extra driver to keep the system from becoming another failed program. The same principle is likely to hold true for ISO 14001 registration. Some companies do not need that external pressure, but many others will find it useful in sustaining their environmental systems.

To determine whether ISO 14001 registration is necessary or may be beneficial to a particular business, one must consider all of these various stakeholders and potential drivers. An understanding of customer requirements, competitive position, local concerns, environmental activist priorities, regulatory benefits, and internal benefits, must be weighed against the cost of achieving and maintaining the registration.

In any case, a business should have a clear idea of the reasons it is pursuing registration. It's wise to consider and track all of these factors and then make an informed decision about EMS implementation and registration. A panicked rush to get that certificate could result in an EMS that meets the minimum requirements of ISO 14001 but is not appropriate or cost-effective for the business. Many companies learned this lesson with ISO 9001 and are still trying to recover from implementing poorly designed or highly bureaucratic systems.

# INTRODUCING ISO 14001

To understand the ISO 14001 standard and interpret its requirements accurately, it's helpful to understand the particular drafting and consensus challenges that were encountered in developing the standard. Consider the difficulty in writing any standard on which more than 40 countries from all over the world must agree. Now add in the major political and regulatory differences in the arena of environmental management. Under these circumstances, it's amazing that such a standard could even be written. In addition, because of pressures from EMAS, ISO 14001 was written in only two years, which is an incredible feat for an ISO document!

Because of these factors, ISO 14001 contains many clauses that represent compromises between differing views. In many cases, the United States, Canada, and Japan were at odds with the European nations. The result is a standard based on a delicate balance of international positions, where some words and phrases have a very distinct intended meaning. The opposite is also true: there are cases where a particular phrase—carefully worded to satisfy both sides—may be interpreted slightly differently in Europe and in the United States. Finally, some segments were left intentionally vague to allow adequate flexibility for all of the industries in all parts of the world that might use the standard.

One result of these differing views is the annex to ISO 14001. The introduction to the annex describes its purpose:

> This annex gives additional information on the requirements and is intended to avoid misinterpretation of the specification. This annex only addresses the environmental management system requirements contained in clause 4.*

Many of the details in the annex's guidance describe the intended meaning of the concise phrases in the ISO 14001 specification. The annex also serves as a "holding place" for certain items where consensus agreement was not possible. Wherever one side would not agree to the standard if a certain requirement was included and another side would not agree if that requirement was excluded, the phrasing was moved into the annex. In this way, particular countries or regions can include parts of the annex in their own national or regional requirements if they wish.

The sometimes specific, sometimes imprecise wordings of ISO 14001 will be interpreted in detail in the following chapters as they occur in the standard; however, there are a few cases that are crucial to an overall understanding of ISO 14001.

## CONTINUAL IMPROVEMENT

The most prominent source of debate in the development of ISO 14001 was the definition of "continual improvement." ISO 14001, section 3.1, defines continual improvement as the "process of enhancing the environmental management system to achieve improvements in overall environmental performance in line with the organization's environmental policy." Although this may seem to be a reasonable and straightforward concept, there are several underlying controversies. Understanding these can help a business gain more benefit from the standard and better understand the registrar's perspective.

Generally, the United States (and some other countries) favor a definition of continual improvement that focuses on improvement of the EMS. Most European countries (and some others) favor a definition more in line with EMAS, requiring improvement of environmental performance. The U.S. position is based on a belief that performance improvement is not an appropriate requirement for an international standard. Many U.S. companies also fear that such a requirement could lead to unrealistic demands on financial and technological resources. These stakeholders are concerned that "continual" improvement of environmental performance could, for example, drive companies to zero emissions before the technologies exist to support that goal. Europeans maintain that the whole purpose of an EMS is to help improve environmental performance, and they therefore define "continual improvement" in this results-oriented way.

---

*© International Organization for Standardization. All rights reserved.

The consensus from this debate is shown in the definition above. Continual improvement, as used in ISO 14001, refers to improvement of the management system itself, which is intended to result in performance improvements. Most important, the improvements are tied directly to the organization's own environmental policy. This allows organizations to set their own goals for performance improvement and to meet regional or national requirements where necessary.

## ASPECTS AND IMPACTS

Months of negotiation were necessary to decide whether the standard should refer to environmental "effects" (as used in BS 7750) or to environmental "impacts." There was a fear (on the part of the United States and other countries) that "effects" could be interpreted too broadly, again resulting in unrealistic demands on industry. In addition, TC 207 wanted to avoid the use of any term with an existing legal definition in any member country. The final determination was that an organization must identify the environmental "aspects" of its business and then determine which of those could have a significant "impact" on the environment.

These terms have been precisely defined in ISO 14001. An environmental aspect is an "element of an organization's activities, products or services that can interact with the environment." Environmental impact is defined as "any change to the environment, whether adverse or beneficial, wholly or partially resulting from an organization's activities, products or services." ISO 14004 provides some examples of aspects and associated impacts. Chapter 6, "Environmental Aspects," describes how to identify aspects and significant impacts.

## ORGANIZATION

Another source of controversy, which continues today, is determining what kinds of organizations can use ISO 14001. All sides agreed that the standard should be broadly applicable to all sizes of companies in all kinds of industries in countries all over the world. In fact, its use is not limited only to companies: it is also applicable to noncommercial groups such as schools, hospitals, and municipal or other government organizations. Some disagreement remains, however, regarding whether a given organization or business can intentionally limit the scope of its application of ISO 14001.

These debates are rooted in the use of ISO 9000 standards for registration purposes. Companies have enjoyed a great deal of flexibility in defining the scope of their own quality systems. Some companies have limited the scope of their quality systems in order to simplify the task of gaining registration. Some have sought registration only for partial plant sites or for corporate-level support functions or single product lines. Other companies have registered multiple plant sites, whole divisions, or their entire operations under a single registration. This flexibility has generally worked well for quality systems, where the main intent is to satisfy customers.

The situation is less clear when considering environmental systems. Environmental impacts can't be contained within a limited scope or part of a plant site. An environmental impact could affect the entire site, the surrounding community, and even the global community. In addition, the stakeholders who may request registration are much more varied and may not be satisfied by a limited EMS scope.

EMAS attempted to solve this dilemma by limiting its applicability to geographic sites, but this seemingly simple scope also raises questions. What happens if a separate business, over which the business seeking registration has no control, is resident on the site? What happens when an industrial site is split into sections and sold to different companies? Moreover, there are numerous scenarios that preclude a simple definition of "site." EMAS has established a committee to consider these and other questions of interpretation.

ISO 14001 resolves this issue by using the term *organization* throughout the standard, rather than "company" or "site." *Organization* is defined quite broadly as a "company, corporation, firm, enterprise, authority or institution, or part or combination thereof, whether incorporated or not, public or private, that has its own functions and administration." This definition covers just about any entity you can imagine! An additional note provides even greater flexibility: "for organizations with more than one operating unit, a single operating unit may be defined as an organization."

Despite the flexibility in the standard, controversy remains over registration scope. Some businesses, especially larger corporations, are in favor of having the same kind of flexibility they have enjoyed with ISO 9001 to define their own EMS scope, with the agreement of their registrar. Other factions—including many environmental groups and members of EPA—support some restrictions on the scope definitions to ensure that EMS registrations are meaningful. The issue ultimately will be resolved by the registrars, the accrediting body, and the users of the system.

## U.S. PARTICIPATION

As was mentioned in Chapter 2, the U.S. TAG process is typically an open and democratic one, and TC 207 is no exception. In fact, the TC 207

U.S. TAG has included broad participation from several major stakeholders, and interest in its activities continues to grow. In early 1996, the TAG membership had grown to almost 600, according to the American Society for Testing and Materials (ASTM), the administrator of the TAG.

Industry is, by far, the largest stakeholder group represented on the TAG. Participation by representatives from a wide variety of industries has been heavy from the very beginning. Most major U.S. corporations, as well as many medium-sized businesses, have sent at least one representative to the TAG meetings fairly regularly.

Consultants, training organizations, and potential EMS registrars have also been actively involved in the development of the ISO 14000 standards, particularly ISO 14001 and ISO 14004. Several professional and industrial associations, including the Chemical Manufacturers' Association (CMA) and Environmental Auditing Roundtable (EAR) have also been active participants since the start.

In addition, several key U.S. government bodies have been involved in the development of the standards. EPA has been very active in all sub-TAGs, especially in the work on EMS and auditing standards. In fact, EPA was directly responsible for several of the requirements in ISO 14001. The Department of Energy (DOE) has several representatives participating in the TAG. More recently, some of the state regulatory bodies have begun to participate, most notably agencies from Pennsylvania and California.

The TAG leadership has made a great outreach effort to ensure that all interested or affected parties have the opportunity to be involved. Some of this outreach has been directed toward prominent U.S. environmental groups. Unfortunately, the participation from this stakeholder group remains sparse, despite these efforts. Only a few environmental groups, including Environmental Defense Fund and the National Wildlife Federation, have agreed to participate and have provided input and feedback.

This diverse participation from different stakeholders was intended to ensure that the resulting standards would meet the needs of all groups to the greatest extent possible. Although the final ISO 14001 document does not incorporate all of the desired aspects of every stakeholder group, an effort was made to reach consensus among all the participants in the U.S. TAG (and then among all the nations represented) to develop a standard that was acceptable to all stakeholder groups.

# PART 2

## POLICY AND PLANNING

> ISO 14001 is written with a commonsense approach to management systems. It follows a basic Plan-Do-Check-Act sequence that leads logically through a cyclical business improvement process. The following chapters proceed through each section of the standard, quoting the relevant requirements of ISO 14001, providing interpretation of those requirements where necessary, and describing how to implement those elements. Interpretations are based on direct involvement in the standard's development process and extensive experience with ISO 9001 implementation and auditing. The implementation guidance is drawn from real examples of both environmental and quality systems in various industries, with a focus on business needs. The key to an effective management system is to keep a strong focus on the unique culture and goals of your own business.

# CHAPTER 5

# ENVIRONMENTAL POLICY

## ISO 14001 REQUIREMENTS*

ISO 14001, section 4.2, Environmental Policy, requires the following:

Top management shall define the organization's environmental policy and ensure that it

a) is appropriate to the nature, scale and environmental impacts of its activities, products or services;

b) includes a commitment to continual improvement and prevention of pollution;

c) includes a commitment to comply with relevant environmental legislation and regulations and with other requirements to which the organization subscribes;

d) provides the framework for setting and reviewing environmental objectives and targets;

e) is documented, implemented and maintained and communicated to all employees;

f) is available to the public.

*© International Organization for Standardization. All rights reserved.

## INTERPRETATION

Since the organization itself defines the scope of its EMS (in the absence of external criteria or limits), this section of ISO 14001 requires a policy for that defined organization (whether a site, a division, an entire company, or any other entity that fits within the standard's definition of an organization). Many large and medium-sized companies have multiple environmental policies: corporate level, business level, and site or facility level. In this case, the policy of interest is the one that reflects the defined scope of the EMS. That policy should be consistent with any policies above it.

As required by subsection *a*, the policy must be "appropriate to the nature, scale and environmental impacts" of the defined business scope. This simply means that the policy should be meaningful for the business. An overly simplistic environmental policy would not be appropriate for a nuclear fuels facility or a chemical plant. Of course, judging appropriateness can be quite subjective.

Subsection *b* requires a commitment to continual improvement and prevention of pollution. Remember that in the official ISO 14001 definition "continual improvement" refers to improvement in the EMS itself, but it is perfectly acceptable for an organization's own policy to include a commitment to performance improvement. The organization must also include a policy statement that focuses on prevention of pollution, which is sometimes referred to as waste minimization (the principle of striving first to avoid making wastes rather than relying on strategies to handle and dispose of them). The presence of this requirement is directly due to the U.S. EPA's involvement in ISO 14001 development.

Note the careful wording of subsection *c*, requiring "a commitment to comply" with applicable regulations and other requirements. The organization's policy statement must reflect a *goal or commitment* of complete compliance, not necessarily a guarantee of 100 percent compliance. This phrasing reflects the complex, sometimes overwhelming nature of environmental regulation in the United States, where, according to many experts, it is impossible for any organization always to be in complete compliance with all regulations.

This subsection also includes the phrase "other requirements to which the organization subscribes." It is easy to gloss over this vague phrase and focus on the regulatory part of the subsection; however, like most phrasing in ISO 14001, it is quite deliberate and has a specific meaning. Other requirements could include any number of additional standards, programs, or guidelines with which the organization has chosen to voluntarily comply. These may be industry-specific programs, global initiatives, or corporate requirements. Examples include Responsible

Care®, Public Environmental Reporting Initiative (PERI), the ICC Charter for Sustainable Development, and many specific codes of practice for various industries. If the organization subscribes to any "other requirements," these should be a part of its environmental policy.

The policy must also provide a "framework for setting and reviewing environmental objectives and targets." This means that the policy must be a part of a cohesive system that includes specific objectives and targets. The detailed requirements for setting objectives and targets are covered in clause 4.3.3 of ISO 14001. There should be a logical link between the environmental policy and these goals.

The requirements to document, communicate, and maintain the policy seem straightforward, but these last subsections are critical to the policy requirements. A policy has no value if it is not used, kept up to date, and maintained as a meaningful part of the organization. Merely posting the policy on a wall will not fulfill this requirement.

Finally, this standard, unlike ISO 9001, includes a requirement that the policy be made available to the public. There is no specific definition of what "made available" means: it is left up to each organization to decide what methods are suitable for its own needs.

## IMPLEMENTATION

If the organization has no current environmental policy, it is wise to begin with a close examination of all of the environmental aspects of the organization to determine where its priorities lie. This type of analysis is required by section 4.3.1 of ISO 14001; detailed guidance on how to conduct such an analysis is given in Chapter 6. This environmental impact analysis can help an organization to take a look at the entire scope of its actual and potential environmental impacts. Once the most significant and critical impacts have been determined and prioritized, an environmental policy is easier to develop.

The results of such an analysis are a critical component in the development of an environmental policy but are not the only input. The policy will serve as the framework for the entire management system, so it must be consistent with and supportive of the overall business goals and mission. Some companies have a fully integrated policy that includes elements of quality, environmental, safety, and financial systems. This single policy is the beginning of a completely integrated system in which all of these arenas are seen as parts of the overall business.

While a single policy has some obvious benefits, it is not the only way to ensure that the organization has an integrated management system. Many effective companies have specific policies for quality, safety, environmental, and other aspects of their business. Having separate policies for these different aspects can work well if there is a single, clear business mission that is supported by the individual policies. Multiple policies may be especially effective in the case of a particularly large and complex organization where a single policy encompassing all of the aspects of the business could easily become too complicated and cumbersome, thereby making it ineffective.

 If multiple policies are used, care must be taken to ensure that the overall message is consistent and that all of the policies are directly linked to an overall business mission.

Whether the policy integrates all elements of the business system or only encompasses environmental aspects, it needs to include certain characteristics to be effective. The policy might be long or short, but it must be clearly written and understandable by all employees. It should include straightforward statements that describe a clear direction for the organization. Defining the path clearly ensures that every individual can contribute to the business goals.

 A well-written policy is relevant to every employee. Regardless of job function or level in the company, every employee should be able to relate the policy to his or her own job.

The process of developing a policy should be led by the top management of the organization (as defined by the scope of the EMS) but should include all employees to some degree. It is usually most effective for top management to create an initial draft policy based on the business's overall mission and the initial environmental impacts evaluation. This draft is then shared among all employees, with feedback and comments encouraged. Based on the input of the organization, revisions are made and a final policy is written.

Many businesses already have an environmental policy of some sort, either as a stand-alone policy or as part of their safety, health, and environmental policy. In these cases, the task is not to create a new policy but to review and possibly revise the existing one. Begin by examining the policy to determine whether it:

- Meets the requirements of ISO 14001
- Is appropriate in light of recent evaluations of environmental impacts (see Chapter 6)
- Meets the criteria for an effective policy described in this chapter

- Is appropriate to the needs, culture, and overall business mission of the organization

When you're satisfied with the content of the policy, circulate it throughout the organization for review and feedback.

Policy content varies dramatically from one organization to the next. The only limitation is that it must meet the requirements of the standard. Each organization's policy will reflect the unique culture and priorities of that organization. Some policies will clearly state all of their critical points in a few sentences. Others will be several pages long. An ideal policy for most organizations will probably lie somewhere in between these extremes—concise enough to be easily understood yet comprehensive enough to cover all critical points. Actual policies from AT&T, DuPont, Kodak, and Duke Power, reprinted in the Appendix, provide examples of the variety of approaches different organizations have taken.

In all cases, policies should describe the organization's overall approach. Detailed goals and objectives do not belong in a policy statement. Once a policy is established, it should be general enough and flexible enough to remain applicable for quite some time. Policies are not generally changed very frequently. Certainly, a policy must be reviewed periodically and occasionally revised to reflect changes in the business or major alterations in the company's direction.

 However, policies that are constantly changing do not provide a stable and consistent direction for the organization.

Developing the policy may seem like a difficult enough task, but this is only the beginning. An effective policy must become a dynamic part of the organization, used and referenced in daily business interactions. The standard requires that the policy be "documented, implemented and maintained and communicated." These few words are the most important in this section of ISO 14001.

A good policy—one that is not just framed and posted but that is actually used—will become the cornerstone of the organization. All business decisions should be measured against the policy to ensure that they are consistent with the direction of the business. New projects, solutions to problems, suggestions, and developments should all be compared to the policy. Many organizations provide training for employees when a new policy is developed or an existing one revised. This is a good start, but the policy will only become a part of the organization when employees see it used and referenced frequently—and this will happen only if management sets the example through its actions.

Finally, ISO 14001 requires that the policy be made available to the public. There are many ways to accomplish this and the methods chosen should reflect the overall goals and culture of the business. In recent years companies as diverse as AT&T, DuPont, Duke Power, and Kodak have published annual environmental reports, often in combination with safety and health reports. These reports typically state the organization's environmental policy, objectives, and the progress made toward meeting objectives. Many include success stories—specific examples where the company has positively impacted the environment. These annual progress reports are usually mailed to employees, stockholders, customers, and regulatory contacts. The example policy statements in the Appendix were excerpted from such reports.

Instead of publishing a separate report on environmental progress, a company might include its environmental policy in its overall annual report. Other communication mechanisms include posting the policy in the local community, sending the policy with a cover letter to interested parties, and including the environmental policy in traditional company communications. If seeking registration to ISO 14001, a company will need to show evidence that it has made the policy available in some such way.

Many of the participants in my company's EMS implementation courses want to know what minimum actions would be required to meet this public availability requirement and still get registered. In just about every class, at least one person says, "Well, our policy is on the wall in our lobby—that's available to the public, isn't it?" Although this type of approach may be deemed adequate by some registrars, there may be some business value in going further. Consider the needs of your own business when deciding how to approach this requirement. Chapter 12, "Communications", further explores the question of external communication.

# ENVIRONMENTAL ASPECTS

### ISO 14001 REQUIREMENTS*

ISO 14001, section 4.3.1, Environmental Aspects, requires the following:

The organization shall establish and maintain (a) procedure(s) to identify the environmental aspects of its activities, products or services that it can control and over which it can be expected to have an influence, in order to determine those which have or can have significant impacts on the environment. The organization shall ensure that the aspects related to these significant impacts are considered in setting its environmental objectives.

The organization shall keep this information up-to-date.

### INTERPRETATION

The organization must define its process for evaluating the environmental aspects of its business and determining its most significant environmental impacts. Aspects and impacts are defined in the standard in the following way: an *environmental aspect* is an "element of an organization's activities, products or services that can interact with the environment (note: A significant environmental aspect is an environmental aspect that has or can have a significant environmental impact)." An *environmental impact*: is "any change to the environment, whether adverse or beneficial, wholly or partially resulting from an organization's activities, products or services."

*© International Organization for Standardization. All rights reserved.

These exact terms and definitions were chosen to avoid any conflict with existing legal and regulatory terminology, especially in the United States. The definition of "aspect" is extremely broad, encompassing virtually all elements of a business—undoubtedly because it is difficult to think of an activity that would not interact with the environment in some way. "Impact" is likewise fairly broad, but the standard requires you to identify only significant impacts. Note that, while aspect and impact are defined, there is no formal definition for "significant." The standard leaves it to each company to decide for itself what "significant" means relative to its own processes and products.

The standard notes some limiting factors in this process of identifying aspects and impacts. The organization must include only those aspects over which it has some influence and control. This helps the evaluation to remain a realistic and practical exercise, without entering into the realm of activities that are impossible for the organization to control.

Great care was taken in the drafting of the standard to avoid defining exactly how this evaluation should be performed. BS 7750 (pre–ISO 14001) and EMAS both include lists of aspects to be considered as part of this evaluation. This level of detail was intentionally left out of ISO 14001 so that each organization could define for itself its own scope of environmental aspects. The Annex to ISO 14001 states that organizations without an existing EMS should undertake an initial review. In reality, most organizations will find some sort of review in these early stages helpful, although the depth of the review may vary according to the work the organization has previously done to evaluate its environmental impacts. Although an initial review is not required, organizations must have a defined process for identifying their aspects and significant impacts.

The purpose of this whole exercise is stated in the standard as well. The identified significant impacts provide part of the foundation for the organization's objectives. Finally, the organization must keep this information up to date. This means that the evaluation process must be repeated whenever there are significant changes in the organization's process, products, or services. The evaluation should also be reviewed periodically as objectives are met (or missed) and as stakeholder needs change.

## IMPLEMENTATION

This impact evaluation forms the foundation for the rest of the EMS. For the system to be credible, the evaluation must be effective and comprehensive. All other system elements are based on the environmental impacts that the organization has determined to be significant. This is one of the most critical, and most difficult, requirements of ISO 14001 to implement.

The difficult part of this section is the how-to. There are many different, equally valid ways to approach this evaluation process. Each organization must carefully consider how it will conduct this process and then define its own procedures for doing so. The process of identifying environmental aspects and significant impacts should be the first step undertaken in defining an EMS since all other elements are based on its results. Figure 6-1 illustrates the major steps in conducting this analysis.

### Define the Scope

The first step in this process is to define the scope of the analysis. The scope has to cover the entire EMS, not just the most obvious environmental impacts, such as manufacturing processes. First one must decide what elements of the facility or business are included, making sure to consider power generation, supply of utilities, any on-site operations that are separate from the main operations, transportation and shipping, and all other support functions.

If the scope of your quality system is intentionally limited (i.e., part of a site, one manufacturing process), you'll probably need to define the EMS in broader terms. It is virtually impossible to limit environmental impacts to one part of a facility or site, so your definition will need to rely in part on physical geography. Chapter 22, "Strategic Planning," provides additional guidance on defining your EMS scope.

### Define the Process

Once you have determined the scope and breadth of the EMS, you will need to define exactly how you are going to identify environmental aspects and significant impacts. What methodologies and tools will you use? Who will be involved? How will the evaluation be documented? What records will be kept of decisions made? Begin by defining the general process to be used; in all probability, you will refine the process as you go through it and test it.

Obtaining valid results from the impact evaluation depends on defining a logical and workable process. This process will be different for every business, based on the type and complexity of its environmental impacts as well as its own culture and approach. You'll need to define how to identify environmental aspects and impacts and how to evaluate the impacts relative to one another. This means that your methodology must define what makes an impact significant. The rest of this chapter provides examples and guidance for various tools and methodologies.

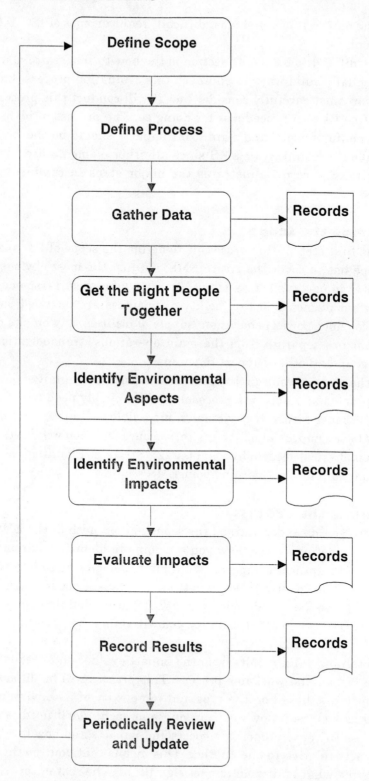

■ **FIGURE 6-1.** Process for Evaluating Environmental Impacts

## Gather Data

Next, you must gather the necessary data. Most organizations will already have some of this information from previous regulatory work, projects, and internal and external communications. In the United States, all organizations covered by SARA Title III have extensive data on their emissions from their required Toxics Release Inventory. Many organizations have detailed information available in their regulatory permits and permit applications. All businesses should have process flow diagrams, drawings, or other basic design data that define their processes and products.

Besides gathering together all of this existing information and data, you may also need to make some baseline measurements, if you have not done so before. Basic information on energy usage and cost, raw materials and supplies used, and amount and type of waste produced will be extremely helpful. In addition, you may want to gather some general information on the environmental impacts of relevant practices. Despite this preparatory work, additional data will probably be needed once you begin the analysis.

## Get the Right People Together

Before proceeding further, it is critical that you bring the right people into the evaluation process. Knowledgeable representatives from every part of the organization—manufacturing, maintenance, shipping/transportation, purchasing, finance, business management, engineering, design/development—should be included. Be careful not to make early assumptions about which areas may or may not be significant in an environmental sense. Most important, recognize that this is not the job of the environmental department alone. Environmental experts are an important resource for this process, but people with detailed knowledge of all parts of the organization must be included.

One large British manufacturing facility learned this lesson the hard way. The company completed a thorough evaluation of its environmental aspects and identified the significant impacts. During a BS 7750 audit, the auditor noticed that the company's fleet of vehicles had not been included as having a significant environmental impact. On further investigation, it was discovered that the site actually had 4,000 vehicles in its fleet! This important environmental aspect had been overlooked partly because the transportation manager had not been involved in the evaluation process.

 Similarly, do not rely too heavily on outside resources. Although your organization may decide to use an outside expert to guide you through the evaluation process, your own managers and professionals know the business best. There will be many decisions to be made regarding the significance of various impacts. While you should rely as much as possible on data and facts, some of these decisions will come down to business judgments that you should make for yourselves.

### Identify Environmental Aspects

Once the right team has been put together, the process should begin with a comprehensive look at the organization's processes, products, and services. One way to identify environmental aspects is to conduct a simple input-output analysis. For each component of the business—purchasing, manufacturing, finishing, packaging, shipping, and so on—make a list of the inputs and outputs. Inputs may include energy, raw materials, water, equipment, packaging, and all sorts of other supplies. Outputs may include products, by-products, wastes, energy, water, scrap materials, and other intended and unintended products.

The varied group of people involved should be able to provide a broad view of the organization. As the team considers each part of the business, care should be taken to evaluate the full scope of activities of the organization. Existing practices should be taken into account as should both normal and abnormal operating conditions and emergencies. Most important, you'll need to think in very broad terms about the environmental aspects of your business beyond the obvious, regulated aspects. Do not try to limit your analysis yet. At this stage, a very comprehensive approach is best.

Although a thorough life cycle assessment approach, using an inventory analysis, would be a good tool to use for this process, simple methodologies, such as the input-output analysis, may work well for your organization. You can also use various diagramming or flowcharting tools to ensure that you have identified all aspects. Fishbone diagrams, commonly used in quality assurance and problem-solving, can help define the aspects of a complex process.

### Identify Environmental Impacts

Once all environmental aspects have been identified, determine what environmental impacts are associated with each aspect. For example, if energy consumption is an aspect of your operation, the environmental impacts might include use of natural resources and air emissions from energy generation. In this process, you may discover that your identification of aspects was not detailed enough. For instance, if you identified a fleet of vehicles as an aspect, you must now consider fuel consumption, exhaust emissions, use and disposal of oil to maintain the vehicles, and other potential impacts.

The task becomes much more complex at this stage. It is critical to remain open-minded and to encourage the group involved to be as broad and comprehensive as possible. This could be especially difficult for environmental professionals in highly regulated industries who are used to thinking primarily in terms of regulations. The identification of environmental impacts must extend beyond the typical air, water, and soil impacts that are so commonly considered and so highly regulated.

U.S. environmental professionals and managers are typically somewhat skeptical at this stage. A common reaction is, "How could there possibly be additional environmental impacts that are not already regulated?" These people are so used to dealing with incredibly complex regulations that they find it hard to believe there could be anything left over that is not already regulated.

ISO 14001 encourages you to think beyond the regulatory requirements to consider a broader realm of environmental impacts. Examples of impacts that are often not directly regulated include noise, odor, traffic, and visual impacts. Although these may seem inconsequential compared to traditional air, water, and soil impacts, you should avoid making judgments about significance at this stage. Just try to define all environmental impacts and let your methodologies determine what is significant.

The Annex to ISO 14001 provides some useful guidance in this identification process. It states[*]:

> The process to identify the significant environmental aspects associated with the activities at operating units should, where relevant, consider,
>
> a) emissions to air;
> b) releases to water;
> c) waste management;
> d) contamination of land;
> e) use of raw materials and natural resources;
> f) other local environmental and community issues.

Other local issues often include some of the environmental impacts traditionally overlooked by businesses, such as noise, traffic, or visual impacts. Be sure that you consider both local and global environmental impacts.

### Evaluate Impacts

Once all impacts have been identified, the most difficult part of the process begins: determining which impacts are significant for your own

---

[*]© International Organization for Standardization. All rights reserved.

business. The definition of "significant" will vary from one organization to another, depending on the relative severity and quantity of environmental impacts associated with the business as well as the degree of control the business has over those impacts. These decisions will seldom be simple or obvious.

 It is especially important not to make assumptions without supporting data.

One business was considering expanding to include a new product line and planned to run this new product at night. Initially the company assumed that the resulting increase in electricity use was a negative environmental impact. When they looked into the situation further and talked with a power company representative, they found that just the opposite was true. By running the process at night, they would be increasing electricity demand at a time when the power company normally had to decrease its output. Such swings in output from day to night frequently result in lower efficiencies and greater pollution—sometimes a local power company even has to shut down one or more plants because of the decreased demand. By allowing the power company to run at a more even pace through the night, this plant was actually making a positive impact on the environment. Make sure that all of your determinations of significance are backed up as much as possible by hard facts.

When determining significance, take several factors into account. Severity of the impact and frequency of occurrence are two of the most obvious. You may also want to consider the relative risk encountered, both in environmental and financial terms. Also remember that the standard allows you to focus on those aspects that you can control and over which you can be expected to have an influence. Control is not always a black-and-white issue, though. You have varying degrees of control over all of your environmental aspects, and you will need to decide which impacts you can reasonably influence. You may use a matrix with a continuous scale, like the one shown in Figure 6-2, to record the degree of practical control your organization has over its various environmental aspects.

 Many tools and methodologies are available to help you through the impact evaluation. Classic quality tools, such as pareto diagrams, why-why diagrams, checklists, and fishbone diagrams, can help you to make sense of complex processes and to assess relative significance. Typical process hazards analyses (PHA) and failure modes effect analyses (FMEA) can help you to identify aspects and impacts related to abnormal or

| For Product X: | Degree of Practical Control | |
|---|:---:|:---:|
| | Strong | Weak |
| Selection of Raw Materials | | ● |
| Product or Process Design | ● | |
| Energy Use | ● | |
| Emissions | | ● |
| Accidental Releases | ● | |
| Persistence in Environment | | ● |
| Method of Disposal/Recyclability | ● | |

■ **FIGURE 6-2.** Sample Worksheet for Determining Degree of Control.
*Source:* DuPont Company, 1996.

emergency situations. Environmental risk assessments can also be helpful. Many companies use weighting and ranking methods to determine relative significance. These can vary from simple rating systems to very complex mathematical formulas.

For instance, you can consider one part of your process at a time and score the impacts relative to one another using a simple numerical ranking system. You might use a scale of 1 to 10, where 10 has the greatest impact. Some organizations prefer a rating system using only 1, 5, and 10 (or low, medium, and high) in order to provide greater weighting to the more significant impacts. Consider each impact in terms of both its severity and its frequency for both normal and abnormal operating conditions. Use the varied knowledge and experience of the group that you have assembled to ensure that all perspectives are included and come to a consensus on the rating for each impact. Be sure to tackle just one area or component of the business at a time at this stage or the volume and complexity of the data could quickly become overwhelming.

Once you've developed a rating for each impact, you will need to apply your own criteria for significance. If you've used a numerical rating system like the one shown in Figure 6-3, you might decide that a total score of 15 is significant. Organizations using a similar system might decide that 12 or 20 is the critical point, given their own unique circumstances. At this stage, you need to consider all impacts within the scope of your organization (rather than just one area), since significance is a relative concept.

Another simple method is a series of checklists with yes/no questions regarding various types of impacts. Include traditional measures, such as whether an impact is regulated, as well as measures that are

| Environmental Area | Raw materials Pre-processing | | Transport of Raw Materials | | Process Step #1 | | Process Step #2 | | Process Waste Recycling | | Packaging | | Distribution/ Transport | |
|---|---|---|---|---|---|---|---|---|---|---|---|---|---|---|
| | S | F | S | F | S | F | S | F | S | F | S | F | S | F |
| *IMPACT RATING* | | | | | | | | | | | | | | |
| Energy | | | | | | | | | | | | | | |
| Air | | | | | | | | | | | | | | |
| Water | | | | | | | | | | | | | | |
| Soil | | | | | | | | | | | | | | |
| Geology | | | | | | | | | | | | | | |
| Landscape, visual | | | | | | | | | | | | | | |
| Noise | | | | | | | | | | | | | | |
| Natural Resources | | | | | | | | | | | | | | |
| Humans | | | | | | | | | | | | | | |
| Local Community | | | | | | | | | | | | | | |
| Climate | | | | | | | | | | | | | | |
| Wildlife | | | | | | | | | | | | | | |

| Score S = Severity F = Frequency | Very High | High | Moderate | Low | Very Low |
|---|---|---|---|---|---|
| | 5 | 4 | 3 | 2 | 1 |

■ **FIGURE 6-3.** Sample Worksheet for Evaluating Significant Impacts. *Source:* Excel Partnership, Inc.

ENVIRONMENTAL ASPECTS ■ 63

sometimes overlooked, such as the views of the local community. You can work through these checklists as a group, characterizing each environmental impact. In this case, the number of "yes" answers would define relative significance.

Whatever method you use, it should be thorough, understandable, and as objective as possible. Try to avoid simply making judgments as to what is significant, since these are bound to be prejudiced by your own background and experience. It is also difficult to judge very dissimilar impacts relative to one another without a common basis for comparison. For instance, how do you compare the significance of air emissions versus water discharges versus noise pollution? By using a defined method, you can ensure that your decisions are based on data, even though there will always be an element of subjectivity involved.

### Record Results

Most businesses find it helpful to use worksheets throughout the evaluation, both to guide the process and to record results. In documenting the results of the overall process, make sure that those environmental impacts that you have deemed significant are clearly identified. EMAS requires a "register" or a list of these. Although ISO 14001 does not require it, many businesses have found it helpful to create such a list to indicate clearly what they have determined is significant.

 In addition to documenting the results of the evaluation, make sure that you have adequate records describing the basis for your decisions. These may be helpful during a third-party audit, but their primary purpose is to help remind your own organization of the processes and criteria used. This information will be particularly useful when you review and upgrade the aspects and impacts periodically or when you need to revisit the evaluation because of process, product, or business changes.

### Periodically Review and Update

Finally, the process you defined at the start must include some way to keep this information up to date. Define a periodic review process, perhaps to coincide with management reviews (see Chapter 21). In addition, make sure that the system ensures that environmental aspects and impacts are reevaluated whenever changes occur in your business.

As you can see, this is an extensive, involved process that can take months to complete. You may get started, find that you need additional information, and then have to suspend the process while the data are gathered. You may find that the methods you initially identified do not suit your organization and must be refined or revised during the process. You may also decide that additional expertise is needed to sort through an unusually complex set of aspects and impacts. In any case, this process and the information that results from it create the foundation for the rest of the management system. All other EMS elements build off this evaluation of significant impacts. It is critical that this process be conducted carefully, thoroughly, and accurately.

# LEGAL AND OTHER REQUIREMENTS

> ### ISO 14001 REQUIREMENTS*
> ISO 14001, section 4.3.2, Legal and Other Requirements, requires the following:
>
> The organization shall establish and maintain a procedure to identify and have access to legal and other requirements to which the organization subscribes, that are applicable to the environmental aspects of its activities, products or services.

## INTERPRETATION

This section is fairly straightforward. The organization must have some established method for ensuring that it is aware of all applicable environmental regulations. The standard has two specific requirements: to identify the applicable regulations and to have access to them. In other words, an organization does not have to have a complete set of the written requirements on site, but must be able to access them when needed.

The full scope of this section must be recognized. It includes not only regulatory requirements but certain voluntary initiatives as well. If an organization has committed to a particular international agreement, industry standard, or similar guideline, it becomes a part of its "legal" requirements, as defined in this section. Examples of these other requirements are given in Chapter 5.

*© International Organization for Standardization. All rights reserved.

## IMPLEMENTATION

Most organizations in the United States should have a head start in complying with these requirements. Applicable regulatory requirements at all levels—federal, state, and local—need to be identified and tracked, and to keep up with these complex sets of environmental regulations, most U.S. organizations already have some sort of regulatory tracking system in place.

Many companies use various information services (provided by industrial associations, regulatory bodies, or commercial firms) to help them to keep up to date on regulatory requirements. Information may be provided by newsletter-type updates, on-line services, or CD-ROMs to give companies access to the details of applicable regulations. Other companies may handle this responsibility on their own or even hire a consultant to track regulations for them. Any of these approaches is acceptable for ISO 14001, as long as it is clearly defined and effective.

Regardless of the methods used, the system must not only identify currently applicable regulations but also keep track of regulatory changes. Changes may occur because of legislative actions or because of changes in the way the company itself operates. The regulatory tracking system and procedures must take both kinds of changes into account.

In larger companies, responsibilities for tracking regulations may be split among corporate, divisional, and site resources. Although local regulations may differ quite dramatically from one site to another, the company may use corporate resources to keep up to date on current federal legislation and regulations, as well as on upcoming changes. If this is the case for your company, your procedures should clearly define the division of responsibilities.

At the opposite end of the spectrum, small companies may find this requirement fairly difficult to meet. Smaller companies typically have fewer resources to keep up with the ever-changing, complex jumble of regulations. Although they need to meet all of these requirements to do business legally in the United States, it is nonetheless an onerous task. These smaller organizations should check regional groups and industrial associations to find out whether any regulatory information services are available to help them.

To show that all applicable regulatory and other requirements have been identified, most organizations need some sort of list or database. Some of this information may be purchased from various services, but the complete compilation will probably have to be pulled together by your own organization. It should include all voluntary environmental requirements to which the organization subscribes, as well as all regulatory requirements. Once again, many U.S. companies will already have some of this information, since it is typically necessary just to keep on top of monitoring and reporting requirements.

✓ Consider who in the business needs to know this type of information. Which people need to have access to the detailed regulations? Make sure that the management system provides the appropriate people with the information they need to do their jobs without burdening people who do not need that kind of detailed information.

Finally, make sure that any "other requirements" included in the system represent a real commitment by the business. By including these in the same section as regulatory requirements, the standard is requiring organizations to treat them the same way. For instance, if a chemical company says it is a part of the Responsible Care® program, it will have to ensure that the program is truly being implemented. Additional plans may be required to implement the program fully and to ensure that the organization is trying to comply with it.

 If an organization wants to register or self-declare its conformance to ISO 14001, it will need to show solid evidence that these additional commitments are given the same attention as legal requirements.

As with many of the requirements in ISO 14001, this section requires procedures. Documenting standard practices is an integral part of the management system. Although most U.S. organizations already do much of what is required in this section, many have never defined their practices. The standard requires that the organization establish and maintain procedures for tracking regulatory and other requirements.

The best approach is to describe current practices, check and monitor these to assess whether they are effective and comprehensive, and update or revise practices where needed. Be sure to define clearly the responsibilities for maintaining the system. The procedure must also be updated periodically so that it always reflects current practice. Chapter 13 includes tips for clear and effective documentation.

# OBJECTIVES AND TARGETS

### ISO 14001 REQUIREMENTS*

ISO 14001, section 4.3.3, Objectives and Targets, requires the following:

The organization shall establish and maintain documented environmental objectives and targets, at each relevant function and level within the organization.

When establishing and reviewing its objectives, an organization shall consider the legal and other requirements, its significant environmental aspects, its technological options and its financial, operational and business requirements, and the views of interested parties.

The objectives and targets shall be consistent with the environmental policy, including the commitment to prevention of pollution.

## INTERPRETATION

Once again, the ISO 14001 standard's authors have provided specific definitions for the terminology used. An *environmental objective* is defined as an "overall environmental goal, arising from the environmental policy, that an organization sets itself to achieve, and which is quantified where

---

*© International Organization for Standardization. All rights reserved.

practicable." A *target* is defined as a "detailed performance requirement, quantified where practicable, applicable to the organization or parts thereof, that arises from the environmental objectives and that needs to be set and met in order to achieve those objectives."

These definitions indicate that the specific targets are directly linked to the objectives, which in turn are linked to the environmental policy. These are all components of the business process and work in conjunction with one another to provide a system for continual improvement. The standard requires that this framework be established "at each relevant function and level" of the organization. This means that some objectives or targets may be focused on a particular portion of the organization. Others may encompass the total company. The full set of objectives and targets should include those functions and levels which have or can have a significant impact on the environment.

ISO 14001 requires that the objectives and targets be consistent with the environmental policy. This makes sense from a business perspective as well. In addition, the standard states that the organization should consider a number of things when establishing its objectives and targets. Regulatory requirements and significant impacts are two such considerations. These will likely form the basis for most of an organization's environmental goals.

This section of the standard specifically grants some flexibility to an organization to do what is right for its own business. The requirement to consider "financial, operational and business requirements" basically means that, to be realistic and achievable, environmental goals must be set in the context of the overall business. The standard is not requiring the organization to set idealistic objectives based only on desirable environmental improvements. This further supports the idea that environment considerations must be managed as a part of the overall business.

Finally, organizations are required to consider "the views of interested parties." ISO 14001 defines *interested party* as an "individual or group concerned with *or* affected by the environmental performance of an organization." Note the use of "or" instead of "and." This was the result of a conscious decision by TC 207, and it creates a very broad definition of "interested party" (the United States supported the narrower definition of "concerned with *and* affected by" but was outvoted). This should not instill panic in an organization, however, since the standard still encourages a realistic set of objectives which considers business needs. There must be evidence that the views of interested parties are considered, but this does not mean that the company must set its goals based on the needs of a single stakeholder.

# IMPLEMENTATION

## What Are Objectives and Targets?

The standard describes the generic definitions of "objective" and "target," but some organizations are still unsure exactly what these mean in practice. Typically, *objectives* are broad environmental goals set for the organization. *Targets*, which support the objectives, are more specific, measurable, and detailed. For example, an organization might have an objective of reducing energy use. A corresponding target might be to "reduce BTUs per pound of production by 10 percent over 1996 usage by December 1997."

In this example, the target is a very specific number that can be measured. Units are included, with a production basis so that the target is reasonable and achievable even if the business expands. There is a base year against which to measure progress, and a specific goal date has been set.

There could be multiple targets for a single objective or multiple objectives for a particular significant impact. In the example cited above, where energy use was determined to be significant, the business could have objectives for reducing energy usage and for researching alternate energy sources. In any case, there should be a clear path leading from the environmental policy (based on an evaluation of significant impacts) to the objectives to the targets.

✓ Many companies already have a defined process for setting environmental goals. If this is the case, build on your existing system. There is no need to start a new "ISO system" just to match the ISO 14001 terminology. As long as your system meets the intent of "Objectives and Targets," as defined by the standard, the exact process or terminology is irrelevant. Ensure that your system meets the intent of the standard and then describe it in your documentation.

## Determine Priorities

Based on the policy and evaluation of significant impacts, the organization must define its priorities. Not all significant impacts will have objectives and targets associated with them every year. All businesses have limited resources with which to work and therefore need to set clear priorities for environmental objectives.

✓ The prioritization process should be based on several factors in order to achieve a balance of realistic environmental improvements and business success. Consider the relative significance of identified environmental impacts: some may require more urgent action than others. Consider the resources that are available. It is wise to choose a variety of objectives, requiring varying levels of time, capital, and human resources. The standard doesn't require that every objective be met every year, but it makes sense to set reasonable objectives since the purpose of an EMS is to improve.

A business's priorities will change as its EMS evolves. If the company cannot yet meet regulatory limits, its goals at the beginning will be focused almost solely on regulatory compliance. When compliance goals are met, an organization can start to look at more advanced objectives, focused on improving performance and refining the EMS. Finally, when an organization has a well-established EMS and has very good control over its regulated processes, it can focus on continual improvement of even broader aspects of its environmental impacts—looking at effects on ecosystems, global impacts, and less obvious forms of pollution.

So the first step for any organization is to use the results of its impact evaluation to determine its process for establishing priorities. Decide what factors to consider and what resources are available. As with the policy, it is critical to assemble the right team for this process. Make sure that all functions in the organization are represented, and then decide what the organization's critical priorities are.

The standard also requires that the views of interested parties be considered. As explained in the "Interpretation" section of this chapter, "interested parties" include many different stakeholders, such as regulatory bodies, local communities, environmental groups, employees, and even shareholders. This does not mean that you have to act on every request from an environmental activist group—only that you must consider all these varied needs when determining your environmental goals.

In order to consider these views, you have to understand what they are. Your organization will certainly have plenty of information about the needs of the regulatory bodies, but some of the other interested parties' views may be less obvious. If you've received environmental inquiries, comments, or complaints in the past, these can be used to help understand which impacts are of the most concern to the local community or to environmental groups. You may also have conducted surveys of employees or the community at some time in the past, and this data will also be helpful.

 Many organizations will find a void of factual information in this area and may need to seek out the views of interested parties so that they can be considered. A July 1993 *Fortune* article, "Who Scores Best on the Environment," describes Dow Chemical's process for understanding the views of interested parties. Each quarter, Dow's senior managers and board members invite representatives from eight environmental groups to meet with them. They spend a day and a half together each time to gain an understanding of the environmentalists' concerns. Obviously, not all companies will be willing to go this far, but some sort of outreach programs may be necessary.

## Set Objectives and Targets

Once you've determined your environmental priorities, set reasonable objectives and targets. Many companies set annual objectives that are reviewed and revised each year, although some objectives will be longer-term, requiring two or three years to complete. Other companies have five- or ten-year objectives, with shorter-term targets each year. The process and timing should be based on what will work best for your own organization.

If you already have defined objectives or goals, you will need to make sure that these are focused on the *significant impacts* of your business, as defined by your impact evaluation. Your existing goals may have been focused only on regulatory aspects. Reassess the scope of your objectives in light of the analysis conducted to determine significance.

It is important to set objectives and targets based on concrete data. If, for instance, a company decides that reducing energy usage is one area in which improvement is needed, the percentage of the reduction should be based on data such as past reductions achieved, current energy usage, and estimated potential reductions from particular projects and/or operational tactics. In fact, it makes sense to approach the setting of objectives, targets, and programs (see Chapter 9) as a single process. It may be necessary to establish plans or programs first in order to determine what objectives and targets might be reasonably achieved.

Finally, you will need to keep records of the process of setting objectives and targets. The records do not need to be overly formal; they could simply consist of minutes of meetings. Be sure to include some indication that you have considered all of the factors listed in the standard, including the views of interested parties. Besides providing evidence to an auditor that you have met the standard, these records will be valuable to your own organization as you continue to review and evaluate objectives and targets and set new ones.

## Corporate Goals Processes

When establishing objectives and targets for an entire corporation (or some other large, complex organization), care must be taken to involve all levels of the organization in the goal-setting process. Input should be solicited from divisions, departments, and individual facilities and plants. The prioritization process should take into account the business needs, significant impacts, and regulatory status of all functions.

One way to accomplish this complex task is first to request that each level (plant, department, etc.) evaluate its own environmental impacts and set its own priorities. Information from these individual processes can then be fed back to the corporate level. At DuPont, representatives from each business work together to determine what the corporation's priorities should be. Based on these priorities, high-level corporate goals are established. These goals are typically quite broad. Particular goals may be applicable to all businesses or to just a few, but their presence at the corporate level indicates their importance and priority for the entire company. For example, elimination of the manufacture of CFCs was one of DuPont's primary environmental goals for 1994. Many plants within the company did not manufacture CFCs and so were unaffected by that particular goal, even though it was important to the company as a whole.

Once corporate goals are determined, the process cascades back down through the various levels in the organization to individual plants, facilities, or groups. Each facility then uses the corporate goals, along with its own significant impacts and priorities, to set its own objectives and targets. If any particular corporate goal affects the facility, it should have its own specific objective and target to help the company achieve its goal.

**Examples of Corporate Goals**   Each company's objectives and targets will be specific to its own significant impacts, regulatory issues, and overall business framework. If an organization has never before set environmental goals, the process may seem somewhat daunting. A few examples from U.S. companies in various industries follow. Keep in mind that these are just a few examples; they may be very different from your own business's goals.

AT&T's 1994 *Environment and Safety Annual Report* reviewed the company's progress toward its corporate environmental goals. Those targets included the following:

- Eliminate CFC emissions by the end of 1994
- Reduce reportable air emissions 95 percent by year-end 1995
- Decrease manufacturing process waste disposal 25 percent by year-end 1994
- Recycle 60 percent of our paper by year-end 1994
- Reduce our use of paper by 15 percent

Each of these targets is specific and quantifiable. Most include a goal date for achievement. The annual report showed that all goals had been met or exceeded. This indicates that the specific targets were chosen carefully to be reasonable and achievable. Most were fairly short-range, with goal dates within one or two years.

DuPont's 1993 *Environmental Progress Report* indicates a slightly different approach. Some of its stated environmental goals were to

- Reduce carcinogenic air emissions by 90 percent from 1987 to 2000 at U.S. sites and by 90 percent from 1990 to 2000 at other sites
- Reduce emissions of 33/50 chemicals, 17 large-volume toxic chemicals identified by the EPA, by 50 percent in aggregate from 1988 to 1995
- Eliminate land disposal of hazardous waste by 2000, or verify that wastes have become nonhazardous
- Equip the oceangoing oil fleet with 100 percent double-hulled tankers by 2000
- Manage corporate property for wildlife habitat enhancement

Several points stand out from these examples. DuPont chose to set longer-term goals in many cases, presumably supported by specific internal short-term targets each year. Regulatory influence is apparent in some goals. Like AT&T's, DuPont's goals are specific and measurable. One exception is the last example listed—to manage property for wildlife habitat enhancement. Some goals, like this one, cannot easily be put into measurable terms. The standard allows this flexibility by defining objectives and targets as "quantified where practicable."

These two examples show how unique each organization's objectives and targets can be. It is critical to define environmental policies, objectives, and targets in the context of the overall business goals and mission. This ensures that the EMS is appropriate to the unique needs of each particular company.

# ENVIRONMENTAL MANAGEMENT PROGRAM

> ### ISO 14001 REQUIREMENTS*
>
> ISO 14001, section 4.3.4, Environmental Management Programme(s), requires the following:
>
> The organization shall establish and maintain (a) programme(s) for achieving its objectives and targets. It shall include
>
> a) designation of responsibility for achieving objectives and targets at each relevant function and level of the organization;
>
> b) the means and timeframe by which they are to be achieved.
>
> If a project relates to new developments and new or modified activities, products or services, programme(s) shall be amended where relevant to ensure that environmental management applies to such projects.

## INTERPRETATION

This section is frequently difficult for American users to interpret because it is based on a usage of the term *program* ("programme" is the British spelling) that is unusual in the United States. This section and terminology come from the British standard, BS 7750. By substituting the word "plan(s)" for "program(s)," the meaning becomes clearer. This section is requiring that detailed plans be developed that describe how

---

*© International Organization for Standardization. All rights reserved.

the objectives and targets will be met. Those plans must include assigned responsibilities, estimated timing, and the methods or means by which the targets will be achieved. Consider these as project plans for achieving the stated environmental targets.

The phrase "at each relevant function and level of the organization" refers to the need for detailed plans that involve all affected areas of the business. For instance, if the company has an overall objective to reduce air emissions by 70 percent in three years, then any functional group, department, plant, or facility that has air emissions should have a plan or program in place. Each individual plan will describe specific steps to be taken for that group, so that each part of the organization contributes to meeting the company objective. The word "relevant" further implies that only areas affected by a particular target will have plans for meeting it.

The last part of this section applies to new or improved processes, products, or services. Anytime a new development is emerging, that development must take environmental management into account. Specifically, the plans or programs need to be reviewed to see whether the process or product changes will affect them.

This is the only place in the standard where design activities are referenced. ISO 14001 describes the basic elements of an EMS. While concepts like Design for the Environment may be very valuable for many organizations, they are specific methodologies and, as such, are not required by the standard. The only requirement for design is that the impact on environmental management programs is considered as a part of any development project.

## IMPLEMENTATION

Environmental management programs are the final piece in the EMS planning process. By this point, you will have evaluated environmental impacts to decide what is significant, identified regulatory requirements, defined a policy, and established objectives and targets by considering a variety of factors. Now comes the time to develop programs or plans to define how you will achieve the objectives and targets. All these components fit together as shown in Figure 9-1 to form the foundation of the EMS.

In developing environmental management programs, consider the concepts of effective project planning. Programs or plans should be carefully thought out and based on the input of the people who will actually be doing the work. Critical steps should be identified, along with timing and assigned responsibility.

As mentioned in the previous chapter, it's almost impossible to establish realistic and meaningful objectives and targets without also con-

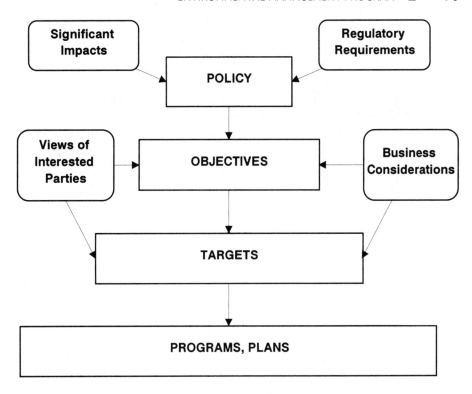

■ **FIGURE 9-1.** EMS Planning Process

sidering how you will achieve them. Although these are two separate sections of ISO 14001, these steps will probably be implemented concurrently in your organization. For example, if you decide that noise reduction is one area where objectives and targets are necessary, you will need to decide how you might reduce noise before you can set a practical target for reduction.

 In other words, you want to avoid choosing a specific target without some basis for it.

Although you may not have detailed project plans in place when you choose objectives and targets, you should at least try to define the general methods and approaches that will be used to achieve each. This will help you to choose realistic and achievable target values. Once the targets are determined, you can go back to fill in the details your programs, including responsibility, timing, and critical steps.

If your company has already tackled some of the more obvious means of waste reduction and environmental control, you may need to take a more creative approach to defining objectives, targets, and programs. Highly regulated industries will have the added challenge of extending their environmental activities beyond the scope of regulatory requirements, perhaps for the first time. The programs that may yield the greatest environmental and economic returns may not be the most obvious ones.

Herman Miller, a furniture manufacturer, reduced its solid waste by 80 percent from 1982 to 1993. The company accomplished this by considering a wide variety of creative approaches that also yielded additional income and cost savings for the company. Herman Miller sold fabric and vinyl scraps to the automotive industry for use as linings in cars and sound-deadening material, respectively. The company found a market for leather scraps in the luggage industry for use as trim on briefcases. Wood scraps are used as fuel in a cogeneration facility, saving $450,000 on gas costs.

These kinds of opportunities exist in just about every business, although the programs and plans to achieve them are seldom obvious. This further emphasizes the need to involve a variety of people from the company in the objectives and programs process to ensure that varied ideas and perspectives are considered.

When determining the timing of and the responsibility for programs, keep the overall business goals in mind, as well as your limitations in both capital and human resources. These environmental programs should fit in as an integral part of your business plan.

 By setting up programs with varied deadlines, responsibilities, and amounts of capital required, you can avoid ending up with a full set of environmental targets all due at the end of the year and all the responsibility of the environmental manager!

As with policy and objectives, particular programs or plans may look quite different from one organization to another. Program formats and styles are left up to each business to determine for itself. Existing capital approval processes, project management software, or other planning methods can be used very effectively for this purpose. Once again, strive to make the environmental plans a part of the overall business planning process.

 Although this section of the standard does not specifically require a procedure, having a procedure in place is the best way of ensuring that programs are developed and maintained consistently over the years. A simple procedure could define overall responsibility for developing programs, coordinating their implementation, and reviewing their progress at a stated frequency.

Responsibilities for reviewing programs when new developments occur can also be included in your procedure. This is critical for ensuring that the EMS is flexible and changes as business needs change. It will also help to ensure that you do not find yourself at the end of the year, with many missed environmental targets and a lot of excuses.

Suppose a plant site had plans for adding a scrubber to one of its stacks to help meet a target of reduced air emissions. If a process improvement involves replacing that old stack with a different technology, then the environmental plans must obviously be revised since they are no longer appropriate. This example can be further extended. If that new process improvement, which is necessary because of equipment failure or revised regulations, requires a great deal of capital investment, the entire set of plans or programs may need to be reviewed and revised because of an unforeseen lack of available capital. Plans and targets that have nothing to do with air emissions may need revision because of this change in resources.

Situations like this are likely to occur in every business once in a while, and more minor changes may occur quite frequently. Your system needs to take these into account by requiring a review of environmental programs whenever changes occur in your organization's products, processes, services, or activities. A good way to ensure this happens is to include a verification that environmental management programs have been reviewed on existing capital approval forms and procedures. It is always more effective to integrate new requirements into existing systems rather than to create new systems.

Additionally, a good practice is to set up periodic reviews of the programs even in the absence of new developments. These can serve as progress checks to ensure that programs are being implemented and that adequate resources are available. As with objectives and targets, the standard requires that programs be established and maintained. "Maintain" means that they are kept up to date and valid.

There is nothing wrong with failing to meet a given target or having to revise programs midway through their implementation. This is bound to occur because of ever-changing business conditions, regulatory requirements, and stakeholder needs. As long as the EMS includes provisions for keeping objectives, targets, and programs up to date, the system will work effectively and will yield improvements over time. Third-party registrars will look for evidence that programs and objectives are reviewed when changes occur and that corrective actions are identified and taken when objectives or targets are not met (see Chapter 18).

# IMPLEMENTATION AND OPERATION

> After establishing a policy and engaging in critical planning activities, it is time to focus on the actual operation of the EMS. The next major section of the ISO 14001 standard, Implementation and Operation, includes a number of subsections that describe the elements necessary for effective EMS operation. The first few subsections cover elements that deal primarily with an organization's most important resource—the people who work within it. These sections include criteria for defining responsibilities, providing training, and ensuring adequate communication. The standard then covers documentation requirements. Finally, both normal and emergency operations are addressed. All these subsections together describe the basic elements necessary to implement and operate an environmental management system.

# STRUCTURE AND RESPONSIBILITY

## ISO 14001 REQUIREMENTS*

ISO 14001, section 4.4.1, Structure and Responsibility, requires the following:

> Roles, responsibility and authorities shall be defined, documented and communicated in order to facilitate effective environmental management.
>
> Management shall provide resources essential to the implementation and control of the environmental management system. Resources include human resources and specialized skills, technology and financial resources.
>
> The organization's top management shall appoint (a) specific management representative(s) who, irrespective of other responsibilities, shall have defined roles, responsibilities and authority for
>
> a) ensuring that environmental management system requirements are established, implemented and maintained in accordance with this International Standard;
>
> b) reporting on the performance of the environmental management system to top management for review and as a basis for improvement of the environmental management system.

*© International Organization for Standardization. All rights reserved.

## INTERPRETATION

This section describes an element that is at the heart of any management system—clearly defined roles and responsibilities. The first statement of this section simply requires that responsibilities are clearly understood by everyone in the organization. Specifically, you are required to document and communicate responsibilities, roles, and authority. Authority is an important element that is frequently overlooked in existing systems. It is common to find clearly defined responsibilities but a lack of defined authority. For instance, each operator may have a very specific job description regarding his or her responsibilities for operating the plant, but does each have the authority to stop the operation if a serious environmental problem is imminent? The standard requires a thorough understanding of both responsibility and authority.

This section of the standard (like all the others) applies to those employees who have a potential or actual impact on the environment and those who have a role within the EMS. Although this seems to narrow the scope of the requirements, you will probably find that most people in the organization have some impact on the environment. The intent of this requirement is to ensure that any environmentally related job functions—not just the roles of environmental professionals and managers—are well defined.

The standard requires that the organization appoint a management representative with defined responsibilities for implementing and maintaining the EMS. There is some flexibility built into this requirement in that one or more management representatives may be designated. Essentially, this person or persons will act as coordinators for the EMS. In a large or complex organization, there may be a management representative for each department or area. The standard only requires that the designee(s) have clearly defined roles and authority for implementing and maintaining the EMS.

## IMPLEMENTATION

### Define Responsibilities

The first step in defining environmental responsibilities is to identify the job functions that could have an impact on environmental management. Consider all aspects of the EMS. Besides the obvious roles of environmental professionals and managers, many others in the organization may need to be included in the EMS, such as

- Engineers in development and production support functions
- Manufacturing operators
- Laboratory and other testing personnel

- Managers who need to consider environmental aspects when making business decisions
- Mechanics who maintain and calibrate testing and control equipment
- Purchasing personnel who deal with suppliers that may have an environmental impact on the organization

It may be tempting to try to limit the EMS, especially if the business is focused on achieving registration. If, however, environmental and business improvement are the ultimate goals of the organization, most or all employees should be considered a part of the EMS and the larger business management system. In any case, well-defined responsibilities are critical to business success. If you are defining or upgrading this aspect of the EMS, it makes sense to apply these same criteria to all business functions. Clearly defined roles will add business value for quality, environmental, safety, and all other parts of the overall management system.

Although it seems very basic, poorly defined responsibilities are a common system weakness. Think of your own organization. When something does not get done, it is often because everyone thought someone else was supposed to do it. Even when responsibilities are fairly well defined, problems can occur if authority is not clear. This is especially true for nonstandard or abnormal operations. It is therefore critical that all members of the organization understand who can make decisions and take action.

A common way to document responsibilities and authorities is to write job descriptions for each job title or function that could impact the environment. Many businesses already have some form of job or position descriptions. To assess whether these are adequate, ask these questions:

- Are all jobs or positions defined?
- Does each job description include environmental aspects of the job?
- Are the descriptions up to date?
- Are they available to employees and clearly understood?

As I have conducted management system audits for different companies, these are the weaknesses that are most commonly identified. The question, "How are your responsibilities documented?" is usually answered with a sheepish look as the auditee scrambles through files to find a job description—written in 1979 for some particular initiative and never looked at again!

Formal job descriptions are not the only way to describe responsibilities. In preparation for ISO 9001, some companies describe the critical functions of each position within a single document, in many cases a part of the quality manual. A single paragraph or short series of bulleted points for each position may be sufficient. My own company, and many others, stay away from separate, detailed descriptions altogether and rely on operating procedures to define specific responsibilities and authorities. Any of these methods can work, depending on the organization's own culture and goals.

## KEY TO SUCCESS

Once roles are well defined and documented in some way, you need to ensure that they are clearly understood by everyone in the organization. This is a critical success factor. The job descriptions or procedures must be available and familiar to each person affected by them. If responsibilities were poorly defined in the past, it may even make sense to hold special training sessions to review newly documented role descriptions.

If writing or upgrading some sort of job description, people should be involved in defining their own positions. Management may even be surprised by the breadth of some self-defined job descriptions. Many job functions expand over time, especially in these times of lean organizations, and management is not always aware of the additional responsibilities that employees have picked up. Writing and reviewing job descriptions together can itself be an improvement mechanism for the organization. The end result should be an organization in which each person understands his or her role and the extent of his or her authority, as well as the general roles of others.

Some organizations go even further to ensure that environmental responsibilities are taken seriously. Two companies, Dow Chemical and Westvaco, have included an environmental category in each employee's annual job appraisal. Because of this, environmental responsibilities are seen as an integral part of each person's job. For this approach to be successful, employees have to understand exactly how their jobs impact the environment. Chapter 11 discusses this type of awareness training.

During an audit or assessment, defined responsibilities are evaluated in two ways. The standard's requirements can be directly audited by asking people about their responsibilities and comparing their answers to the documented roles. Additionally, other nonconformances found by an audit will have resulted from a lack of well-defined responsibilities. Sometimes these are obvious and are noted by the auditor, but in other cases, a more extensive root-cause analysis, conducted by the organization itself, will reveal the connection (see Chapter 18). Either way, it is clear that poorly defined roles can lead to all sorts of problems.

### Provide Adequate Resources

A related cause of problems in many organizations is a lack of resources. The standard requires that management ensure that adequate resources are available for the EMS, but this is not always easy to do. This requirement includes all types of resources—money, time, people, and technology. It is management's direct responsibility to understand what resources are necessary for routine operations as well as special projects and to ensure that those resources are available.

The availability of resources is of particular importance when establishing objectives and targets and setting plans to meet them. No organization will have the resources to achieve all that it wants immediately. Objectives and targets must be prioritized to use available resources wisely.

This means that establishing objectives and programs should not be the responsibility of the environmental professionals alone. Management, representing all critical functions of the organization, must be involved in determining priorities and developing programs or plans. This is the only way that resource needs can be fully understood and met.

Once again, this requirement is most commonly audited indirectly. Although records will indicate whether resource issues were considered during planning activities, the real evidence of adequate resources is that objectives and targets are routinely being met. If resource availability changes because of unexpected organizational changes or capital expenditures, then programs and plans should be revised to reflect the actual resources available. Records of this sort of program review will assure auditors that resources are being managed proactively.

### Designate Management Representative(s)

The management representative requirement is a familiar one to those organizations with ISO 9000 experience, although it contains some minor differences from ISO 14001. While ISO 9001 and 9002 specifically require that a single person be responsible for the quality system, ISO 14001 allows for more than one management representative. The main reason for this flexibility is to permit large or complex organizations to have multiple EMS coordinators. It remains good practice to designate one person who is ultimately accountable for the implementation and maintenance of the EMS, even if there are multiple area coordinators. Doing so helps to prevent things from slipping through the cracks because of a lack of assigned responsibility and authority.

## KEY TO SUCCESS

One of the most difficult and critical decisions to be made in the course of implementing an EMS is the choice of management representative. The role of this person is pivotal to the system's success or failure. A well-suited management representative can help to ensure that systems are focused on business needs and that the work of implementing an effective system gets done in a timely manner. A management representative who is poorly suited for the role can hold up effective implementation of the system for many months or even years.

I assisted about ten different sites within one company in their ISO 9000 implementation. Of these sites, the smallest had about 20 employees. Typically, such a small site has a much easier time implementing a management system simply because its organization and procedures are much less complex than larger sites. This particular site, however, ended up being the last in the company to become registered to ISO 9002, and the delay was due entirely to the lack of an appropriate management representative. At the beginning of their effort, the site's manager told me that they needed to hire a new process engineer anyway, so whomever they hired would also act as management representative.

It was more than six months before they finally found an appropriate candidate and filled the position. In the meantime, their ISO 9000 efforts floundered. Then, when the new engineer had been brought on board, he found his hands full with the backlog of process engineering work to be done. The pressure involved in restarting the ISO 9000 work was immense. He knew almost nothing about the organization and had to start from scratch in understanding the internal processes and practices before he could help to document them. He had also missed attending the early training sessions along with his coworkers, so his background was different than theirs. Eventually, he left the company, and the site was again left without a management representative. Once again, the managers assigned the task to a new person, the recently hired laboratory supervisor. He struggled with some of the same issues as his predecessor, although he was eventually able to lead the site through a successful registration.

To avoid difficulties, it is crucial for you to understand the role of the management representative and the kinds of skills necessary for success in that role. Anyone in the organization can act as the management representative; the standard doesn't require a particular level or functional role. The best choice is not always the most obvious one. Several DuPont sites had management representatives who were production operators on special assignment. They were well-qualified people who had the right sets of skills and the motivation to do the job effectively. The personality and skills of the particular person selected are often more important than his or her title or position in the organization. The particular skills, capabilities, and resources an effective management representative needs are summarized in the following paragraphs.

**Adequate Available Time** This is one of the most important criteria. Before appointing a management representative, management must have a realistic understanding of the time that will be required to fulfill the role. A survey of ISO 9000 registered sites and businesses within DuPont showed that the management representatives spent an average of 80 percent of their time implementing the quality system. A full third of the sites surveyed said that, prior to registration, their management representatives spent 100 percent of their time on implementation. ISO 14001 preparation could be even more demanding because of the extensive planning requirements.

**Communication Skills** The management representative must be able to communicate effectively to both higher and lower levels within the organization. He or she must have the confidence and skills to communicate clearly with upper management, especially when problems occur or additional resources are needed. In addition, the management representative must be someone who has credibility among all employees to enable him or her to communicate effectively within the organization's various levels and functions.

**Authority** The standard specifically states that the management representative must have the authority to carry out his or her defined role. This means authority in a positive sense—the capability of making decisions and taking action. The management representative's authority is not necessarily a function of his or her position in the organization; authority can also be granted by those at higher levels. If the management representative does not already have authority by virtue of occupying a high-level position, then it must be clearly communicated to all employees that this person has been given authority by management to get this job done. In addition, some people are simply more comfortable with authority than others. Authority is of no use if the person is afraid of using it.

***Organizational Skills*** The same skills needed for effective project planning and implementation are needed to implement or upgrade an EMS. The management representative must be able to coordinate and direct a large amount of work taking place all over the organization. In one small chemical plant that I did consulting work for, the management representative was an engineer who was very intelligent, hardworking, and easy to get along with. Unfortunately, he did not possess the organizational or communication skills needed to do this job effectively. He was overwhelmed, the plant was frustrated, and he ended up leaving the company for a different job. Implementing an EMS is an enormous, ongoing job that requires strong leadership and coordination skills.

***Broad Knowledge of the Organization*** Although the management representative will not actually do all of the implementation work alone (see Chapter 22), he or she will have to coordinate work throughout the entire organization. This means that, to be effective, a management representative must have a broad knowledge of the business and its various functional groups or departments. Additionally, he or she must have a good understanding of the organization's culture to make sure that the management system adds value instead of just bureaucracy.

Of course, the management representative must also have at least a general knowledge of the business's environmental impacts and the applicable regulatory requirements. However, he or she does not need to be a regulatory expert. In fact, that kind of in-depth knowledge of one facet of environmental management can sometimes prevent someone from viewing the EMS more broadly.

It will not always be possible to find a management representative with all of these characteristics, but you can compare potential candidates against these criteria to try to find the optimal person to coordinate your EMS. Many companies choose someone who is already in a similar role—the environmental coordinator or environmental manager, for instance. This works well so long as the person has the kind of skills discussed above and can maintain a broad focus, beyond traditional regulatory considerations. Because of their environmental background and responsibilities, such people are usually well suited to the kinds of decisions and work needed to pull the EMS together.

I know of several companies that have chosen their ISO 9000 management representatives to coordinate the EMS implementation. This can also work well, given certain conditions. The quality system should already be well established and functioning smoothly enough to allow the management representative adequate time to devote to the EMS.

The ISO 9000 coordinator will have a very thorough understanding of the basic management system elements, many of which can be expanded to include environmental activities. This is definitely a benefit to the company; however, the EMS management representative will also need to have a basic understanding of the organization's environmental issues. He or she should have some initial training in the regulatory framework under which the organization works. Beyond that formal training, the management representative should be able to rely on an environmental expert within the organization to assist him or her in matters related directly to environmental issues. Finally, the management representative should be involved in the early planning stages of the EMS—especially the identification of environmental aspects and evaluation of significant impacts—to gain a more in-depth understanding of the company's own environmental issues.

In the training courses that my company conducts, people frequently ask whether they should hire an "expert" to be their management representative and to implement their EMS. This is seldom a wise choice. Many of the course participants who ask this question seem to feel that the most critical skill for the management representative is an in-depth understanding of the requirements of ISO 14001. In reality, it is much easier for someone within the organization to learn about ISO 14001 than it is for an outsider to learn about your organization's unique culture and practices.

 The most effective management representative will come from within your own company—someone who knows the people and understands the working environment. The goal is to upgrade existing management systems to meet the ISO 14001 standard and meet your own business needs, not to implement a generic ISO 14001 system.

If the chosen management representative comes from within the organization and meets the general criteria discussed above, there are several ways to gain the expertise needed in ISO 14001. The management representative can attend training courses and conferences, read books and newsletters, and network with other EMS coordinators both within and outside the company. The organization can also use a consultant to assist with its EMS implementation. Keep in mind, however, that an outside consultant cannot replace a competent management representative. The consultant's role is to provide guidance and expertise, but the organization will still need to do much of the work itself to define best practices.

# CHAPTER 11

# TRAINING, AWARENESS, AND COMPETENCE

## ISO 14001 REQUIREMENTS*

ISO 14001, section 4.4.2, Training, Awareness and Competence, requires the following:

> The organization shall identify training needs. It shall require that all personnel whose work may create a significant impact upon the environment have received appropriate training.
>
> It shall establish and maintain procedures to make its employees or members at each relevant function and level aware of
>
> a) the importance of conformance with the environmental policy and procedures and with the requirements of the environmental management system;
>
> b) the significant environmental impacts, actual or potential, of their work activities and the environmental benefits of improved personal performance;
>
> c) their roles and responsibilities in achieving conformance with the environmental policy and procedures and with the requirements of the environmental management system, including emergency preparedness and response requirements;
>
> d) the potential consequences of departure from specified operating procedures.

*© International Organization for Standardization. All rights reserved.

> Personnel performing the tasks which can cause significant environmental impacts shall be competent on the basis of appropriate education, training and/or experience.

## INTERPRETATION

This section is an extension of the previous one, which required defined responsibilities. It basically requires that all personnel whose work might affect the environment are properly qualified, trained, and adequately aware of the environmental management system.

*Training,* as used in the standard, is interpreted broadly to include all forms of training and does not necessarily refer to traditional classroom training. On-the-job training, job experience, and background education are all acceptable types of training.

The first sentence of this section summarizes the entire scope of its requirements: identify training needs. This means that qualifications and training requirements should be determined and documented for every job type that could have a significant impact on the environment. Much of the rest of the section expands on this basic requirement.

Subsections *a* through *d* expand on this requirement by describing the particular types of awareness training that are necessary. Essentially, these sections state that any employee whose work has the potential to impact the environment should be aware of the EMS and its policies and procedures as well as the responsibilities of his or her own job. Specifically, employees must understand how their jobs could affect the environment, what procedures must be followed, and how the environment could be affected if procedures are not followed.

The last sentence tends to cause some anxiety, but its meaning is really quite straightforward: all personnel whose jobs can affect the environment should be competent. This does not mean that the organization must set up complex testing methods to determine competence. It means that you must determine what qualifications are necessary for each job, including education, experience, and training. Then you must ensure that each employee meets the qualification requirements for his or her own job.

## IMPLEMENTATION

### Determine Scope of EMS

Figure 11-1 shows the major steps in implementing and maintaining an effective training system. The first step is the same as that for defining responsibilities: determine the scope of the EMS. The standard

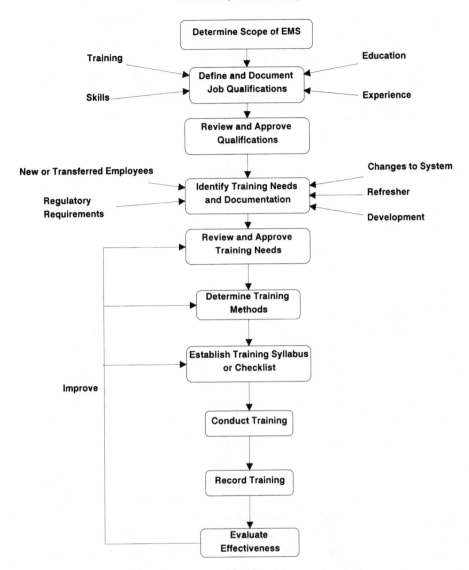

■ **FIGURE 11-1.** Implementing a Training System

specifically says that this section is applicable only to those employees "whose work may cause a significant impact on the environment." This determination will be based, in part, on your previous analysis of significant impacts. Note also the use of the word "may." Both potential and actual impacts must be considered.

As with defining responsibilities, defining the scope of training in a broad way is best for business improvement. Ensuring that employees are properly qualified just makes good business sense.

In defining this scope, do not forget about contractors. If their jobs could significantly impact the environment, then their qualifications and training requirements must be defined just as those for other employees. In this case, you should require that any contracting organization meet the same management system requirements that your own employees must meet, leaving it up to the contractor's management to define their own training needs.

The core requirement for training is to identify training needs and qualifications for all jobs within the scope of your EMS. Many of my clients have found this to be a difficult task, usually because training needs have been poorly defined in the past. Industrial plants frequently have well-defined qualifications and training programs for skilled operators but little or no defined training requirements for others in the organization.

### Define Job Qualifications

Begin by defining qualifications. There are three general approaches that can be taken. Frequently, top management asks that each supervisor or manager define the qualification requirements for each person in his or her group. In other cases, the responsibility is passed along directly to the employees themselves, and each person is asked to define the requirements for his or her own job. A third method is for a representative group of managers to define categories of job types and then to develop qualifications for each that can be applied across the organization. This third method is likely to result in the least amount of paperwork and the best overall descriptions, although it requires greater initial effort to bring a group together and work as a team.

Regardless of the methodology used, everyone in the organization should have a chance to at least review the qualifications for his or her own job. As in defining responsibilities, this is the best source for accurate and realistic information.

As a general rule of thumb, include the qualifications that would be used if a new person had to be hired for the job. Criteria should include level and type of education, amount and type of experience, previous training, and special skills. Be careful not to be so specific that you will have trouble complying with the qualification requirements in the future. A common pitfall is to describe the qualifications of the current person in the job rather than the minimum qualifications that would be acceptable. Qualifications can be quite flexible. For example, a production supervisor's job could require a high school degree plus ten years of production experience, a two-year college degree related to the field plus five years of production experience, or a four-year degree in the field plus two years of experience. Remember that you are defining your own qualifications. They will be unique for your business.

Once qualifications have been defined and reviewed by the employees whose jobs are affected by them, they should be approved in some way. Chapter 14, "Document Control," provides detailed information on how to accomplish this. For the qualifications to remain useful it is important that they be documented, approved, and dated. There are no requirements for formatting; qualifications can be documented in whatever form works for your own organization. Some companies include job descriptions (roles and responsibilities) and qualifications in the same document.

If your organization already has some sort of defined job qualifications, the task is even easier. Simply review existing qualifications to ensure that they

- Cover the entire scope of the EMS,
- Include any particular requirements related to environmental skills or knowledge,
- Are up to date, and
- Are approved and controlled.

### Identify Training Needs

With qualifications defined, reviewed, documented, and approved, the next step is to define training needs. Various situations where training could be necessary include:

- New employees
- Transferred employees or cross-training opportunities
- Ongoing development
- Refresher training
- New or revised procedures, processes, and systems
- Regulatory requirements

Remember that ISO 14001 lists some very specific awareness training requirements in relation to the EMS.

Once again, specific training needs should be identified for each unique job function and could be developed by managers, supervisors, or employees.

✓ Do not forget to include training needs for supervisor and manager positions. Too often, training is focused solely on lower levels of personnel, but anyone whose job could impact the environment must be included as a part of the training system.

For each job function, consider the skills and knowledge needed to do the job. Use whatever process worked well for defining qualifications, and once again include input from all affected employees. Alternatively, you could define qualifications and training needs simultaneously. The process depends entirely on your own organization—how people work best and how well qualifications and training needs have been identified in the past. If you already have these requirements defined and documented, the whole process will be reduced to a review and update of existing documents.

Like qualifications, training needs must be approved and documented. They could be separate documents or a part of some other existing documentation. Qualifications and training needs can also be documented together for each job function. Keep in mind that there is no specified format. What is important is that the system you develop works for your business.

### Determine Training Methods

The next step is to determine the training methods that will work best for your identified training needs. Different types of training may be necessary, based on your goals. Training can provide information, help people to acquire or improve skills, and build awareness. Various training methodologies can be used for each of these goals.

Generally, training comes in several forms:

- On-the-job or demonstration training
- Internal classroom training
- Commercially available training

Choose the type of training that is best suited to the audience and the knowledge or skills being taught. If you decide to design your own classroom training, there are numerous instructional approaches that can be used. Many excellent books, journals, and training courses are available to assist in selecting appropriate training methodologies.

### Establish a Training Syllabus or Checklist

Once the general type of training has been determined, the next step is to establish a training syllabus or checklist for each training need. This should be done even for those needs that you will fulfill with outside training. A checklist of critical items to be included can help you to evaluate commercial training offerings.

If you plan to conduct your own classroom training, you will need a detailed syllabus and training plan. The plan should define learning objectives, including whatever specific skills, knowledge, and/or awareness the training is meant to provide. The syllabus can provide a detailed account of how you will provide these. In many cases, an internal training resource person will be developing the syllabus and course plan. If your organization does not have those kind of resources, you may need to rely more heavily on external training.

Although on-the-job training can work very well in certain situations, it must be adequately defined and documented. A checklist is a simple yet effective tool that can be used for both purposes. The blank checklist serves to define the required knowledge and/or skills that the trainee must gain. As the training period proceeds, the trainer (usually an experienced worker or supervisor) fills in the checklist to track progress. Afterwards, the completed checklist becomes a record of the skills and knowledge attained, the trainer(s) involved, and the dates that the various elements of training were completed.

### Provide Training

Once the training needs and programs have been fully defined and documented, compare the identified needs with the skills and knowledge of the people in those jobs. If there are any gaps between needs and present skills, these will have to be filled with training. In most cases, it is adequate to indicate that the people who currently hold each position are qualified for their jobs based on past experience. The exception is training that is particular to any new or revised aspects of the EMS. At a minimum, you will have to conduct awareness training to ensure that all employees understand the environmental policies, objectives, and significant impacts of the organization and of their own jobs.

Most organizations will need to expend quite a bit of effort to meet the standard's requirements for environmental awareness training. I have yet to find an organization that had done this type of extensive training prior to ISO 14001. Since the standard requires awareness of the environmental impacts of each job, a single overview for all employees will not be sufficient.

There are several ways to accomplish this goal. You could create customized training sessions for various departments within the organization based on the unique environmental impacts of each. An alternative is to provide training for managers and supervisors and require that they train the people in their own groups, as appropriate, based on the environmental impacts of each group.

✓ Perhaps the most effective approach is a combination of these other approaches. The environmental management representative, along with management, could develop an overview training session that covers some basic information about the organization's EMS and its significant environmental impacts. Following this overview session, each department or group manager could conduct additional focused sessions to cover the environmental impacts of each job type. The defined job descriptions can provide a basis for these more detailed discussions.

### Record Training

A critical component of any management system element is good recordkeeping. Any training conducted should also be recorded. Records can be kept in any way that suits your organization. I have seen some excellent training-record databases in use. Other businesses use paper records quite effectively.

Use whatever works best for you, with one caveat.

Do not include training records in personnel files. Many companies start out this way and later realize that the records are inaccessible to auditors, other employees, and anyone else since they are a part of confidential files! The records must be accessible to be a useful part of the system. Chapter 19, "Records," gives additional guidance on the details of an effective records system.

### Evaluate Effectiveness and Improve

Finally, build a mechanism into your training system for continual improvement. Consider how you will evaluate the effectiveness of your training programs. A periodic review of qualifications and training needs works well, but the ultimate test of training effectiveness is the use of the new knowledge or skills in the workplace. Some highly skilled jobs will require competence testing immediately after training and refresher training programs at defined intervals. For other jobs, an evaluation six months after the training program can help to identify any gaps. Have the employees retained the knowledge and skills learned? Have new methods been applied correctly?

A review of root causes and corrective actions (see Chapter 18, "Nonconformance and Corrective and Preventive Action") can reveal how many incidents or nonconformances are attributable to a lack of training. Many evaluation and review techniques are possible. Define yours and then act on the results to improve the system.

You may have noticed that the process of establishing a training system fits the Plan-Do-Check-Act model. Much of the effort is spent early, in the Plan phase: defining scope, establishing job qualifications, and identifying training needs. This investment of time should result in less time spent later correcting problems that result from inadequate or ineffective training.

All of these elements of the training system should be described in a procedure. Besides being a requirement of the standard, a procedure is the best way to define and describe all of the pieces that make up your total environmental training program. Describe the main components of your system—qualifications, training needs, syllabi, checklists, records, review—in a simple procedure, and provide references to related documents.

Although ISO 14001's requirements deal only with environmental training, any kind of training program will include these same basic elements. It makes sense to establish one training system that meets your business needs and to use that system to identify, conduct, and record all training. If necessary, you can indicate quality-related or environmental-related training needs with special symbols on your single set of training documents. In the case of training, there is no benefit to maintaining separate systems.

# COMMUNICATION

### ISO 14001 REQUIREMENTS*

ISO 14001, section 4.4.3, Communication, requires the following:

With regard to its environmental aspects and environmental management system, the organization shall establish and maintain procedures for

a) internal communication between the various levels and functions of the organization;

b) receiving, documenting and responding to relevant communication from external interested parties

The organization shall consider processes for external communication on its significant environmental aspects and record its decision.

## INTERPRETATION

This section is fairly straightforward, requiring defined processes for both internal and external communication. *Internal communication* refers to methods of keeping employees within the organization up to date on relevant environmental issues. The Training section already requires initial awareness training on the environmental policy, significant impacts, and environmental management system. Communication requirements deal with ongoing efforts to keep employees informed about the system and the environmental aspects of the business.

*© International Organization for Standardization. All rights reserved.

The requirements for *external communication* are more limited. Organizations are only required to have a process in place for responding to any inquiries received from interested parties. Remember that the definition of "interested party" is quite broad in the standard, encompassing anyone affected by or concerned with your environmental performance (see Chapter 8). The standard requires that you have a defined process in place for responding to such inquiries and that you keep records of these communications.

Note that this definition of interested parties includes regulatory and community bodies. This means that your procedures must include mechanisms for communicating with local authorities, for emergency planning with the local community, and for maintaining communication with state and federal agencies.

Finally, this section of ISO 14001 includes a rather unusual requirement in the last paragraph. You're required to *consider* broader external communications on your significant aspects and to record your decision. You could consider this and decide not to pursue further proactive communications. The requirement seems pretty odd unless you understand the background. It results from extensive debates within TC 207 regarding public reporting. Since EMAS has very detailed and rigorous requirements for public reporting, most European delegates wanted some similar requirement in ISO 14001 to make the standard more compatible with the EU's regulation. The United States and others were adamantly against any kind of additional reporting requirements in an international standard. The result is the requirement only to consider further external communications and to record your own decision.

## IMPLEMENTATION

### Internal Communication

Most organizations already have some internal environmental communication processes in place. DuPont, for example, uses E-mail, environmental incident reports, company newsletters, regulatory bulletins, an annual progress report, and other mechanisms to keep its employees regularly informed of environmental information. As in most companies, this occurs as an integral part of normal business communications. The missing piece is likely to be defined procedures.

If you already have communication methods in place, your task is to ensure that these methods are effective and then to define and document them. The simplest way to find out if they are effective is to test them. Ask a random sample of employees from a cross section of the organization about some recent changes to the EMS, past environmental improvements, or other environmentally related information that you think they should know given the existing communication processes. If everyone seems well informed, just document your processes. If your questions are met with blank stares, you need to make some improvements before you document existing systems.

If existing internal communication is lacking, consider what types of communication are most effective within your own company. Is E-mail the system people rely on most heavily? Do employees tend to pay more attention to paper memos? Is critical information commonly transmitted through each supervisor during daily or weekly meetings? Consider your own culture and environment and choose the methods that will work best for you. Specifically, you want to establish means for communicating the following:

- Revised objectives, targets, or programs
- Changes to EMS procedures and practices
- How process or product changes affect environmental aspects and significant impacts
- Regulatory changes
- Environmental problems or incidents

Most likely, you will use several communication methods, depending on the urgency and importance of the information.

You must also consider who needs to know these various types of environmental information. While a lack of communication is certainly a problem, inundating every employee with excess information is not the solution, and it could even make things worse. When constantly presented with irrelevant information, employees may begin simply to ignore that information (remember "the boy who cried wolf"?). Your goal should be to ensure that those who need environmental information get it or know where to find it. Some, like environmental professionals, will need to be included in all communications. Others, like operators or managers, may need to hear only those pieces of information that are relevant to their jobs.

After determining what your processes are, document them in a simple procedure. Describe what types of information you communicate to which audiences and what methods you use.

✓ Alternatively, you may not need a dedicated communications procedure if your communication practices are adequately described throughout other procedures. You might have existing procedures for incident reporting, daily and weekly group meetings, document control, and tracking regulations. If each of these adequately addresses communication

**108** ■ IMPLEMENTATION AND OPERATION

aspects, then there is no need for a new procedure. Your EMS manual or other system description can simply reference these procedures. Chapter 13, "EMS Documentation," has additional tips for effective documentation.

### External Communication

You can approach external communication in the same way. Look at your current practices and determine whether they are effective. In the case of external communication, the scope is much narrower. How do you respond to outside inquiries regarding environmental issues?

One company I worked with had never really considered this activity as a distinct process. The company's informal policy was that whomever received a request for information forwarded it to whoever they thought could best respond. That was it. Although the company never perceived this as a problem, there were no records of any inquiries or responses, no documentation, and no standard policies on how to respond. Various people in the organization could have been responding to outside inquiries in vastly different ways. Some inquiries may never have received responses. There was no way to tell.

This is why the standard requires an established, defined process. Contrary to popular opinion, ISO's goal is not to create as much paperwork as possible but to help organizations manage their systems more effectively. If you do not have a defined process for responding to environmental (or other) inquiries, you will need to establish one.

 It's a good idea to designate a single contact point for all inquiries. That person can still pass inquiries along to the people best qualified to respond to them, but having a single contact ensures that records are kept of all inquiries and that each is responded to appropriately and in a timely manner.

A simple log can be used to record inquiries and track responses. If you get requests for information frequently, you can also establish a standard letter that can be easily customized for responses. Many companies have a brochure or annual environmental report that is enclosed with any responses.

Finally, you need to consider more extensive external communications. This means that the environmental manager or coordinator should meet with the top management to decide what its policies on proactive communication will be. Many U.S. companies send annual environmental (or safety, health, and environmental) reports to a wide variety of stakeholders, as described in Chapter 5, "Environmental Policy." If you already have extensive mechanisms in place for external communication, then you have already made this decision and you should simply describe your practices in your procedures.

At a minimum, any U.S. company that manufactures or handles hazardous materials is already required to report detailed emission data to the EPA through SARA Title III, which is then reported to the public. Some state regulatory agencies have additional public reporting requirements. Although U.S. industry is already required to make this type of information public, many companies have initiated their own external communication programs to provide a more positive type of publicity. Newspaper headlines featuring SARA Title III emissions numbers rarely focus on environmental improvements made!

Once again, once you have determined what your practices should be, document them in a simple, straightforward procedure. The procedure should include responsibilities, critical steps, reference to records kept, and a description of the major external communication mechanisms. If you decide *not* to provide more extensive external communications, state so specifically, making it clear that you have *considered* doing so, as the standard requires.

Unlike most other ISO 14001 requirements, there are no corresponding ISO 9001 requirements for communication. From that perspective, little integration of systems is necessary or possible. However, you can still ensure that your environmental communication processes are an integral part of overall business communication processes. As mentioned earlier, you do not need a separate "ISO 14001 Communications" procedure. In fact, management systems are most effective when they are seamlessly built into existing organizational structures. That way, people do not have to worry about doing the "environmental part" of their job and the "safety part" and the "quality part." It's all one job within one system.

# ENVIRONMENTAL MANAGEMENT SYSTEM DOCUMENTATION

### ISO 14001 REQUIREMENTS*

ISO 14001, section 4.4.4, Environmental Management System Documentation, requires the following:

> The organization shall establish and maintain information, in paper or electronic form, to
>
> a) describe the core elements of the environmental management system and their interaction;
> b) provide direction to related documentation.

## INTERPRETATION

That's it. Fewer than 30 words to describe the requirements for documentation. Since many people assume documentation is the central purpose of ISO management system standards, this brevity may come as a surprise. Actually, the concise wording is deliberate and makes a very important point: most of the decisions concerning EMS documentation are left up to you. Each business can use its own unique way of describing its systems.

*© International Organization for Standardization. All rights reserved.

Although it emphasizes flexibility, the section does state a few explicit requirements. First, you are required to document "the core elements" of your EMS. This can be interpreted to include all of the areas covered by ISO 14001. This documentation must describe the EMS elements, explain how those elements interact within the comprehensive system, and provide references to more detailed documentation, where appropriate.

What is documentation? While it may sound like a simple concept, many people struggle with an exact definition once they begin to implement their system. In this context, documentation provides a written description of your EMS. As the standard states, it can be in paper or electronic form. Further, documentation can take many varied formats, including procedures, instructions, flowcharts, checklists, plans, standards, and manuals. It's up to you to decide how you will describe your system. Typically, a business ends up with a variety of different types of documents, which together define its EMS.

The Annex to ISO 14001 contains a few very interesting points of interpretation that further highlight the degree of choice in documentation. The Annex specifically states that your EMS documentation may be integrated with documentation of other systems. It further states that a single EMS manual is not required by ISO 14001. This is an especially interesting point, since the 1994 revisions to ISO 9001, 9002, and 9003 now require a quality system manual as an essential piece of documentation. Prior to 1994, many ISO 9000 registrars were requiring their client companies to submit a manual even though it was not a requirement of the standard. It still remains to be seen whether EMS registrars will place the additional requirement of a manual on their clients.

## IMPLEMENTATION

For any business implementing a management system, one of the biggest challenges is effective documentation. The system must be adequately documented not only to meet the requirements of the standard but also to ensure that environmentally related work is done consistently and effectively. If you are considering registration, the third-party auditors will base much of their assessment on your documented system.

A lot of emphasis has been placed on documentation, but it does not have to be the overwhelming task that people fear. During the last phase of ISO 14001 approval, after two years of careful negotiation and delicate international compromise, the Draft International Standard (DIS) was circulated for balloting. One member of the U.S. Technical Advisory Group voted "no" on the standard, but his was the only no vote of the 128 U.S. votes. One of the comments he made to support his vote was that docu-

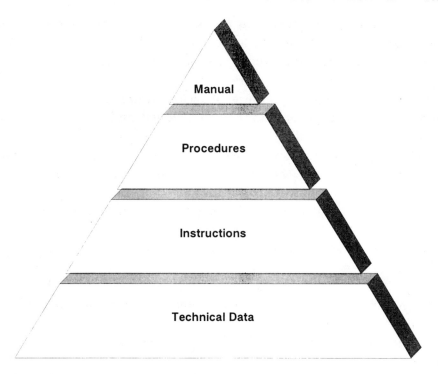

■ **FIGURE 13-1.** Documentation Pyramid Model

mentation and document-control requirements would create "a paperwork nightmare" for U.S. businesses. It's a shame that so many companies believe this myth.

Documenting a system may be a big job if little or no documentation already exists; however, you do not need to develop complex and cumbersome documentation just for the purpose of ISO 14001. Unfortunately, many businesses have taken this approach with ISO 9001 and now have paper-heavy systems that get in the way of business improvement. If done effectively, the process of documenting your system can add great value to your business rather than creating a bureaucratic nightmare.

### A Documentation Model

Although there are no specific requirements for the format of your documented EMS, there is a basic system model that has become widely accepted as best practice. It describes the documentation of an effective management system in the shape of a pyramid (see Figure 13-1). In this type of model, documentation and the amount of detail increase as you progress down the pyramid.

At the very tip of the pyramid is a manual or similar type of document. This is a brief document, typically 20 to 40 pages, that summarizes the management system. The manual is quite general, provides an overview of the entire system, and references more detailed documents. Although ISO 14001 does not require a manual, it is still a very effective way to describe the overall system and will work well for most companies.

Procedures are the next level of documentation shown in the pyramid. These are more detailed than the manual and describe the basic flow of materials or information in a work process. Work processes include running a manufacturing operation, ordering supplies, identifying training needs, or any other activities that affect the environment. ISO 14001 specifically requires procedures in many areas.

The most detailed type of documents in a management system are sometimes referred to as instructions, although they could take many different forms, such as checklists, flowcharts, syllabi, or detailed forms. These are the step-by-step instructions that are needed for some tasks. Instructions are needed when it is critical that a certain job be done a certain way every time. Not all jobs or work processes need this level of detail.

Finally, the pyramid is supported by a collection of technical data—all sorts of information of both internal and external origin. In an EMS, these could include regulations, standards, computer and equipment operating manuals, detailed product specifications, and other relevant information.

Although not every area of your organization will need every level of documentation, you do need to consider each of these types of documents for all areas of your EMS. Remember that your own documentation does not have to fit the model described here. You may refer to these documents by different names, have additional levels, or even take an entirely different approach. Throughout the process of implementing and documenting an EMS, remember that the standard is not prescriptive. How you document your system is for your company alone to decide.

One small British business run by a husband-and-wife team got registered to ISO 9002 with some very unusual documentation. They were in the business of testing fire extinguishers. Most of their documented system consisted of two index card files. One contained cards listing individual customers and their requirements. The other listed the types of equipment and how to test each. This was all the documentation they needed to be effective. Remember that you have the flexibility to do what is right for your business.

### How to Get Started

A common approach for companies preparing for ISO 9001 or ISO 14001 registration is to start by writing a manual. This is also an *ineffec-*

*tive* approach most of the time. The manual is supposed to be a summary of the system, and few organizations already have a complete and comprehensive management system in place. Anyone who has started out by trying to document this incomplete system in a manual soon finds out that it's like writing a work of fiction! A lot of work and effort goes into trying to describe system elements that have not yet been developed.

The best way to start is to find out where you are starting from. A comprehensive initial assessment of the EMS will help to identify which elements you already have in place and which elements are missing or need improvement. This type of assessment could be conducted by your own trained auditors, as a part of the EMS audits required by ISO 14001 (see Chapter 20). If you have not yet trained internal auditors, you could ask an outside party, such as a consultant, corporate audit function, or auditors from another facility in your company, to conduct the audit for you. The gaps identified by this initial assessment will tell you where to focus your efforts.

In each area where improvement is needed, begin by analyzing work processes. If, for example, the audit shows gaps in your emergency response procedures, you may need to look at the processes of identifying potential incidents and emergencies, defining and documenting emergency plans, and testing the plans.

✓ Whatever the work processes are, the first step is to get together the people who are involved. This is critical to all documentation efforts: the people developing the documents should be the people who actually do the work and use the documentation. If different shifts are involved, representatives from each shift should be included. This may seem costly, but the payback is that you develop accurate and effective procedures *the first time around*.

Once a team is assembled, its members need to map out what they do and agree on how the process currently works. Flowcharting is a valuable tool at this stage. You do not need to use process mapping experts or complex flowcharting rules involving dozens of different symbols. Simple block flow diagrams will work fine. The key is to write down the critical steps that occur and who is responsible for each one. It is also helpful to note where there are existing documents and records. A sample flowchart for the process of responding to inquiries from external interested parties is shown in Figure 13-2. Note that responsibilities are shown for each step and that records are indicated on the right-hand side of the chart.

**116** ■ IMPLEMENTATION AND OPERATION

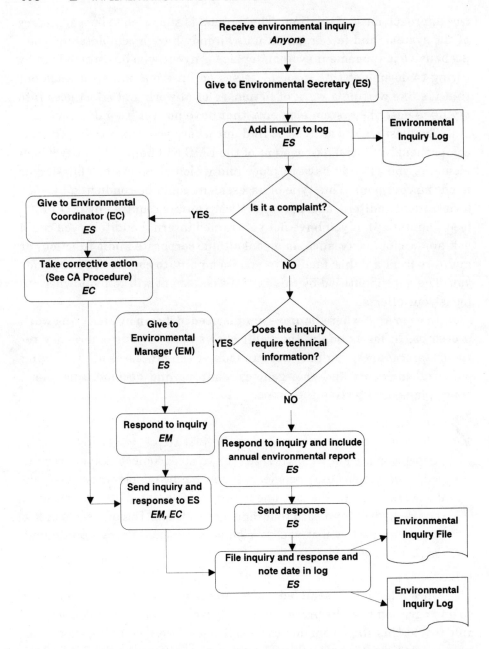

■ **FIGURE 13-2.** Sample Process Flow Diagram: Responding to External Inquiries

If the audit has identified areas where there are no existing practices, then the task is a little more difficult, but it still follows the same basic steps. For example, maybe your audit shows that you do not have any environmental objectives or goals and have never defined a process for developing them. Once again, the first step is to get the right people together—in this case, the organization's environmental professionals plus management from all critical areas of the organization. Using the ISO 14001 requirements as a baseline, discuss and determine how your own business will go about establishing environmental objectives. Decide who should be involved, what criteria will be used to define them, how they will be documented and kept up to date, and how often they will be reviewed and revised. Use a simple flowchart to work through and document the practices to which you all agree.

Once the work is flowcharted, look for areas where the process can be simplified or improved. Whether this is a brand new process for you or something you have been doing for years, there will probably be opportunities to streamline and simplify it. Often, just drawing a flowchart of the process makes improvement opportunities obvious.

One group I worked in was having problems with long response times for customer inquiries. We assembled all the different people involved and flowcharted the processes for responding to customer requests. The resulting diagram was a mess, with many different people involved and lines crisscrossing all over the chart! We immediately saw ways to simplify the process and ended up reducing our response times dramatically. If an activity looks overly complicated on the chart, it will probably be difficult to perform consistently and effectively. Simple systems work best. When the team has agreed to a simple and effective work process, you are ready to document it.

## Procedures and Work Instructions

✓ It is sometimes easiest to start in the middle, with the general procedures. Based on the flowcharts that have been developed, it is a simple task to document procedures and practices. An organization may choose to use the flowcharts as references and to develop written procedures from them, or the flowcharts themselves—showing the various roles and responsibilities—may serve as the documentation. A flowchart can also help to visually describe a more complex process, with extra details described in accompanying text. One chemical company I worked with includes a simple block flow diagram as the first page of every procedure; this practice makes every documented procedure understandable at a glance.

Most important, there is no need to scrap the old system. If some documentation already exists, use the results of the internal audits and the work process analyses to determine how the documentation should be upgraded or improved. Some of the current procedures may be adequate and need little work.

 It is much easier to start with whatever documents already exist (even in the form of memos or informal notes) than to start with a blank sheet of paper.

 Above all else, make sure that your procedures and other documentation are focused on your business needs. Over the past six years, I have seen quite a few organizations that customized their documentation to the ISO 9001 standard rather than to their own business environment. Some of these companies established very rigid systems, with one procedure corresponding to each section of the standard. The result is often an artificial system that is not integrated into any existing business framework. This type of system is cumbersome and difficult for employees to get used to and adds little value to the business.

Just because ISO 14001 requires that you have procedures for particular aspects of your EMS does not mean that you must have an exact number of procedures that correspond to the standard's sections. Chapter 12 described a way of meeting the communication requirements by using existing procedures. That same approach may work for many of the standard's requirements. In addition, when the standard says that a "procedure" is required, you could meet that requirement by using a variety of different types of documents—including checklists, flowcharts, and forms—rather than through a formal text-based procedure.

Once your critical EMS processes are documented, the same teams can decide if more detailed instructions are needed for the tasks or activities involved. If it is important that a task be done the same way by every person who does it, then detailed instructions are important. If more flexibility and creativity are warranted, the general procedures will probably be sufficient. This is a decision that each work group must make for itself.

 Consider the amount and level of detail of documentation necessary for jobs in your own organization. In defining any type of job or task, there should be a balance between documented instructions, training, and qualifications (see Figure 13-3). For instance, for a job requiring particular skills, such as a laboratory technician, you might require certain educa-

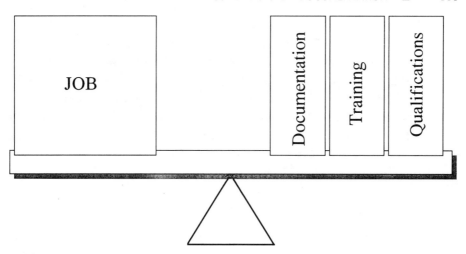

■ **FIGURE 13-3.** Balance of Documentation, Training, and Qualifications

tion or experience as background qualifications, provide training for certain skills, and document any critical steps that are complex or that change frequently. Consider training and qualifications when deciding how much you need to document.

Detailed instructions are typically needed for areas such as operational control, laboratory analysis, and instrument or equipment calibration. In many cases, these types of instructions already exist in the form of Standard Operating Practices, laboratory test methods, batch sheets, or calibration instructions. In that case, each work team's task is to review the existing documents and decide if any upgrades or improvements are needed. This is where getting input from all shifts is especially critical. Many times, each shift has its own way of doing things. Representatives from all shifts need to work together to share ideas and choose the most effective way of doing each job. This process alone can create great improvements in business processes.

Another consultant told me about a business he has worked with that believes in the practice of circulating drafted documents to all people involved. One particular instruction, recently revised by one group of workers, was circulated to the remaining workers for approval. All had approved the changes and the document was ready to be issued when one person returned from a four-week vacation. He decided to test this new involvement approach and brought everyone's attention to the fact the he had not yet reviewed the changes. In keeping with their practice of employee involvement, the document's authors gave it to him for review.

After reading the document, the worker exclaimed, "I don't do it this way." Although everyone else had already agreed to the new procedure, the worker protested and insisted that he did things differently and could not support the revised practice. The group finally evaluated his way of doing the job and found that this one person's method was actually much more effective than the newly documented practice to which they had all agreed. Changes were made to reflect the more effective method, and the organization estimates that the improved practice has saved them more than a million dollars.

**The Manual**

The authors of ISO 14001 (at least those in the United States) deliberately avoided requiring an EMS manual in order to give businesses plenty of flexibility. Whether you choose to have a formal EMS manual or not, however, you are required to document some sort of system description. For the sake of simplicity, I'm going to call this description a "manual," but don't ever tell anyone I said you *have* to have one!

Once the two lower levels of documentation are in place or planned, it's time to describe the overall system. It may be helpful to work on a rough draft of the manual earlier in the process so that it can act as a guiding document in showing how the system fits together and what elements are still being implemented. Many organizations struggle with writing this brief document because they try to do it before the system has been defined. Keep in mind that the manual should remain in draft form until it accurately describes what really happens in the organization—not some ideal future state.

Once the basic practices of the EMS are documented, or at least defined, it becomes a much simpler task to summarize the system elements in a manual. There are many different ways to write a manual, and whatever works and makes sense for your organization is fine. Two types of approaches are typical.

One approach uses the format of the ISO 14001 standard and addresses each element of the standard as a separate section of the manual. Although this clearly shows compliance with the standard, it may not make much sense to people internally. Most ISO 9001 quality manuals have been written this way, and they often serve mainly as a registration tool and are of little use to the organization. This approach works somewhat better with ISO 14001, since its sections are arranged in a logical order that follows a basic business improvement model.

The other variation is to format the manual in a way that makes sense for your organization—by functional group, following the process or service flow, or whatever. I have found that many people have never even considered an approach that differs from the standard's format, but it can be very effective. In particular, this approach may be appropriate for businesses that want a single, combined management system manual rather than separate manuals for quality, safety, environmental, and so on.

Most organizations are still worried about satisfying the third-party auditor. To help external auditors, simply create a cross-reference matrix, like the one shown in Table 13-1, to show how the standard's re-

**■ TABLE 13-1** Sample Cross-reference Matrix of ISO 14001 and Environmental Manual

| ISO 14001 | ABC Company Environmental Manual | | | | |
|---|---|---|---|---|---|
| | Intro-duction | Organi-zation | Management Responsibility | Environmental Department | Core Systems |
| Policy | X | | | | |
| Environmental Aspects | | | X | | |
| Legal Requirements | | | | X | |
| Objectives/Targets | | X | | | |
| EM Program | | | X | | |
| Responsibility | | X | | | |
| Training | | X | | | |
| Communication | | | X | | |
| Documentation | X | X | X | X | X |
| Document Control | | | | | X |
| Operational Control | | | | | X |
| Emergency Response | | | | X | |
| Monitoring/Measurement | | | | | X |
| Corrective Action | | | | | X |
| Records | X | X | X | X | X |
| EMS Audit | | | | X | X |
| Management Review | | | X | | |

quirements are addressed by your manual. This type of matrix can also be used to show how procedures relate to the standard's requirements. Multiple matrices could be used to show how a combined manual addresses the requirements of ISO 14001, ISO 9001, and other standards.

 Whatever approach you choose, consider who the primary audience is as you develop the manual or other documentation. Too many organizations write their documents for the registrar rather than for their own internal use. Although registration may be a goal, remember that you will have to live with this management system for a long time (maybe forever). Although you can always revise documents and improve them later, it is much easier and less costly to do it right the first time.

Recall that the standard requires you to provide references to additional documentation. The most effective way to do this is to include references within each section of your manual or system description. If you are describing your emergency response process, you might add a sentence like the following:

 Details of our emergency response program can be found in the site Crisis Management Manual, which is maintained by the Safety, Health, and Environmental Manager.

Complete references are a critical component of the manual. With them, the manual becomes a valuable reference tool for both employees and outsiders (auditors, regulatory bodies, etc.), leading them to the detailed documentation.

 *KEY TO SUCCESS*

### DOCUMENTATION GUIDING PRINCIPLES

The documentation for your business will be different from any other business's documentation. It may have the same general structure as other system's documentation, but it should uniquely fit your own organization's needs. There are some basic guiding principles to remember about management system documentation.

#### *Balance Internal and External Needs*

Before starting to revise or develop a document, consider how it will be used. Externally, it may have to provide evidence of compliance with ISO 14001 to third-party auditors. You may also want to share certain documents, including your manual, with your customers to show them how you manage environmental issues. Internally, a document may be used for training, as a daily reference, and as a guide for people new to the job. Considering these uses early will help you to develop documentation that meets your business's unique needs.

### Involve People in Documenting Their Jobs

Another guiding principle is to involve the people who actually do the work in revising or developing documentation. A common mistake is for a coordinator or a small group of people to try to document the entire system. Although this seems much easier and quicker in the short term, it rarely works out well. People who need to use the documentation will have difficulty accepting it since they had no input—and it probably will not be an accurate reflection of what really happens. Involve a representative group in determining the content of the documentation, then a smaller group or single person can work on the actual writing. Once a draft is available, circulate it broadly to everyone involved for review and make it clear that feedback is welcomed.

### Use What You Have

Make use of existing documentation wherever possible. Too many organizations make the mistake of treating ISO 14001 as a new project and creating a whole new set of documents. This approach will be greeted with skepticism and contempt by the organization—with good reason.

The experience of one plant that I audited illustrates the importance of involving people and using existing documents. I was conducting an ISO 9002 pre-assessment for a plant some years ago, when ISO 9000 was still very new. The audit team began its assessment by reviewing the site's documentation. The plant had a very complete quality manual and a four-inch thick binder filled with procedures that covered every imaginable activity that had anything to do with the quality system. Our team of four auditors reviewed it all carefully and found only a few very minor points to comment on. Then we began the actual audit. It quickly became apparent that a small group of area coordinators had written all the procedures themselves over the course of the previous few months. They had almost literally locked themselves into a conference room and worked diligently to put all that documentation together. Although copies of this binder of procedures had been carefully distributed to anyone who might need them, no one outside of this small group was really aware of the details of what was written.

I was auditing an operator in the control room and asked him how he knew when to take samples of the process. He looked a little nervous and said, "Uh, we have a procedure for that," and dutifully began paging through this huge binder. After a few minutes of watching his unsuccessful hunting, I said, "OK, I know these procedures are new. How do you personally know when to go out and take your samples on a daily basis?" He brightened up and said, "Oh! We have this sample schedule." He pulled out a one-page, laminated schedule from the control desk. That simple, single sheet of paper—not a newly written, strictly formatted procedure—should have been the controlled document.

### *Keep It Simple!*

Do not make your documentation more complex than it needs to be. The real test of a management system is how well it works. If a job does not require detailed instructions, then do not write them. If a job skill relies on training and qualification rather than on documented procedures, then state that. If a computer documentation system works better at your site than a paper system, use it. It's up to you and your organization to make these decisions about how to run the business most effectively.

# DOCUMENT CONTROL

> ### ISO 14001 REQUIREMENTS*
>
> ISO 14001, section 4.4.5, Document Control, requires the following:
>
> The organization shall establish and maintain procedures for controlling all documents required by this International Standard to ensure that
>
> a) they can be located;
> b) they are periodically reviewed, revised as necessary and approved for adequacy by authorized personnel;
> c) the current versions of relevant documents are available at all locations where operations essential to the effective functioning of the environmental management system are performed;
> d) obsolete documents are promptly removed from all points of issue and points of use or otherwise assured against unintended use;
> e) any obsolete documents retained for legal and/or knowledge preservation purposes are suitably identified.
>
> Documentation shall be legible, dated (with dates of revision) and readily identifiable, maintained in an orderly manner and retained for a specified period. Procedures and responsibilities shall be established and maintained concerning the creation and modification of the various types of documents.

*© International Organization for Standardization. All rights reserved.

## INTERPRETATION

This is one of the sections that is likely to be least well understood by users of the standard. Those familiar with ISO 9000 will immediately understand the concept of document control, which is an integral part of any management system, but may have some difficulty interpreting the exact words here since they differ from those used in the ISO 9000 standards. People with no ISO 9000 experience will probably have no idea what is even meant by document control.

Let's start with the basics. The idea behind document control is to develop a system that will ensure that critical documents are kept up to date and are available where needed. That's really the basic requirement here, although it's hidden in all the verbiage. The authors of the standard are more prescriptive here than in other sections of ISO 14001, so there are some specific how-to requirements.

First, as in most other sections of ISO 14001, this section requires procedures—in this case procedures that describe your document control system. The scope of that system must include "all documents required by this standard," which means the documents that support your EMS. These can include checklists, blank forms, manuals, regulations, procedures, process information, and many other kinds of documents.

In my training and consulting experience, I have found that people frequently have trouble understanding the difference between documents and records. Generally, documents describe intended actions while records are a history of what has already happened. Even more important, documents can change and so must be controlled to ensure that the current revision is in use. Records cannot change since they reflect what has already happened (although they may be added to). The distinction between documents and records is not always perfectly clear. For example, objectives and targets serve as a record of your environmental goals, yet they may be revised. The bottom line is that if a document is part of your EMS and may be revised, it must be controlled.

This scope will include some documents that are created and revised externally. For example, copies of the regulations or standards (including the ISO 14001 standard) used by your organization must be included. Although you are not responsible for making changes to these documents (even though you might like to!), you are still responsible for keeping your internal copies up to date whenever revisions are issued.

Items *a* through *e* in this section, which contain fairly detailed requirements for the document control system, are mainly self-explanatory. Your system will need to ensure that documents are available where they are needed, that they are reviewed and revised when needed, and that obsolete copies are not used inadvertently. Your procedures must describe how you ensure that these things happen and who is responsible for review and approval. The standard also addresses the use of obsolete documents for historical or legal purposes. This just means that it is acceptable to keep obsolete documents, as long as they are clearly identified as obsolete so they will not be used inadvertently.

The rest of this section is fairly clear, except for the statement that documents must be retained for a specified period. This requirement does not make much sense and seems more appropriate for records. Documents, by their nature, will not have a defined retention time. Document control ensures that a document is valid until it is superseded by its next revision. I have talked to several other U.S. TAG members to try to understand the intent of this confusing statement. The best explanation that I have heard is that this requirement actually refers to any obsolete documents retained as a history (which would actually make them records). It is still quite confusing to me, however; at best, it is a misplaced requirement that should be in the Records section of ISO 14001.

You should now have a good understanding of what the words mean in this section, but you are probably still unsure as to how to actually do all of this. The most difficult part of document control is figuring out what your organization's own system should look like. There are a lot of bad examples out there and few really effective systems.

## IMPLEMENTATION

Document control: the mere words send shivers through most people. Like documentation itself, document control is often assumed to be a complex and cumbersome undertaking. Once again, it doesn't have to be.

Consider the following basic principles of documentation and document control:

- Documentation is a critical element of environmental, safety, quality, and other management systems.
- When processes are documented and implemented, it is possible to determine with confidence how things are currently done and to measure current performance.
- Documented standard practices are essential for maintaining gains from improvement activities.
- Documentation may exist in many different formats: procedures, manuals, checklists, forms, instructions, flowcharts, drawings, and so on. Documents may be maintained in paper or electronic systems. Regardless of format and media, all documents critical to the operation of the management system must be controlled.
- Personnel using a particular document must be able to find out whether it is the current revision.

- Simple document control systems typically work better than complex ones.

The first step in establishing a document control system is to identify the documents that need to be controlled. A common mistake is to focus only on procedures when defining the document control system. The system needs to be broad and flexible enough to apply to all EMS documents. These could include the following:

- EMS procedures
- Environmental policy
- Objectives, targets, and programs
- Checklists
- Blank forms
- EMS manual or other system description
- Instructions, methods, or operating procedures for any groups whose work affects the environment
- Reference manuals
- Regulations
- Standards (internal and external)
- Process information, flowcharts, and drawings

These are just some examples: you need to look at the documents that your own organization uses as a part of the EMS. As a rule of thumb, if it is important that the current version of a document be in use, then it should be controlled.

You may already have some elements of a document control system in place for some types of documents. If you have implemented ISO 9001, you have a comprehensive document control system for quality-related documents. Even without ISO 9001, many businesses have revision and approval processes defined for their operating procedures or instructions. When you begin to develop a document control system for your EMS, begin with these existing elements. It is much easier to improve and expand an existing system than to define a new one.

The system you define must include certain elements in order to ensure effective control and to meet the standard. Figure 14-1 shows the basic elements of a document control system. These are the steps that a controlled document will follow whenever it is revised. Let's take a closer look at what is involved in each of these steps.

### Write/Revise Document

The need to write a new document or to revise an existing one may come from several sources. Any time your products, processes, or systems change, documentation must be revised to reflect those changes.

DOCUMENT CONTROL ■ 129

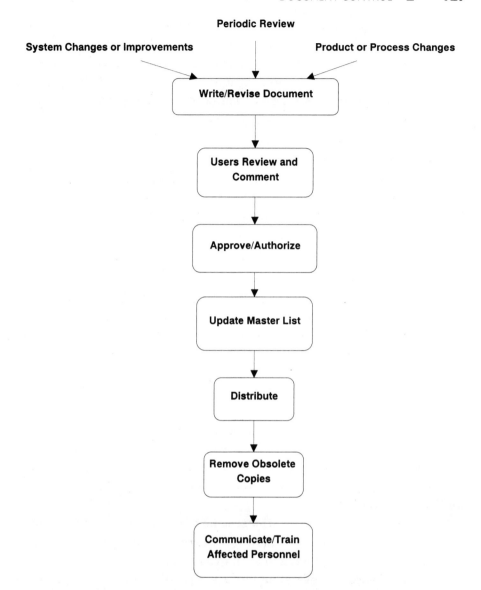

■ **FIGURE 14-1.** Basic Elements of Document Control

Improvements to the system, initiated by audits, management reviews, corrective actions, or incident investigations, often result in document revisions.

Even if major changes or improvements have not taken place, it is good practice (and a requirement of ISO 14001) to review critical documents in some regularly scheduled way to ensure that they are still accurate and effective. One plant that I worked with established annual reviews of every document in its system, then found that it could not keep up with this requirement.

**130** ■ IMPLEMENTATION AND OPERATION

 Two to five years is a typical, reasonable review period. It is most effective to establish different review periods for different types of documents based on their importance and how often practices are likely to change. Operating procedures might be reviewed every one to two years, while management review and audit procedures may change much less frequently and only need review every three to four years.

Anyone in the organization should have the freedom and authority to initiate or suggest a change to a document. Some companies use simple forms to encourage everyone to suggest changes when appropriate. This is critical to ensure that documents are accurate and up to date.

 For example, if an operator finds a better way to perform a particular task but does not initiate a change to the procedure, the system begins to break down, even if that person's job is being done more effectively in the short term. Without a procedural revision, other operators may not know of the improved technique; this could result in inconsistencies in operation. Moreover, the written procedure will no longer reflect actual practice and will be of no value for reference or for training new operators.

Each document or type of document typically has a designated "owner" to maintain it. This person is responsible for making revisions to the document, initiating periodic reviews, and ensuring that the document control procedures are followed throughout the revision, approval, and distribution processes.

I've seen several organizations, some quite large, designate a single document control coordinator to fulfill this role for all documents within the system. One plant I worked with even hired someone for this newly defined role. There are several problems with this approach. For one thing, it may be too big a job for just one person. If your organization is fairly large, controlling all documents from one central place can make the system somewhat cumbersome and less efficient. It's also unlikely that a single person will have a good understanding of all areas within the organization, and such an understanding is vital when revising documents.

The approach that seems to work best is to designate area coordinators to act as central points for document control (and other functions) within their own areas or departments. This way, you get the ease and efficiency of a single contact point within each area, while defining narrower and more manageable scopes. Chapter 22 provides more detail on the concept of area coordinators.

### Users Review and Comment

Once a new document has been drafted or substantial revisions have been made to an existing document, the draft should be circulated to those people who will be affected by the proposed changes. Affected personnel should review the new document or revisions and return comments to the document owner. In this review, personnel should ensure that the proposed documentation accurately reflects actual practice. This may seem like a lengthy process, but it can prevent having to make additional changes after a document is issued. Even better, it can help you avoid producing documents that have little practical value because they do not reflect actual practice.

### Approve/Authorize

Once the new document or revisions to an existing document have been reviewed by users, the document proceeds to a designated approver or authorizer. The approver reviews the document and indicates his or her approval, as described within the document control system. A signature is a common way to indicate approval, but other means, such as electronic approvals, may also be used.

The approver of the document must have the pertinent background information and knowledge to enable him or her to conduct a meaningful review of the document. The organizational level of the approver should be appropriate to the level of detail in the document.

A common mistake is to designate a long list of approvers for every document. A plant that I worked in had four manager-level approvers, plus an authorizer, for every change to standard operating practices or standard operating conditions. This often resulted in massive backlogs: I and other process engineers often ended up going around to each manager, trying to find a particular procedure we had started circulating weeks earlier. Documents should be approved by those who have the specific knowledge to evaluate the changes. Do not be afraid to grant some authorizing authority to people below manager level.

In one 200-person plant that I consulted with, the plant manager insisted on approving every document. This was a chemical plant that manufactured small batches of hundreds of different products and had more than 500 operating procedures that were planned for upgrade as part of the plant's ISO 9001 registration efforts. In addition, like any other organization, the plant had system procedures, training checklists, forms, and plenty of other documentation. I described this document volume to the plant manager and explained that he would have little time for any other activity were he to review and approve every document personally. He quickly decided it was not such a good idea after all!

## Record Document Revisions

 Anytime a document is revised, you will need to record that the new version is now the most current. How you do this depends entirely on the system you set up. A common practice is to establish a master list.

The master list is simply a list of the controlled documents and their latest revision dates. The function of the master list is to show document users the latest revision status of each controlled document. An organization may have many different master lists for different types of documents or for documents in different areas. For instance, procedures may be on one list and forms on another. The system may be easiest to maintain when each area keeps its own master list(s).

ISO 9001 requires a master list "or equivalent document control procedure." The authors of ISO 14001 specifically avoided the mention of a master list, but you will still need some method for verifying which document revision is the latest. An alternative to creating a master list is to specify that the document owner will maintain "master" documents that are, by definition, the latest versions. That way, if someone is unsure of the most recent revision, he or she can go to the document owner for that information. A master list just makes this information more readily accessible to users.

Another means of document control—a method that is becoming more prevalent—is electronic control. This is a good option if you have an adequate computer system and if everyone (or almost everyone) in the organization has access to the computer. The consulting and training group I was a part of at DuPont used electronic document control very effectively. Most of our group was located in the office, and we had a computer network that allowed us to share documents. Each functional area had a coordinator who had revision privileges for his or her area's documents. Everyone in the group had read and print privileges for all documents. When a document was revised, the coordinator would replace the old document with the revised one on the network and send an electronic mail message to the group. That E-mail notification was important in case anyone had printed a copy of the document. The coordinators also maintained master lists on the server as a handy reference in case someone was unsure whether a printed document was the most recent.

Besides recording the revision status of a document, you may also want to record the nature of the changes. This can be done by keeping a revision log for each document, by retaining obsolete copies as records, or by noting where revisions were made on the document itself. If you keep obsolete copies, be sure they are appropriately identified so that they will not be used by mistake.

### Distribute

Once the revision and approval process is complete, the revised document must be distributed to every person or location that currently holds a copy of that document. Distribution lists should be maintained for each document or class of documents. The effective functioning of a document control system depends on a distribution process that ensures that every person who needs the document has the most recent version.

The system will be more effective and easier to maintain if distribution is limited to those people or locations that will actually use the document. Avoid issuing extra copies to people for information only. If someone really needs an informational copy, you can issue an uncontrolled copy. This just means that he or she will not be added to your distribution list and will not receive future revisions.

You can also consider distributing a single copy to a group or area rather than sending individual copies to every employee. This usually works well for operating areas, maintenance, laboratories, and small office areas. Individual copies should be distributed only in cases where all employees need them. Such documents might include, for instance, specific instructions that each employee has to carry with him or her.

 Distribution is an important part of document control, but it can easily become cumbersome if it is overcontrolled. A common—but not necessarily good—practice is to use document transmittal forms as a positive verification that document users have received their new copies of a document. Some systems even require users to return the obsolete copies to the coordinator. This process creates a lot of extra paperwork that may not be necessary for all organizations.

An alternative method is to rely on all employees to replace obsolete documents with revised ones as a part of their job responsibilities. This eliminates the double-check of the transmittal form. When the document control system is being developed or revised, make it clear to all employees that this is an expected part of their role. Internal audits can then serve to verify that this responsibility is being carried out. Auditors can simply check distributed copies against the master list to ensure that obsolete copies have been removed. You may still want to use transmittal forms for off-site copies to verify that documents were successfully delivered through the mail.

Another common practice that makes distribution more complicated is the inclusion of multiple attachments to each copy of a document. I've worked with various businesses that attach distribution lists, approvals, revision histories, and other extras to every copy of every document that is distributed. This creates a lot of unnecessary paperwork and makes the documents themselves difficult to use. You might end up with a one-page form or a simple procedure that has five pages of attachments! I've seen such things, and they are not very effective.

The best way around this problem is to keep all these extras on file with the master copy (whether paper or electronic). There is no reason for users to receive distribution lists, approvals, and revision histories if they know they are on file and they can see them if they need them. Revision histories become particularly cumbersome since they grow over time. Advise users of the most recent revisions and maintain the full document history elsewhere.

If documents are maintained electronically, distribution is much simpler, involving only updating the document file in the computer system and perhaps printing a single master paper copy. The key is to ensure that anyone who needs a document has access to it. In our business in DuPont, we had many consultants who worked out of their homes and could not connect to the in-house computer system. Although the electronic system was used for the office, paper copies were printed and distributed to the consultants.

 A caveat is necessary, however: do not even consider electronic systems if most employees are not accustomed to using the computer. In that case, stick to using the computer for revisions and distribute copies on paper.

### Communicate/Train

Any change to a controlled document could impact the proper functioning of the business and its critical processes. The organization must have some method for advising users that a document has been changed and for providing training if the change is significant. This is especially critical if the documents are electronic and are accessed only by computer. If a file is updated electronically, users may not know it has changed. Also, people do not usually refer to a procedure regularly once they have become familiar with it, so there must be a way to notify users of changes so that they will refer to the revised procedure.

Methods of communication may include an E-mail or voice-mail notice to users, a cover sheet explaining changes with paper copies, or some indication of changes within the body of the document itself. If a cover sheet is used, this sheet can act as both a notification and a history of revisions (see example in Figure 14-2). Some organizations prefer to high-

## DOCUMENT CHANGE SHEET

**Document Name:** ADM01 - Document Control Procedure
**Document Owner:** Environmental Coordinator

| DATE | NATURE OF CHANGE | PAGE NO. |
|---|---|---|
| 3/12/95 | Original issue | |
| 4/3/95 | Changed Environmental Coordinator to Environmental Manager | 2 |
| | Added Section 5 - Urgent approvals | 4 |
| 7/23/95 | Removed requirement for special paper | 2 |
| 3/18/96 | Annual Review: | |
| | Clarified responsibilities of Environmental Manager | 2 |
| | Simplified Document Change Request form | 5 |

*Form Revised 2/5/95*　　　　　　　　　　　　　　　　*Page 1 of 1*

■ **FIGURE 14-2.** Sample Document Change Sheet

light changes within the text of the document so that users do not have to refer to a second piece of paper. This can be done with a special mark in the margin that does not interfere with the text itself.

If changes are significant and could have an impact on the environment or the business, you may want to provide additional training for employees. This can be done in a number of ways, depending on the extent of training needed. A short meeting can serve to communicate the changes and highlight their importance. More extensive changes—which might be necessary with the introduction of a new product or service or a major process change—could require on-the-job training, special classroom training, or even off-site training.

## *KEY TO SUCCESS*

After auditing and reviewing dozens of document control systems, I have seen just about every unnecessary complexity possible. For one workshop in an Implementation training course, I pulled together a sample document control procedure for course participants to simplify. Everything in that example came from real systems that I had seen, but when combined together in a single procedure, the result was a paper-heavy, overcontrolled system. Participants always have trouble believing that all the elements of that example procedure are real, but most of those elements are actually fairly common. Here are some tips to help you avoid these common problems.

### *Keep Formatting Simple*

Although standard formatting is not required by either ISO 9001 or ISO 14001, many businesses develop such formats as a part of their document control systems. This is especially true of system procedures, but sometimes organizations specify a certain format for instructions, forms, and other documents as well. While this can give documents a consistent look and ensure that critical components are included, it can also create unnecessary complexities.

One common component of a standard format is a header. Some organizations require a standard header on every document; others require them only for procedures. Often, they become overburdened with unnecessary information. I have seen headers that take up almost a quarter of the page!

If you decide to specify a header for documents, keep it simple and include only information that is needed. Some headers include the company name, division name, and plant name—on every document! This is unnecessary for internal documents. Others include a revision date, an issue date, and/or a revision number. These are redundant. ISO 14001 requires a revision date on each document, and that should be sufficient to identify the current version.

Required information on documents should include a unique document title, revision date, and page number. Some organizations also include a document number and/or the name of the approver. In a large business, the name of the department or area can be helpful, although this information can also be incorporated into a simple numbering system. This basic information can be put into a header or a footer and can be formatted differently for different types of documents (e.g., procedures, forms, checklists).

Another aspect of formatting involves the actual body of the document. It is common practice for organizations to specify certain sections or topics, especially for procedures. Typical sections include purpose, scope, responsibilities, references, definitions, and steps. This type of format can help document writers, but it can easily become cumbersome.

Standard formatting can work well for procedures but is usually unnecessary and limiting for other types of documents. For procedures, any required sections should be clearly defined and useful to the users. Purpose and/or scope are a helpful way to define the use of the procedure. If both purpose and scope are used, procedure writers should have a clear idea of what information is required for each. Some organizations list the responsibilities at the start of a procedure so that it is evident to whom the document applies. This section can also be used to define abbreviations for various positions to make the text of the procedure simpler.

References are a good idea in cases where it is frequently necessary to use other documents in conjunction with a procedure. This section can be used to reference related procedures, forms, or other documents. Be careful with requiring a reference section, though. I have seen systems in which a reference section was "required" but was almost always left blank. Other systems use a reference section to note which parts of the ISO standard are applicable, but this type of information is not needed by the user and just takes up space. A cross-reference matrix is a better way to show how you have met the standard's requirements (see Chapter 13).

If you choose to specify some standard formatting, remember: the simpler, the better. Allow procedure writers to use the section headings that make sense for their documents and to omit those that do not apply. Limit the number of section headings and clearly specify how the required ones should be used. Avoid required formats for most documents to allow the documents to match the tasks. Include required document control information in a simple one- or two-line header or footer.

### *Identify Controlled Documents Simply*

One of the most common problems that I have seen is document identification systems that are both unnecessary and costly. Most organizations assume that they need to identify "controlled" and "uncontrolled" documents in some way. Many stamp every document with a rubber stamp. Others use a special paper, such as letterhead or other embossed paper, for controlled documents. Some use both. Stamping every document or using embossed paper add unnecessary costs to the system.

The theory is that these techniques allow users to tell at a glance whether a document is controlled. These types of systems usually employ complicated methods of distribution to ensure that obsolete documents with a stamp or on special paper are retrieved and recorded. Together, these methods, which seek to "idiot-proof" document control, can create overly complicated and expensive systems. This type of over-control builds on itself: some facilities go to great lengths to control access to the special paper or the stamps. In most organizations, all of this is unnecessary.

Before assuming that you need this extra level of assurance, take a look at the other control mechanisms that are in place. Once you have established reasonable distribution systems, have provided a master list or another simple way for users to check on the latest document revisions, and have trained users on how the system works and what their responsibilities are, it is unlikely that additional control mechanisms will be needed.

The key is to train people on their responsibilities within the system. Ensuring that changes are communicated well provides further assurances. The document control system can be tested out through internal audits.

If you still decide to use some sort of unique identification (many of my clients have felt uncomfortable setting up a system without including these tactics), then use the simplest and least costly method. For instance, there is no need to purchase and use both "controlled" and "uncontrolled" stamps: since a document is either one or the other, only one stamp is needed. A single colored stamp on the front page of every controlled document is probably the least costly method, but review your system carefully to be sure you really need it.

Another aspect of document identification that can easily get out of hand is document numbering systems. One 200-person plant site that I worked with created a system for numbering every controlled document using a 15-digit number. The system's creators were adamant that every part of that number was absolutely necessary, and I could not talk them out of a single digit! Complicated numbering systems are quite common and are usually unnecessary.

Documents do not need to have any numbers so long as each has a unique title by which it can be identified. Many businesses find that a simple numbering system for some documents helps in keeping track of the documents. If numbers are needed, I recommend a simple alpha-numeric code that can be easily understood by all employees. The group I worked with at DuPont identified procedures using a three-letter code to designate the department originating the document plus a consecutive numbering system (e.g., MKT-1, ADM-4, etc.). Many forms and other documents were identified by title alone.

If you find that you need a more complex numbering system because of the volume of documents, consider whether all those documents are necessary. Many organizations overdocument their systems based on misconceptions of ISO 9001 or ISO 14001 requirements. Strive for a simple system where the documents are useful *and* are used.

### *Keep Clear Records of Document Revisions*

While the standard has no requirements for keeping records of document revisions, it is good practice to do so. This type of record will show the history of the document and possibly prevent the organization from repeating past mistakes. However, once again, it is easy to go too far and to create excessive paperwork.

The two most common methods of tracking document revisions are to keep obsolete copies of documents or to record document changes in a log or similar record. One or the other method should be selected for each document type. It is redundant both to keep a log and to retain obsolete copies.

In most cases, a log of document revisions is sufficient and is easier to maintain. Retaining obsolete copies of documents can easily become a paperwork nightmare. Not only is it necessary to identify each document as obsolete and to file or catalog it, but storage space will quickly become a problem.

A revision history can be a simple log listing the date of each revision and describing the changes that were made. As noted earlier, this log sheet can act as both a change notice for users and a history of revisions (see example in Figure 14-2). If used as a change notice, copies of the revision history should accompany distributed documents but not become an integral part of the documents. This way, the user can refer to the sheet to see what changes have been made and then throw it away. If the change sheet is an integral part of the document, it will add unnecessary paperwork to an otherwise useful document. A permanent record of changes can be kept by the document originator.

In some cases, it is useful to keep full copies of obsolete documents. This may be true for complex or especially critical documents that are frequently revised, such as operating instructions, laboratory methods, and product specifications. In these cases, it may be helpful to refer back to a more detailed history of changes than a log could provide.

Since this practice can result in a large volume of records, however, organizations should carefully consider which obsolete documents will be needed. Over the long term, it may be a good idea to review these document-change policies occasionally to find out whether the obsolete documents are being used and whether a change history could work instead.

Finally, recognize that either method of tracking changes (the obsolete documents or the change histories) creates some records. All records related to the EMS have to meet the requirements described in ISO 14001, section 4.4.3. One of the most critical of these requirements is to establish retention times—that is, to define how long these records will be kept. This can also help to keep the system from becoming paper heavy. See Chapter 19 for details on record management.

## Establishing the Document Control System

The Plan-Do-Check-Act model is as applicable to establishing a document control system as it is to other aspects of the EMS. Plan and design your system, put it into practice, then check to see how it is working so that it can be further improved. Review the system with a critical eye to ensure that it is as simple as possible and does not include unnecessary complexities.

*KEY TO SUCCESS*

The best way to test the newly defined system is to use it. Do not wait until it is "perfect" to put it into use. Since document control procedures affect all other elements of a management system, they should be defined early in the implementation process. When new or revised document control procedures are implemented, make it clear to everyone in the organization that comments and feedback are welcome and necessary in order to test the system. Based on this feedback, plus internal audit results, the system can be improved. Your ultimate goal is to create a document control system that is geniunely useful and is not seen merely as something that "ISO is making us do."

# OPERATIONAL CONTROL

> ### ISO 14001 REQUIREMENTS*
> 
> ISO 14001, section 4.4.6, Operational Control, requires the following:
> 
> The organization shall identify those operations and activities that are associated with the identified significant environmental aspects in line with its policy, objectives and targets. The organization shall plan these activities, including maintenance, in order to ensure that they are carried out under specified conditions by
> 
> a) establishing and maintaining documented procedures to cover situations where their absence could lead to deviations from the environmental policy and the objectives and targets;
> 
> b) stipulating operating criteria in the procedures;
> 
> c) establishing and maintaining procedures related to the identifiable significant environmental aspects of goods and services used by the organization and communicating relevant procedures and requirements to suppliers and contractors.

## INTERPRETATION

Although the wording of this section is a bit convoluted and difficult to follow, the requirements are fairly simple and logical. The first sentence

*© International Organization for Standardization. All rights reserved.

takes you back, once again, to your earlier evaluation of significant environmental aspects and impacts. Each of the aspects you identified as significant is affected by certain parameters within your processes. These processes need to be controlled so that the resulting environmental impacts will be controlled.

However, this does not mean that you are required to control processes in order to minimize environmental impacts. Notice the careful wording, which states that you need to control operations "associated with the identified significant environmental aspects in line with [your] policy, objectives and targets." The specific reference to your own EMS means that you must control those aspects that you have decided are critical and controllable for your own business. When you established objectives and targets, you considered the operational and financial needs of your business. Operational control applies within the limits that you determined for yourself.

The standard refers to "operations and activities." This term is used in a broad sense to apply to all critical functions in your organization. It applies not only to "operations" in the traditional sense of manufacturing processes but to a broad array of business processes. For example, it could include design, purchasing, engineering, construction, maintenance, and finance as well as production or manufacturing. The standard also applies to the activities found in nonmanufacturing businesses.

The standard requires that control be achieved through planning, documented procedures, and specific operating criteria. It states that an organization should "plan these activities . . . to ensure they are carried out under controlled conditions." This is just another way of saying that you have to consciously consider environmental aspects as a part of your overall operations or process control systems. Maintenance is specifically included as one function that affects the control of environmental impacts.

Although this is one area of the standard where "documented procedures" are specifically required, there is still plenty of flexibility for an organization to document in a way that suits its own business needs. ISO 14001 requires documented procedures only "where their absence could lead to deviations from the environmental policy and the objectives and targets." It's up to you to determine where procedures are necessary, based on your evaluation of significant impacts, your own policy and objectives, your knowledge of the activities and processes, and the extent of training and qualifications of personnel.

"Operating criteria" refers to specifications, limits, control points, and other important parameters that must be specified to ensure control of the significant environmental aspects. This will mean different things to different businesses. A plant may have standard operating conditions that include upper and/or lower limits on critical plant control points. A service company may have procedures that define critical tasks and performance criteria for those tasks.

These requirements for procedures and specified operating criteria do not mean you need a new set of environmental operating procedures. ISO 14001 neither requires nor advocates developing new procedures just to meet the standard. You just need to ensure that existing procedures and operating criteria include environmental aspects.

Subsection *c* brings suppliers into the realm of operational control. This is the only place in the standard that references the environmental impacts that suppliers might have on your environmental performance. The requirements are somewhat loosely defined.

First, you are required to identify the supplied goods and services that can affect your significant environmental impacts. In other words, which suppliers can affect your environmental performance, based on your earlier evaluation of what is significant? Once you have identified the environmentally critical suppliers, you are only required to communicate your environmental requirements to them. There are no requirements to evaluate or monitor suppliers' environmental performance. Certain countries wanted this section left intentionally vague to prevent companies from forcing their suppliers to implement ISO 14001.

## Implementation

It is unlikely that many organizations will be implementing these requirements from scratch. Some degree of operational control is necessary for any type of business to ensure consistency and quality of products and services. There may be many businesses, however, that have never fully considered the environmental implications of their operations.

As with other parts of ISO 14001, it is best to begin with existing systems. Consider the controls that are already in place within your organization. These could include the following:

- Written instructions, procedures, or methods
- Training for operations personnel
- Product or service specifications
- Computerized control systems
- Preventive and predictive maintenance programs
- Testing and monitoring
- Control or operating limits
- Target or on-aim control parameters
- Statistical process control

Your business may use any combination of these or other methods to control its processes and activities to ensure that the end product or service is what was intended.

Once you have identified what "operational control" means for your business, go back to your earlier evaluation of significant environmental impacts. You need to determine which operational parameters can control these impacts, within the scope of your environmental policy, objectives and targets. Your existing operating controls probably focus on quality, safety, and perhaps the regulated environmental aspects of your business. Now you will need to make sure that they also incorporate controls for significant environmental impacts.

As with defining your impacts, policies, and objectives, it is critical that the right people are involved in determining appropriate environmental controls. Representatives from all major functional groups within the organization, as well as the organization's environmental professionals, should be involved. People with expertise in quality and safety should also be involved to ensure a balanced approach.

Begin with the environmental impacts you defined as significant and that you incorporated into your objectives and targets. Decide which parameters within your operations or activities can control these impacts. For instance, in a chemical plant one of the significant impacts with an associated target might be the amount of $NO_x$ gas emitted from the process. In examining the process, you will identify certain variables that can determine the amount of $NO_x$ gas produced, such as reaction temperature, amount and purity of raw materials, and reaction time. Based on this analysis, you will then identify process controls to ensure that the amount of $NO_x$ stays within defined limits. In this example, you might monitor and control reaction time and temperature and act to ensure that raw material specifications take environmental as well as quality considerations into account. While this example is one that would already be covered by environmental regulations, you may not have previously considered the operating controls in the context of environmental policies, objectives, and impacts.

The specifics of operational control will vary greatly from one business to another. A service company will have very different types of controls than the manufacturing business in the previous example. For example, a delivery company may have identified vehicle emissions as one of its most significant environmental impacts. In reviewing the activities and processes involved, the organization may decide that effective scheduling of deliveries is one way to reduce its vehicle emissions. The details of that scheduling process, including procedures and training of the scheduler and drivers, define its operational controls.

Alternatively, another company in the same business may decide that using an alternative fuel is the most effective way to reduce this particular environmental impact. This business may specify certain fuel types and purity levels, define its fuel requirements, and even make changes to its vehicle fleet to allow use of an alternative fuel. Each of these delivery services would be in conformance with the standard since it has established a way to control that impact within the context of its own EMS.

The elements of the EMS interact in many ways and are not stand-alone components. You can see from the examples cited above that environmental policy, objectives and targets, and programs are entwined with operational controls. Environmental plans or programs will likely include some operational controls. It's best not to get too concerned with categorizing these various elements into ISO 14001 terms since they are so intricately related. Focus on your own business needs and systems.

As mentioned earlier, most companies already have some sort of controls over their critical activities. The key to meeting ISO 14001 requirements is to ensure that those existing controls include environmental considerations.

In reviewing these controls, each organization will probably encounter conflicts where quality, safety, environmental, or economic goals cannot all be met. For example, the customer may want a product that is best achieved with low process temperatures, whereas higher temperatures may help to reduce emissions. Delivery-service customers might demand the fastest service possible, which may make many options for reducing environmental impacts unfeasible. In these cases, some difficult decisions will have to be made to determine what operating conditions will produce an optimal result. Sometimes environmental performance may need to be sacrificed for quality performance or vice versa.

However, there are often alternative approaches that can help to optimize all types of performance. Finding these alternatives can require a lot of creativity and a willingness to look beyond the obvious or usual choices. This is where it is especially critical to ensure that a broad cross-section of people is involved. Encourage this team to take an open-minded approach to finding innovative solutions that will improve both the environment and the business. These are often the situations with the greatest potential for business and economic improvement.

United Parcel Service (UPS) illustrates this point. The company wanted to reduce the air emissions from its delivery trucks, much like the hypothetical delivery service cited above. At the same time, competitors were offering the faster service its customers wanted. UPS decided to switch to compressed or liquified natural gas instead of the usual gasoline in its trucks. Although the equipment retrofits were costly at the start, UPS is now saving money since natural gas is significantly cheaper than gasoline. The company has managed to improve its environmental performance *and* to reduce its fuel costs without jeopardizing customer satisfaction.

One common method of controlling operations and activities is to use written procedures. In fact, this is one of the only sections of ISO 14001 where "documented procedures" are specifically mentioned. In most cases, organizations already have some sort of instructions or procedures for detailed operating tasks. When enhancing procedures to include environmental aspects or creating new procedures, you may wonder how much needs to be written down.

It's common for companies to overdocument their systems because they think that the standard requires everything to be written down. ISO 9001 offers some sound advice on this topic. In section 4.2.2, Quality Procedures, the standard states that

> the range and detail of the procedures that form part of the quality system depend on the complexity of the work, the methods used, and the skills and training needed by personnel involved in carrying out the activity.*

When determining how much needs to be written into procedures, consider the qualifications, skills, and training of the people who will be performing the activity (see Chapter 13, "Documentation"). Then write down those steps and details for which documentation is really necessary. For instance, an airline pilot does not need detailed instructions on how to fly the plane (you hope!). Each pilot has been trained and has gone through an extensive qualification process, including an enormous amount of in-flight experience. Despite these rigorous qualification criteria, however, pilots still use a written checklist prior to takeoff to ensure that nothing is overlooked or forgotten. This is because safety is absolutely critical to the task of flying a plane.

This same thought process can be applied to your own operational practices. Look at your defined job qualifications and training requirements, consider the potential environmental impacts, and decide what critical pieces of the job need to be documented. Then use your existing documentation, where possible, to include these additional environmental elements.

Since operational controls are related to significant aspects, objectives, and targets, they are likely to change over time. As the process and business change and environmental impacts are reevaluated, different operational controls are needed. As targets are reached and new ones are

---

*© International Organization for Standardization. All rights reserved.

established, operational controls may again be affected. A review and revision process should be an integral part of your operational controls.

Another critical component of operational control involves working with suppliers. The first step is a familiar one: begin with your identified significant environmental impacts. Determine which of your supplied goods and services affects these impacts. A similar group of cross-functional representatives should work on this process, including someone—perhaps the purchasing representative—who is familiar with the suppliers.

The scope of this section includes more than just raw material suppliers. It encompasses all suppliers of goods and services, including equipment, utilities, information, transportation, and others. Contractors are also included in this definition.

This identification process should discriminate between varying degrees of significance and take into account the entire organization. A supplier with a significant impact on one particular department may not be significant relative to other site impacts. As with the process of identifying environmental aspects, the organization's own definition of significant needs to be clear. In addition, records should be maintained to describe the basis for decisions made.

Once you have determined which suppliers can impact your environmental performance, you will need to decide what to do about these suppliers. The standard only requires that you communicate "relevant procedures and requirements." The requirements set for each supplier should relate to the significance of that supplier's environmental impact on your business.

For a critical raw material supplier, you may consider tightening your specifications on impurities. You could also require the supplier to notify you before making any significant product or process changes. Besides focusing on the product itself, you may want to know more about how a critical supplier manages environmental impacts in its own business. You could audit the supplier's environmental management system, send the supplier a self-evaluation questionnaire, or even ask the supplier to consider ISO 14001 registration.

Although you have all of these options and more, the standard does not require these kinds of specific actions. Consider the relationship you have with critical suppliers and set requirements that make sense for your business and theirs.

✓ If you have a quality system in place, you probably already have a comprehensive program for working with your suppliers. Integrate environmental requirements into other supplier requirements so that there is only one set of comprehensive requirements for each supplier. Use existing means of communication and contacts to define any new environmental requirements.

If you decide to evaluate some suppliers' environmental systems, consider whether these assessments can be built into existing mechanisms. If self-evaluations or on-site audits are used, environmental requirements could be integrated into the forms or checklists. Finally, make sure that your own purchasing department understands any new requirements well enough to communicate them to suppliers. Environmental professionals or managers may have to help them get started or provide technical support.

The extent of operational control is left for each organization to determine. It will not necessarily be feasible to control all parameters within all processes so that environmental impacts are minimized or eliminated. The goal is to choose the most significant impacts based on your policies and objectives and to implement operational controls that will help to improve the environment and your business.

# EMERGENCY PREPAREDNESS AND RESPONSE

> ## ISO 14001 REQUIREMENTS*
>
> ISO 14001, section 4.4.7, Emergency Preparedness and Response, requires the following:
>
> The organization shall establish and maintain procedures to identify potential for and respond to accidents and emergency situations, and for preventing and mitigating the environmental impacts that may be associated with them.
>
> The organization shall review and revise, where necessary, its emergency preparedness and response procedures, in particular, after the occurrence of accidents or emergency situations.
>
> The organization shall also periodically test such procedures where practicable.

## INTERPRETATION

The requirements of this section are straightforward and are described quite clearly. Most industrial businesses in the United States already meet some or all of this section's requirements, because of the regulatory

---

*© International Organization for Standardization. All rights reserved.

requirements of EPCRA, the Emergency Planning and Community Right-to-Know Act, as well as requirements established by state agencies. In addition, many industry-specific standards and codes of practice, such as the chemical industry's Responsible Care® program, require comprehensive emergency planning, response, and communication systems.

The standard uses the term "emergency preparedness and response procedures," but these may exist in many organizations by other names. Many plants have emergency response plans that fulfill the same requirements. Other businesses use what they refer to as crisis management plans. It doesn't matter what you call them, as long as you have some written documents that satisfy the requirements detailed in this section of the standard.

Those requirements state that you must have methods in place to identify potential emergency situations, to respond in case an emergency or accident does occur, and to mitigate any environmental impacts that may result. Note that this applies to any accidents or emergency situations, not just to environmental releases. Many different types of emergencies could result in environmental impacts.

The standard specifically requires that these procedures or plans be kept up to date (as a part of your documented EMS, these are a part of your document control system anyway). ISO 14001 does make special mention of the fact that these should be reviewed after any accidents or emergencies occur, when you will be able to best determine the effectiveness of your existing response procedures.

## IMPLEMENTATION

As with all other sections of ISO 14001, the most effective way to start is to consider what you already have in place. Pull together all procedures, plans, methods, and records of your existing emergency planning and response program.

Once again, bring together representatives from all major functional areas of the facility. Review the existing emergency planning and response information against the standard's requirements, regulatory requirements, industry requirements, and your own internal needs. Determine whether the written procedures and plans accurately describe your current practices and whether they are effective.

Consider whether your plans and procedures have ever been tested in a practice drill or during a real emergency. The standard requires that the procedures be tested, to the extent that is reasonable and practical. Look back at records of any previous incidents or emergencies to determine whether your written plans and procedures were, in fact, used and whether they worked effectively.

Based on this data and analysis, make revisions to your existing plans and procedures, as necessary. Remember that the format and style of documentation is up to you. If you have response plans or manuals already in place, there's no need to rewrite them into a generic EMS procedure format. This will only cost you money, time, and effort—and may even diminish effectiveness. Stick with a format that's familiar and effective for your organization.

If you are in a nonregulated industry that has no existing emergency response plan, you will need to develop one from scratch. Begin by deciding what types of accidents, incidents, or emergencies could result in environmental impacts. Your base analysis of environmental aspects and significant impacts will be a valuable reference and starting point.

Your aspects identification should have considered both normal and abnormal functioning of your systems. Extend the abnormal scenarios to consider what types of emergencies could occur.

✓ There are numerous methodologies available to aid you in conducting a thorough review of potential problems. These include everything from simple what-if processes to more complex Failure Mode Effects Analyses (FMEAs) and in-depth process hazards reviews. Choose a methodology that is appropriate for the relative magnitude and significance of environmental impacts for your business.

Once you have identified potential emergencies, decide on the best response to each. Contact your local fire department and emergency organization to find out how they would respond in case of the emergencies you have identified and how you will need to work together to ensure that the response is appropriate and timely.

✓ Although the scope of ISO 14001 is limited to environmental impacts, it makes sense to include safety and health impacts as a part of this process. The same steps are involved, so you can save some time and effort by considering all impacts at the same time. In addition, some single accidents or incidents will result in safety, health, and environmental effects, so the responses may be similar or concurrent.

In determining appropriate responses to potential emergencies, consider the following actions:

- Individual employee actions required (especially if employee safety is threatened)

- Emergency personnel and/or management actions required
- Local emergency response personnel to be notified
- Authorities to be notified
- Actions to be taken to deal with immediate and urgent situations
- Actions to be taken to mitigate both short- and long-term environmental impacts on both the local and global environment

It's critical that these actions and plans be determined by the full representative group rather than by a single environmental professional. Environmental impacts and necessary actions could affect all groups within the facility, so all should at least review the suggested plans.

Once the basic plans are developed, they need to be documented. Many organizations find that a manual or three-ring binder works best. It's important that the plans are clearly written, easy to understand, and easy to access and use during an emergency. A three-ring binder with color-coded or tabbed sections meets these criteria. Of course, if you have identified only a few potential emergencies of the sort that will probably be fairly simple to deal with, then you may only need a simple plan or procedure written in a few pages.

Generally, a comprehensive emergency response plan includes the following components:

- Description and map of facility, including location of emergency response equipment (hydrants, fire extinguishers, absorbent materials, etc.)
- Emergency organization and specific responsibilities
- Emergency services available on site and in local area (site response team, fire department, etc.)
- Employee communication and training for planning and response to an emergency
- External communication with local authorities, regulatory bodies, and the community for planning and response to an emergency
- Specific actions to be taken for different types of emergencies
- Information on hazardous materials, including environmental impacts
- Testing and drill procedures
- Process for keeping plans up to date

You could also choose to put preparatory information, such as training, communications, testing, and revision processes into a separate procedure and keep your actual emergency response plan or procedure very simple and uncluttered so it will be easy to use.

Of course, if your business has relatively minor environmental impacts to begin with and few potential environmental emergencies, your response plan or procedure could be very simple. It might consist of an evacuation plan for employees in case of a fire or a gas leak, along with contacts for local emergency personnel.

In addition to these plans or procedures for response to emergencies, you must document your methodology for identifying potential accidents and incidents. Base this procedure or description on the methods used for your initial evaluation of potential emergencies. Be sure to include a defined process for periodically reassessing these, especially when the products or processes of your business change.

Once the emergency plans or procedures are defined and documented, make sure that they have been well communicated both internally and externally. All employees need to know about the types of potential emergencies that could occur and the appropriate responses. This will ensure that the plans are effective and will help to protect employees' own safety and health. Even if you have well-established emergency response plans in place, it's a good idea to survey employees to evaluate previous communication programs. Make sure that employees know how to respond to protect themselves and the environment.

Externally, several types of communication may be necessary. EPCRA focuses on emergency planning and communication with the community and local emergency response organizations. State and local regulatory agencies may require additional communication during planning or in case of an emergency.

✓ You may also want to consider communication and response to the media if an emergency occurs.

Finally, decide on the most effective ways to test your plans or procedures. Practice drills work well. They give employees, emergency response personnel, and management a chance to walk through their planned actions as though an emergency were occurring. Experience and familiarity with procedures and equipment will greatly aid in the effectiveness of your response. A combination of announced and unannounced drills is usually best. During an unannounced drill, you have a chance to see how well people remember the critical steps to take, since they may be unaware that it's only a drill.

Generally, an emergency planning and response plan covers an entire physical location. This could require different organizations to work together on a combined plan if, for instance, two different divisions or companies share a single facility. If your EMS covers a large scope, you may need multiple levels of emergency response plans. A corporate or divisional EMS will require a separate response plan for each site.

In addition to site plans, a large company or division may need corporate or divisional plans. Although members of management in corporate headquarters will not have responsibilities for physically responding to a site emergency, they may have critical responsibilities for reporting to authorities, communicating with other parts of the organization, or dealing with the media.

Your emergency planning and response procedures have to be tailored to your own organization's needs. An auditor will expect your plans and procedures to be consistent with the types and magnitude of environmental risks within the organization. The purpose is to avoid or mitigate potential harm to people and the environment. Like other elements of the EMS, this just makes good business sense.

# PART 4

# CHECKING AND CORRECTIVE ACTION

The Plan-Do-Check-Act process introduced in Chapter 1 provides the framework for the entire ISO 14001 standard. We have now looked at the Planning and Implementation requirements; the next four sections of the standard deal with Checking and Corrective Action. These cover parts of both the Check and Act portions of the improvement cycle.

As systems are defined and put in place, it makes sense to establish measuring processes so that you can find out how well various elements of the system are working. If there are any real or potential problems, you will want to act to eliminate them. This ongoing process of measuring progress and improving the system is described in the following sections.

# MONITORING AND MEASUREMENT

> ## ISO 14001 REQUIREMENTS*
>
> ISO 14001, section 4.5.1, Monitoring and Measurement, requires the following:
>
> The organization shall establish and maintain documented procedures to monitor and measure, on a regular basis, the key characteristics of its operations and activities that can have a significant impact on the environment. This shall include the recording of information to track performance, relevant operational controls and conformance with the organization's environmental objectives and targets.
>
> Monitoring equipment shall be calibrated and maintained and records of this process shall be retained according to the organization's procedures.
>
> The organization shall establish and maintain a documented procedure for periodically evaluating compliance with relevant environmental legislation and regulations.

## INTERPRETATION

The purpose of this section is to measure various performance indicators to determine whether the environmental programs that you have put in

*© International Organization for Standardization. All rights reserved.

place are achieving your stated goals. There are three key requirements described in this section: measure your environmental performance, calibrate equipment used for environmental monitoring and measurement, and evaluate your compliance with environmental regulations.

ISO 14001 provides some general guidance on what to measure to judge environmental performance. The standard states that your monitoring and measuring system must include key characteristics and operational controls related to significant environmental impacts, as well as progress made toward achieving your objectives and targets.

If you are familiar with ISO 9001, you will notice a significant difference in the way that ISO 14001 deals with calibration. While the ISO 9000 standards include a very detailed set of requirements around equipment calibration, ISO 14001 merely requires that monitoring equipment be calibrated and maintained and that records be kept. No further details are provided.

Similarly, the requirements for monitoring regulatory compliance are very simply stated, with little detail. You need to set up some sort of procedure to evaluate your own compliance with applicable regulations. This sentence is the direct result of the EPA's involvement in the development of ISO 14001. Although 100 percent compliance is not explicitly required by the standard, EPA insisted on a requirement for organizations to conduct some sort of compliance auditing to track their own progress.

Finally, it's important to take note of some phrases that provide organizations with the flexibility to meet their own business needs. Monitoring and measurement are required "on a regular basis." Calibration must be in accordance with "the organization's procedures." Compliance evaluation must be done "periodically." Each of these phrases allows the businesses that use ISO 14001 to establish procedures, processes, and schedules based on their own internal needs.

## IMPLEMENTATION

### Performance Measurements

The main steps involved in establishing a monitoring and measurement system are shown in Figure 17-1. The first step in meeting the ISO 14001 requirements is to determine exactly what should be monitored and measured. This is also one of the most difficult tasks. Since every business has its own unique processes, products, activities, and services, every business will have a unique set of indicators for measuring its environmental performance.

ISO 14031, Environmental Performance Evaluation (EPE), is still in the early drafting stages but provides some good advice and guidance

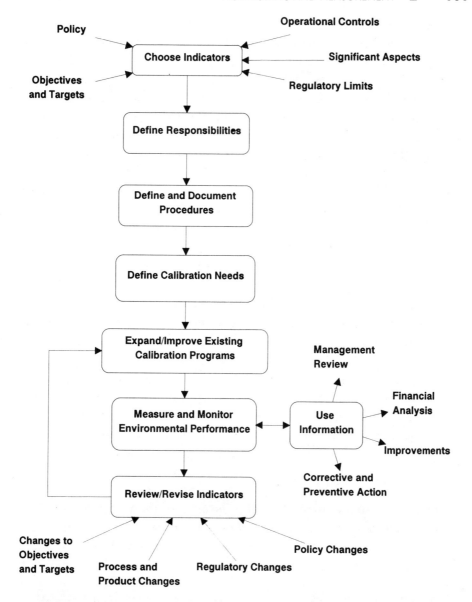

■ **FIGURE 17-1.** Establishing a Monitoring and Measurement System

on establishing a system to measure environmental performance. This draft standard divides measurement of environmental performance into three general areas: management system, operational system, and state of the environment.

The management system evaluation area includes measurements relative to the EMS itself, including progress toward objectives, training and communication, and resource allocation. Operational system measurements encompass the core facilities and systems that create the organization's products and services. These could include energy and material usage, waste management, supplier impacts, and actual outputs of the system (air emissions, water discharges, etc.).

Finally, the draft of ISO 14031 describes state of the environment as measures of the actual quality or condition of the local and global air, water, and soil and their impacts on ecosystems. The draft standard points out that it is difficult to isolate a single organization's contributions to the overall environmental condition, so these types of measurements are often left to local, national, or international public bodies or scientific organizations.

Based on guidance from the draft ISO 14031, your own environmental measurements are likely to focus on your operational and management systems. This brings us back to your initial analysis of significant aspects. In meeting the requirements for operational control, you had to determine which parameters within the various business functions needed to be controlled. These parameters were directly related to your significant environmental aspects and your environmental policy, objectives, and targets. You will want to monitor many of these same parameters as indicators of environmental performance.

Although you may have a separate compliance auditing program, regular monitoring of compliance parameters will likely be an integral part of your measurement system. Since regulatory requirements were considered early on in conjunction with significant aspects and objectives, inclusion of these should be a natural part of the process described here.

As with operational control, keep in mind that the scope of your measurements should extend beyond the obvious manufacturing parameters. Key characteristics of your operations and activities could include supplier performance, transportation and shipping parameters, financial factors, and others. The measurements you choose should relate to the critical functions of your own business.

Besides defining operating parameters, you will need to establish metrics for tracking progress toward environmental objectives and targets. This can be done as an integral part of the objective-setting process. As objectives and targets are chosen, decide how achievement of them will be measured. Since targets should be quantifiable, you should be able to choose performance indicators fairly easily.

For example, if one of your objectives is to implement a recycling program, you may have set a target to collect two tons of white paper for recycling by year's end. You will measure progress toward this goal by tracking the amount of paper collected for recycling on an ongoing basis. If you have a weekly pickup by a recycling company, you can track it on a weekly basis. If you transport the paper to a recycler yourself once a month, you will set up a monthly measurement. Even a simple and straightforward example like this one will vary depending on the exact details of the business.

ISO 14004, the EMS guidance standard, provides some good advice on developing performance measurements. It states that performance indicators should be "objective, verifiable and reproducible . . . relevant to the organization's activities, consistent with its environmental policy, practical, cost-effective, and technologically feasible." The early draft of ISO 14031, the EPE standard, offers additional guidance. It advises that chosen indicators be simple and understandable. These are sensible guidelines for assessing chosen measurements.

You need to consider not only *what* to measure but *how* to measure. For any potential indicator, ask yourself the following questions:

- Do we have or can we develop a reliable method for measuring it?
- Will the method produce repeatable results?
- Will this measurement be cost-effective for the information we will gain from it?
- Are there any alternate measurements that can provide similar information at less cost or in a more reliable manner?

Additionally, pay attention to the *number* of indicators. Too many environmental measurements will create information overload. The result will be that critical information is lost in a jumble of data. Obviously, having too few indicators will not provide enough information for making good business decisions.

Once you have chosen your performance indicators, it's critical to establish solid systems for tracking them. Most importantly, this means defining responsibilities and establishing procedures to describe the monitoring and measurement program.

## KEY TO SUCCESS

Defined responsibilities are especially critical here. Since measuring performance is not a necessary element of daily business, it's one of those things that can easily be overlooked. People get caught up in the day-to-day urgencies of their own jobs, and these types of improvement-focused activities don't get done. To avoid this potential pitfall, designate specific responsibilities for tracking, analyzing, compiling, and reporting data related to environmental performance. These responsibilities can be split among various people, as long as accountability is clearly defined.

Procedures go hand-in-hand with defined responsibilities. Procedures for measuring environmental performance should clearly define the following:

- What indicators are being measured
- Frequency of monitoring/measurement for each indicator
- Who is responsible
- How data are analyzed or compiled
- How the information is reported

As with any other procedure, do not limit yourself to traditional views of what procedures must look like. Your "procedures" in this case could consist of various lists of indicators for each area or department, with frequency and responsibility also listed. These could be supplemented by a brief procedure that describes some overall aspects of the monitoring program.

Although ISO 9001 does not explicitly require a similar measurement system, measuring progress is a critical component of any management system, and many organizations have some sort of measurement program for quality. In fact, to meet the preventive action requirements of ISO 9001, you are required to collect and analyze quality-related data, which amounts to the same thing. If you have a well-defined system for quality metrics that works effectively for your organization, simply apply it and expand it to environmental measurements.

### Calibration

The standard requires that you have a calibration system in place for equipment used to monitor and measure environmental performance. ISO 14001, its informative annex, and ISO 14004 give no additional guidance. *Calibration* in this context simply means measuring a known, standardized quantity to determine whether a piece of equipment is measuring accurately. The underlying concept is to ensure that the measurement results are reliable and believable. Just about everyone in industry has experienced the "sample until you get the answer you want" method of testing, and despite its allure, it's not very dependable!

The good news is that many companies already have some form of calibration system in place. Companies registered to an ISO 9000 standard have comprehensive systems implemented. Environmental permits frequently include specific calibration requirements. OSHA's process safety management standard requires calibration of measuring equipment. Many plants have extensive preventive maintenance programs in place to avoid unplanned downtime. Any of these systems can be expanded to include equipment used for environmental measurements and monitoring.

ISO 9001 provides very detailed requirements for establishing a comprehensive calibration program. Although these details are not required by ISO 14001, they are mostly commonsense elements that can be used as guidance for any calibration program.

Generally, ISO 9001 requires that any equipment or instruments used to measure quality related parameters are controlled, calibrated, and maintained. More specifically, the calibration program must include the following elements:

- Measurement uncertainty is known and is consistent with the desired measurement capability;
- Quality related measurements are identified, including the degree of accuracy required for each;
- Appropriate equipment, capable of the necessary accuracy and precision, is chosen for each measurement;
- Equipment is calibrated at prescribed intervals, or prior to each use;
- Calibrations are done using equipment traceable to national or international standards or using some other well-defined basis;
- Calibrations are done using defined procedures that include details of equipment type, unique identification, location, frequency, method, acceptance criteria, and action to be taken if the equipment is found to be out of calibration;
- Calibration status is indicated by records, physical indicator, or other means;
- Calibration records are maintained;
- Environmental conditions and facilities are suitable and appropriate for the calibrations and measurements being carried out;
- Handling and storage of measuring equipment does not compromise its accuracy and fitness for use;
- When a piece of equipment is found to be out of calibration, the validity of the results of previous tests on that equipment is evaluated;
- The capability of software or test hardware (templates, jigs, etc.) is verified before use and rechecked at prescribed intervals.

At first glance, these requirements may seem overwhelming or excessive, but they are all reasonable and necessary elements of a good calibration program. Just keep in mind the main purpose of calibration: to ensure that measurements are meaningful and accurate. You do not want to make business decisions based on faulty information.

If you already have a calibration system that meets ISO 9001, just expand it to cover equipment used for environmental measurements. Such equipment includes both laboratory instruments as well as in-process measuring equipment. Some of these may be the same pieces of equipment used for quality purposes. You could choose to create a separate list or procedure for environmental measurements or you could just add to existing lists or procedures. The degree of integration is up to you and should be based on your own company's culture and circumstances.

If you have existing calibration systems that may not meet ISO 9001, begin by evaluating them against the criteria listed above. If particular elements are missing or ineffective, improve the system. Then it can be applied to environmental measurements. In any case, calibration of instruments used for environmental purposes should just be a part of your overall equipment maintenance program; a separate "ISO" program will just be more difficult to maintain and create excess work.

If you have virtually no formal calibration system, you'll need to develop one, at least for environmental measurements. Establishing a comprehensive calibration program is a big job and there are no shortcuts, but the effort will pay off in more reliable data and less retesting and redundant measurements. The following steps outline the main tasks in defining a calibration system:

1. *Identify measurements to be made.* This process was covered earlier in this chapter. You may also want to include critical quality and safety measurements as well. Trivial or seldom-used measurements may be excluded. If it's important that the measurement be accurate and reliable, it should be included in the calibration system.
2. *Identify equipment, instruments, hardware and software to be used.* For each measurement identified, list the means that will be used to measure it. This could include laboratory instruments, in-process equipment, weighing scales, computer software, templates, rulers, thermometers, and timers.
3. *Identify the testing methods to be used.* Just as important as the equipment itself is the method or procedure for using it. Define how each measurement will be made, relying on industry standards or existing written methods wherever possible. Where written methods do not exist, define and document your own.
4. *Determine the accuracy and precision required or desired.*[*] For each measurement, define how accurate and precise the information should be to meet your needs. Keep in mind that increased accuracy and precision are typically more costly due to specialized equipment

---

[*] Accuracy is defined as how close the measured value is to the actual value. Precision is defined as the repeatability of the measurement or how close repeated measurements will be to each other.

or methods, so try to set realistic expectations without going further than is really needed.

5. *Determine the accuracy and precision possible.* Now consider the capability of the equipment and methods being used to determine what levels of accuracy and precision are possible for each measurement.

6. *Compare desired versus available accuracy and precision and make changes where necessary.* If your desired accuracy or precision is greater than that available, you have three choices. You can look into improved methods or alternative equipment to improve the reliability of the data. You can accept the currently available conditions and proceed with the understanding that the data is less reliable and should not be used as a primary factor in critical decisions. Finally, you could look for alternate ways to get the information you need using different measurements.

7. *Define calibration procedures.* In step 3 you defined and documented the actual measurement methodology. Now you need to define the procedures and processes that will be used for your overall calibration system. Include responsibilities, frequencies, and other elements referenced in the ISO 9001 requirements. Determine frequencies based on your need for the information and the importance of the data.

8. *Use the system.* Implement the calibration system and follow your procedures and methods for a period of time to determine whether they are effective and appropriate for your business.

9. *Keep records.* Even ISO 14001's limited calibration section requires that records be kept. These can be in paper or electronic form, in whatever format suits your own needs.

10. *If equipment is found to be out of calibration, take corrective action.* Three types of action need to be taken if you find an out-of-calibration instrument or piece of equipment. First, adjust or repair the equipment so that it reads accurately. Then look at the measurement data taken since the last calibration to determine if they were valid, since you do not know how long the equipment has been out of calibration. Finally, determine why the equipment was out of calibration and take steps to prevent it from recurring (see Chapter 18, "Corrective Action").

11. *Improve the system as necessary.* Improve the calibration system based on feedback and calibration and measurement results. You may need to revise methods, change calibration frequencies, conduct additional training, or revise procedures. The improvement process will be ongoing.

### Regulatory Compliance Evaluation

The standard also requires that you periodically evaluate compliance with environmental regulations. Most businesses in regulated industries already do this in one way or another. The size and complexity of your compliance monitoring program will depend on the extent of applicable regulations that you identified earlier.

Compliance evaluation can be accomplished in two ways: ongoing monitoring and/or periodic audits. Many companies use both methods to form a complete program. Monitoring of parameters that are critical to regulatory compliance will just be a part of your overall monitoring and measurement program, as defined above. Parameters to be monitored may include effluents, operational controls that relate directly to regulated emissions, and the composition of waste streams.

To complement these types of monitoring, many organizations have established compliance auditing programs. Environmental compliance auditing is very different from management systems auditing and requires different knowledge on the part of the auditors. Systems audits are covered in detail in Chapter 20.

An environmental compliance audit compares actual environmental performance and actions against the very detailed requirements of environmental regulations, including the federal, state, and local regulations applicable to a particular site or facility. Waste handling, water discharges, and air emissions are the key components typically covered in a compliance audit. Actions and results of these components will be compared to details in permits, regulations, and your own company's defined standards and limits.

Since the U.S. system of environmental regulations is extremely complex and detailed, compliance auditors must have extensive knowledge of the applicable regulations to audit effectively. The audit can be organized so that auditors with a particular expertise, such as solid waste management, can focus on the regulations with which they are most familiar.

Any type of audit follows through the four basic stages shown in Figure 17-2: Preparation, Evaluation, Reporting, and Corrective Action. The activities within these stages are essentially the same for all types of audits and are covered in detail in Chapter 20.

There are a few elements of compliance auditing that differ from systems auditing. During the preparation stage, auditors need to ensure that they have up-to-date knowledge of all applicable regulations. This may involve some additional preparation to understand particular local regulations, site permit requirements, or corporate standards.

During the auditing phase, a compliance audit will focus very heavily on paperwork and records. Although these are an important component

■ **FIGURE 17-2.** Audit Stages

in systems audits as well, compliance auditing will rely almost exclusively on the paper trail, since that is what regulators will look at most heavily. Personnel interviews in a compliance audit will typically be aimed at clarifying or supplementing records. Because of this, compliance audits will usually focus mainly on environmental personnel, whereas an EMS audit must include interviews with many different people in various functions throughout the organization.

An internal system of compliance audits requires certain elements to be comprehensive and effective. These include

- Defined audit procedures, including preparation, auditing, and reporting
- Qualifications and training for auditors
- Defined audit criteria (i.e., what the site is being audited against)
- Specific schedule for audits
- Defined responsibilities

Once again, these elements are necessary for all types of audits and are covered in detail in Chapter 20.

Note that the standard does not require that compliance evaluation be done internally by your organization's own people. To meet the requirements for evaluating compliance, you could use an outside service to conduct compliance audits for you. If you choose to do this, just make sure that the external service you choose meets the criteria described above and in Chapter 20 for an effective auditing program.

## KEY TO SUCCESS

You have now determined the measurements needed, established a calibration system to ensure the data are valid, evaluated your compliance status, and gathered a lot of information. What do you do with this information? The standard does not say much about what to do with this data once you have compiled it. A later section on Management Review (see Chapter 21) references the use of this information, but for real business success you will need to go further. As with all other sections of ISO 14001, you should not establish this measurement system just to satisfy the standard; there should be some inherent value to your business.

In this case, there's an obvious value in merely knowing how well you are doing relative to your stated goals. This can be expanded to correlate environmental improvements with financial or business results. All managers of all businesses want to know the impact of their companies' systems on the bottom line. After all, the primary goal of any business is to make a profit. You can use your monitoring and measurement system to link financial performance with environmental performance. This is simply a matter of translating the environmental data collected into financial terms. Energy use, yields, product purities, and waste amounts all translate easily into cost information. This kind of analysis can then help you to make better decisions about your environmental objectives and programs in the future.

### Benefits of Performance Data

A few well-known companies have publicized their environmental improvements and successes, with bottom line results. 3M has saved more than $500 million since 1975 by reducing emissions by more than 1 billion pounds through its "Pollution Prevention Pays" program, which is based on employee suggestions. IBM saved $32 million in energy costs from 1990 to 1991. Baxter International, a medical products manufacturer, saved $21.7 million in 1994 through its pollution prevention efforts. Without well-defined, thorough measuring systems in place, these companies would have great difficulty quantifying the savings and benefits of their environmental programs.

Additionally, good monitoring systems can help you prevent problems from occurring. Data may show trends that indicate gradually reduced performance, even though a failure, incident, or noncompliance has not yet occurred. The measurement systems should link directly with preventive action systems (see Chapter 18) in order to make use of this valuable data and to avoid the costs inflicted by these types of problems. The economic benefit of catching noncompliances or releases before they occur may alone be enough to pay for the costs of establishing and maintaining a monitoring program.

The measurement data can also be used to allocate resources and to identify future business opportunities. By quantifying your environmental performance, you can determine where resources will bring the most benefit, both environmentally and financially. You can also pinpoint areas where further improvement is possible or necessary and focus on finding alternative solutions.

✓ Finally, environmental performance data can be very useful for both internal and external communications. Let your employees know how the EMS is working. They will be interested in the results of the programs, plans, and systems that they have been working so hard to implement. If your measurements show significant environmental improvements, use this information for its public relations value. Let the regulators, local community, and other interested groups know of your efforts and results. See Chapter 12 for more information on external communications.

There is a lot of work involved in establishing an effective and useful measurement system, but it can be a critical tool for business success. With reliable data based on important performance metrics, you can quantify environmental and business improvement; communicate successes; provide valuable input to environmental objectives, targets, and programs; and make sound business decisions based on facts.

# NONCONFORMANCE AND CORRECTIVE AND PREVENTIVE ACTION

> ### ISO 14001 REQUIREMENTS*
>
> ISO 14001, section 4.5.2, Non-Conformance and Corrective and Preventive Action, requires the following:
>
> The organization shall establish and maintain procedures for defining responsibility and authority for handling and investigating nonconformance, taking action to mitigate any impacts caused and for initiating and completing corrective and preventive action.
>
> Any corrective or preventive action taken to eliminate the causes of actual and potential nonconformances shall be appropriate to the magnitude of problems and commensurate with the environmental impact encountered.
>
> The organization shall implement and record any changes in the documented procedures resulting from corrective and preventive action.

## INTERPRETATION

To those familiar with the language of ISO 9001, this section may seem disjointed and incomplete. Because of the precariousness of international consensus around this standard and the sensitivity of U.S. environmen-

*© International Organization for Standardization. All rights reserved.

tal professionals to certain wordings and liabilities, several key components of corrective action are implied rather than explicitly stated, which, makes this section more difficult to understand as a cohesive system. The annex provides a slightly more logical approach. Unfortunately, in this case, ISO 14004 is severely lacking and provides no further guidance.

Let's begin with the definition of nonconformance, which is conspicuously absent from ISO 14001, its annex, or ISO 14004. Since this is a management system standard, nonconformance should be interpreted broadly to include all types of system problems. This section is not limited to regulatory noncompliances but applies to any instance where actions or results differ from defined intentions.

A nonconformance results whenever a problem occurs in any part of the EMS. For example, a piece of equipment that is out of calibration, a process parameter that is outside prescribed operating limits, and an out-of-date procedure are all system nonconformances, even if these instances have not resulted in a regulatory noncompliance. These elements are a part of your defined system, so each has a role in managing the environment. If any of these or other elements of the system is not operating as intended, it has the potential to result in environmental problems, so corrective and preventive action is required.

Similarly, results of the system may be nonconformances. If a compliance audit indicates that a water discharge has exceeded its defined limits, a stated environmental target is missed, or someone in the local community complains about an unusual odor from your facility, these are also nonconformances that require corrective and preventive action.

Finally, your own internal monitoring systems may point to a need for corrective and preventive action. Internal EMS audits, compliance evaluations, document reviews, and management reviews all frequently identify nonconformances that need to be corrected and/or prevented. All of these different examples act as triggers for your corrective and preventive action system.

Now that nonconformance has been defined, we can take a closer look at what the standard requires when one occurs. The Annex to ISO 14001 provides a clearer picture of the process of corrective action. According to the Annex, the basic elements of investigating and correcting a nonconformance are these[*]:

a) identifying the cause of the nonconformance;
b) identifying and implementing the necessary corrective action;
c) implementing or modifying controls necessary to avoid repetition of the nonconformance;
d) recording any changes in written procedures resulting from corrective action.

[*]© International Organization for Standardization. All rights reserved.

This list outlines a basic problem-solving sequence that can be broadly applied to all types of nonconformances.

Letter *c* of the Annex excerpt above begins to define preventive action. Although the title of this section of ISO 14001 includes the word "preventive," it is not further defined within the text. There are two levels of preventive action. One is that alluded to in the Annex: when a problem occurs, you need to fix the immediate problem and also prevent it from recurring. This is also implicit in the standard's reference to corrective or preventive actions taken "to eliminate the cause of actual and potential nonconformances."

The second level of preventive action is the process of analyzing data to detect potential problems or nonconformances and taking action to prevent these from occurring. This is barely hinted at in this section but is implied in the standard's focus on monitoring, measurement, and continual improvement and is a direct requirement of ISO 9001. Preventive action of this type is directly linked with your systems for monitoring and measuring.

The language of this section, like that of many other sections, explicitly allows each business to consider its own needs and respond appropriately. The second paragraph states that actions taken "shall be appropriate to the magnitude of problems and commensurate with the environmental impact encountered." This means that you have the flexibility to respond with different levels of corrective action, depending on the extent of the environmental risk and the relative severity of the problem. You are not required to spend millions of dollars to correct a problem with a minimal environmental impact.

The last sentence of this section (and its associated Annex section) refers to changes in documented procedures. This means that besides correcting the immediate problem encountered, you also need to make permanent changes to your management system to prevent the problem from recurring. These changes may include revisions to procedures but could also encompass changes to training systems, job qualifications, defined responsibilities, or policies. In short, this includes all of the elements that make up the management system.

## IMPLEMENTATION

As with all management system elements, there are two implementation components to a corrective action system. The first is to understand the process and purpose of corrective action and how it works most effectively. The second is actually to implement an internal system for that corrective action process.

Figure 18-1 shows the basic steps of the corrective action process. This process is the same whether you are responding to a quality noncon-

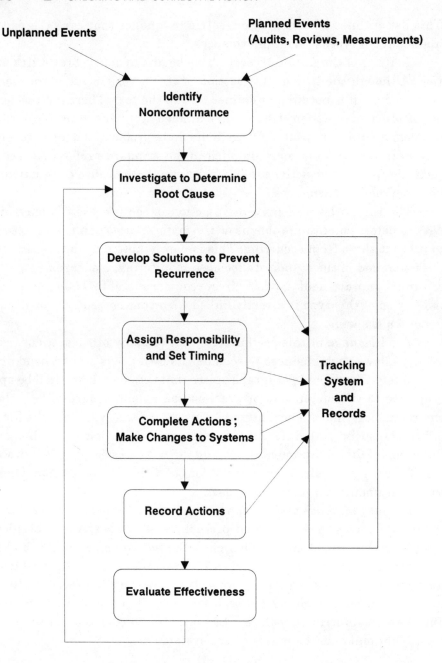

■ **FIGURE 18-1.** Corrective Action Process

formance, a safety nonconformance, or an environmental nonconformance. The ultimate purpose of any corrective action is to prevent the problem from recurring. In the case of preventive action, you want to prevent a potential problem from occurring in the first place. In this way, corrective action and preventive action drive continual improvement by eliminating problems for good.

### Identify the Nonconformance

The need for corrective or preventive action is initiated by a planned or unplanned event. Examples of planned events that are meant to detect current or potential nonconformances include audits (internal or external), management reviews, analyses of measurement data, and identification of potential emergencies. Each of these activities is covered in detail in Chapters 20, 21, 17, and 16, respectively. Unplanned events may include environmental incidents and resulting investigations, customer or community complaints, regulatory noncompliances, and any other problems or nonconformities that may occur throughout the business. As noted in the "Interpretation" section of this chapter, this also includes system nonconformances.

 It's important that the original identification of the nonconformance describe the problem and circumstances very clearly and completely. This will facilitate the later investigation to determine cause. Many organizations use a simple form, which is widely available to employees, to record problems or nonconformances. The form is then passed on to a manager or a central contact for corrective action.

 *KEY TO SUCCESS*

Every person in the organization should have the responsibility and authority to identify actual or potential problems needing corrective action. When auditing management systems, I have found that a common problem with corrective action systems is that they are applied too narrowly. For instance, a facility may use its corrective action system only for out-of-limits discharges or emissions and audit results. Other nonconformances are handled on an ad-hoc basis.

The best way to avoid this problem is to ensure that every employee understands that the required response to a problem of any sort is to take any necessary immediate action and then to record the problem for input into the corrective action system. Communication and training are necessary to help employees understand their responsibilities. If a problem is taken care of without entering it into the corrective action system, that is a nonconformance that requires its own corrective action. While this may seem to be a paperwork exercise, its real purpose is to eliminate problems rather than just fixing them in the short term.

### Investigate to Determine Root Cause

Once a problem has been identified, some sort of investigation or analysis is necessary to determine exactly how and why the problem occurred. It is important in this step to broadly analyze all related and associated systems, issues, and records and not to focus too narrowly on the specific area where the nonconformance occurred.

### KEY TO SUCCESS

This type of investigation is a critical component of continual improvement. Very often, during audits of corrective action records, I find that the actions recorded are superficial ones designed to fix the immediate problem rather than to eliminate the root cause. This not only results in audit nonconformances but also can have a very negative impact on your ability to improve the business.

For example, if a water discharge exceeds the site's allowable limits, the immediate action will be to adjust the process to bring the discharge within limits (and possibly to notify the local authority, if the limit is regulated). This will solve the immediate problem but it will not prevent the problem from occurring again. This approach is at the heart of many companies' worst organizational problem: they spend all of their time fighting fires, leaving no time to work on higher value improvements.

The solution is to approach every problem with an open mind and to investigate thoroughly to discover why it happened in the first place. Only after you have conducted such an investigation can you take steps to really prevent the problem from recurring. The catch-22 for many organizations is that you don't have time to investigate every nonconformance because you're spending all your time responding to the daily problems and urgencies that continue to occur. There is no easy way out of this vicious cycle except to make real corrective and preventive action an organizational priority. Once you begin to eliminate problems, you will be spending less time responding to them.

Be careful not to assume you know the cause of the problem without investigating. Recurring problems are typically rooted in one or more systems problems that may require further investigation to uncover. It's all too common to blame a problem or incident on some person's actions, but very few problems are really caused merely by human behavior. The real root causes are almost always in the underlying systems. For example, you need to look deeper to find out if there was adequate communication and training, if responsibilities were clearly defined, and if the written procedures accurately reflect best practices. "I talked to the employee and he agreed to be more careful next time" is not adequate corrective action!

The right people need to be involved in determining the cause of the nonconformance and in developing solutions. The person who identified the problem may or may not be the right person to investigate it. In some cases, you will have to form a multifunctional problem-solving team.

✓ To make sure that the right people are involved, identified problems should all go to a central contact point for the group or area. That contact can assign a person or team to investigate.

When it comes to the actual investigation, gather all pertinent data. Work process analysis methods such as flow-charting or process mapping are useful for understanding the entire system to determine all possible causes of a problem. Use recognized quality tools and methodologies to assure that the true root causes of the nonconformance are found. These could include fishbone diagrams, why-why diagrams, data analysis tools, and other methods.

### Develop Solutions to Prevent Recurrence

Once you have investigated and identified the root causes of the nonconformance, the next step is to figure out how to eliminate those causes. This may be as simple as revising a procedure or providing additional training, but many times solving a problem is not so straightforward.

Once again, the right people must be involved. These could be the same people who investigated the problem. In fact, many times the investigation and solution processes are merged. Be careful of this approach, however, because it's very easy to begin developing solutions before the root cause has been thoroughly investigated. For more critical or complex problems, it's best to approach investigation as a separate process from developing solutions.

 For these more complex issues, brainstorming can be an effective tool. The idea behind brainstorming is to come up with as many ideas as possible without evaluating them (yet). For this to work, there needs to be an open environment that encourages creative thinking without judging the ideas. Once a range of ideas and solutions have been identified, you can begin to compare and evaluate them.

When it comes to deciding how to solve the problem, you have a large degree of flexibility to respond in a way that is appropriate to the magnitude of the problem. The standard allows you this flexibility (as described in the "Interpretation" section above), and it makes sense from a business viewpoint that you will not want to respond to all problems in the same way or with the same amount of effort. In determining your response, ISO 14001 requires that you consider the severity of the environmental impact or environmental risk, and good business sense requires that you weigh the costs and benefits against those risks.

Solutions should be prioritized using appropriate risk-benefit analysis. Criteria for establishing priority may include

- Severity of the nonconformance (degree of impact on the environment and/or the business)
- Probability and potential of recurrence (frequency)
- Cost of correction
- Penalty or risk if not corrected

If a decision is made *not* to correct a nonconformance, given an assessment of the factors listed above, that decision must be adequately recorded, including the risk analysis that was made and the reasons for the decision.

Finally, as you consider solutions, remember to focus on long-term elimination of the problem. For many nonconformances, there may two levels of corrective action: immediate, short-term action to mitigate environmental impacts and longer-term, more permanent system changes to prevent the problem from recurring.

### Assign Responsibility and Timing

For each solution to a nonconformance, develop a specific action plan, including responsibilities and timing. Some organizations do a good job of investigating nonconformances but have problems implementing their solutions because of a lack of planning. If the actions are not specifically assigned to individuals, it's unlikely they will actually get done. If you ever hope to break out of that cycle of quick fixes and recurring problems, corrective action has to become a priority.

When determining timing, choose a reasonable time frame based on the urgency and importance of the problem. In his best-selling book *The Seven Habits of Highly Effective People*, Stephen Covey explains that all activities can be categorized according to their urgency and their importance. Most of us spend much of our time on activities that are urgent—whether or not they're important.

Long-term corrective and preventive actions typically fall into the category of important but not necessarily urgent. You have already taken care of the urgency by stopping the leak, fixing the equipment, or bringing the emissions back within limits. Preventing the problem from recurring sometime in the future is often lost in a new flurry of urgent activities. It takes conscious planning to ensure that the followup takes place.

## KEY TO SUCCESS
### Use a Tracking System

Because of this normal tendency in both people and organizations, it's critical to put together specific plans that spell out responsibilities and expected timing. In addition, there needs to be some sort of followup or tracking process to ensure that the plan is actually implemented.

The importance of a tracking system was illustrated most clearly to me when I heard about one plant that nearly lost its registration because of problems in its corrective action system. Although the site had a well-defined system that seemed to be effective during the initial assessment, in the first surveillance audit the auditors found dozens of incomplete corrective actions. The system was working well at identifying nonconformances and solutions, but these were not being acted on. With a tracking system in place, along with a few other changes, the site was able to reduce its backlog, improve its system, and keep its registration.

Figure 18-1 shows several of the corrective action steps that feed into a tracking system. The tracking system accomplishes two important things: it provides a way of tracking progress toward completing corrective actions and provides a record of the actions taken. I've seen effective tracking systems in both paper and electronic form; the best type of system depends on your own organization.

Some organizations rely on the same simple form for employees to initiate corrective action, to track progress, and to serve as a record. One example of a form that works well is shown in Figure 18-2. Notice that it includes space for assigned responsibilities and timing. Another important feature is that it has space to record both short- and long-term actions. This allows employees to record the actions taken immediately while also serving as a reminder that longer-term prevention must also be addressed.

■ CHECKING AND CORRECTIVE ACTION

## COMPANY ABC CORRECTIVE ACTION FORM

Date: _____

Description of Problem/Nonconformance: _____

_____

_____


Assigned To: _____

Estimated Completion Date: _____

Root Cause (Results of Investigation): _____

_____

_____

_____


Immediate Action Taken: _____

_____

_____


Long-term Action Taken to Prevent Recurrence: _____

_____

_____

_____


Follow-up (Has the problem been eliminated?):

_____          _____
           Signed                             Date

*Revision Date: January 15, 1996*

■ **FIGURE 18-2.** Sample Corrective Action Form

These paper forms are typically collected and filed by a central contact, who tracks the progress of the corrective action. For instance, when a due date draws near, the coordinator can contact the responsible person to ask whether the actions have been completed. A quick review of the records can reveal which actions are still pending.

A few organizations use a fully computerized system that has the same basic features as the paper form. Most corrective action systems that I have seen rely on a combination of the two, typically using a paper form, which is easily accessible by all employees, along with a computer database used mainly by the coordinator(s) to track progress. This type of database can be extremely useful if it is well designed. Table 18-1 lists important features to look for in this type of system.

## Complete Actions

Now it's time for the assigned people to complete the corrective actions and, hopefully, to eliminate the problem. Remember to make permanent changes to your management system wherever needed. These may include procedure revisions, changes in defined responsibilities, or changes to training procedures or syllabi. If the corrective action has included an actual process change, this will likely result in procedural changes as well.

### ■ TABLE 18-1 Elements of a Corrective Action Tracking System

Whether a paper or electronic tracking system is used, it should have the capability to do the following:

- Record the corrective action number and title
- Categorize the nonconformance (e.g., audit finding, safety, quality, environmental)
- Record a description of the problem, responsibilities for resolution, root causes identified, recommended actions, actions taken, and assessment of the effectiveness of the solution
- Group multiple corrective actions under a single record or file
- Assign responsibilities for a single corrective action to multiple personnel (although one person should be accountable for completion)
- Assign a due date for each corrective action
- Update the status of the corrective action

In addition, it is helpful if the system has the ability to generate reports, including reports on

- All incomplete corrective actions
- Status of all corrective actions within a given category
- All corrective actions associated with a particular category
- Past-due corrective actions
- All corrective actions assigned to a particular person

Occasionally, the actual actions taken may be different from the recommended actions based on the initial investigation. This can happen when something has changed in the organization or process since the nonconformance occurred. You may also be midway through the corrective action when you suddenly find that the proposed solution will not eliminate the problem. This is an indication that the investigation may not have uncovered the true root cause. Regardless of the reason, there is nothing wrong with taking a different action than was recommended as long as the reason for the change is adequately recorded.

### Record Actions Taken

The process does not end when the corrective actions have been taken. It's important to record changes made and actions taken. These records provide evidence for auditors (both internal and external) that the corrective action system is being followed. More important, these records could be valuable to your own organization. If a problem recurs or a similar problem occurs later, you can go back to see what actions were taken previously and why.

The record of actions taken may be written on the corrective action form, entered into a computer database, or noted on a log. The format of the records is up to you. Any EMS records kept should be maintained in accordance with the requirements described in Chapter 19.

If the corrective action includes changes to the system (as most will), communication and/or training may also be necessary. If a procedure has changed, you need to let the people who use it know of the change, especially if they do not often refer to the written procedure. Some corrective actions will be based on communication, as when a procedure is correct but has not been followed.

### Evaluate Effectiveness

The final step in the corrective action process is to make sure that you really did eliminate the root cause of the problem. This can be accomplished in a variety of ways, but the simplest is to include corrective action followup in internal audits. The internal auditors then need to verify that the actions were taken and that they have been effective in preventing the problem from recurring. If you would prefer to keep corrective action followup separate from internal audits, the coordinator or internal auditors can followup at designated intervals.

To assess effectiveness, there needs to be some time lag between the corrective action and the followup or audit. I've seen records which show a followup check the day after the action was taken. At that point, it's difficult or impossible to tell whether the action will really be effective in the long term.

As with all other steps, there should be some evidence of this followup. The example form in Figure 18-2 uses a signature and date to indicate this final check. This is a common way to record the verification, but some organizations prefer more detailed written comments.

### Setting Up the System

With an understanding of how corrective action should work, it's time to actually develop and implement the system. As with most EMS elements, you will need a procedure that defines your own practices. This procedure should include the following:

- Responsibilities for identifying, tracking, and recording corrective actions
- Description of the tracking system used
- Examples of the events in your business that would trigger a corrective action
- References to tools or methodologies used for investigating nonconformances and problem solving
- References to relevant procedures, such as internal auditing, management reviews, monitoring and measurement, and emergency planning

Since an effective corrective action system uses the same process regardless of the type of nonconformance, extensive integration with other management systems is possible. Quality, safety, and environmental nonconformances can all be resolved using the same system. If you already have some sort of corrective action system for ISO 9001, QS-9000, or OSHA's 1910.119, simply improve and expand it as necessary to include environmental nonconformances. A single system will be less confusing and more effective for the entire organization.

Some companies prefer to track various types of nonconformances separately, even though they are all corrected using the same basic process. If this is the case for your organization, simply define how your own system works in your procedure. Many databases can track and report on different types of nonconformances separately if some sort of identifier is used to categorize them.

I know that all of these steps sound like an enormous amount of work, but consider the potential value. If you could just take care of all of those recurring problems and all that daily firefighting, you would have the time and money to do the things you really want to do for your business. An effective corrective action system can help you do exactly that. This is one of the most powerful and valuable elements of a management system. Use it to its full potential.

# RECORDS

> ### ISO 14001 REQUIREMENTS*
> 
> ISO 14001, section 4.5.3, Records, requires the following:
> 
> The organization shall establish and maintain procedures for the identification, maintenance and disposition of environmental records. These records shall include training records and the results of audits and reviews.
> 
> Environmental records shall be legible, identifiable and traceable to the activity, product or service involved. Environmental records shall be stored and maintained in such a way that they are readily retrievable and protected against damage, deterioration or loss. Their retention times shall be established and recorded.
> 
> Records shall be maintained, as appropriate to the system and to the organization, to demonstrate conformance to the requirements of this International Standard.

## INTERPRETATION

Although records are involved in most elements of a management system, this section of ISO 14001 specifically addresses the maintenance of those records. It states that you need to have procedures that describe how you manage all the different records kept in conjunction with your EMS.

*© International Organization for Standardization. All rights reserved.

Records and documents are often confused (even the ISO standards fail to use the terms consistently!). Remember that a record is a *history* of something that has happened; therefore, it cannot be changed. A document, by its very nature, is likely to be changed. Because of this distinction, documents must be controlled so that the most recent version is always in use. Records simply need to be maintained (filed, stored, etc.) in case you need to refer to them later.

One difference between ISO 9001 and ISO 14001 is that ISO 9001 specifically identifies many of the records that you are required to keep. Many of the individual clauses of the standard state that records shall be maintained and provide a reference to the Records clause of the standard. ISO 14001 has very few specific references to required records. The Records clause itself mentions training, audit, and review records, but most other sections only imply the need for records.

This means that it will be up to your own organization to define which records are necessary to "demonstrate conformance to the requirements of this standard." Besides training, audits, and reviews, records of the following will likely be needed:

- Environmental aspect and significant impact identification/evaluation process
- Considerations made in setting objectives and targets
- Internal and external communications
- Decision whether to provide external communication on significant aspects
- Document revisions
- Operational control
- Identification of environmentally significant suppliers
- Identification of potential emergencies
- Testing of emergency response procedures
- Monitoring and measurement data
- Calibration of equipment
- Corrective actions
- Regulatory compliance evaluations/audits

This is a generic list, based only on ISO 14001. You will need to look at your own organization to develop a complete list of EMS records (see "Implementation" section, below).

The standard requires records to be "legible, identifiable and traceable." "Legible" is just plain common sense. "Identifiable and traceable" means that if you choose a record from a file or database, you can tell what it is associated with. For example, a date and product or process designation would allow you to know exactly what the record pertains to.

"Readily retrievable" has created all kinds of fun for third-party auditors. I have occasionally heard tales of auditors who defined this to mean that the record could be found within five or ten minutes. They then ask for a certain record and monitor their watches while the auditees go off on a game-show-like chase. A more sensible interpretation is to consider how the record is actually used by your own business. If it's something you need to access frequently, can it be easily and quickly located? If it's a record that is rarely used by your organization, it may be stored in a separate office or even on microfilm or computer backup tapes. Use your own needs to determine what "readily retrievable" means, not some auditor's irrelevant rule of thumb. (And find a new auditor!)

The standard requires that retention times be established and documented. "Retention time" simply means the length of time you will keep the record before disposing of it. The pros and cons of minimum and maximum retention times, along with legal implications, are discussed in the "Implementation" section.

## IMPLEMENTATION

Figure 19-1 shows the major steps in establishing a comprehensive system for environmental records. This is a fairly straightforward system to implement, and you may find that much of it already exists in your organization. As with other parts of the EMS, it's common to find that pieces of the system exist but are not connected in a cohesive way.

### Identify Records

Begin by identifying environmental records that are explicitly or implicitly required by ISO 14001, as well as any additional records that are important and useful to your own organization. The list of implied records requirements in the "Interpretation" section is a good starting point.

### KEY TO SUCCESS

You should not be keeping a record to satisfy ISO 14001 that does not also have some value to your business, and as you look through the records indicated on your list you should check that they will be useful in some way. If you feel there are records that are being kept only to satisfy the standard or that are creating an unnecessary paperwork burden, take another look at the words in the standard to reevaluate the requirement. Many times, assumptions are made about the standard's requirements based on hear-

**190** ■ CHECKING AND CORRECTIVE ACTION

say or overly prescriptive auditors. Examine the standard's actual words and find a way to meet that specific record requirement without creating an organizational burden.

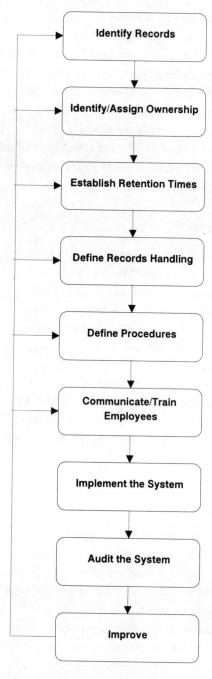

■ **FIGURE 19-1.** Establishing a Records System

There may be additional records that are not required by ISO 14001 but that are important to your business. Be sure to include these records, which you may already be maintaining. It's a good idea to handle all of your environmental records under a single system. This is less confusing and emphasizes that the EMS is simply a part of your business and not a stand-alone project.

Many businesses find it helpful to create a list or lists of environmental records as the basis for their procedures. Depending on the size and complexity of the organization and its culture, you can create a single list of all environmental records or separate lists by area, department, or function.

### Identify/Assign Ownership

A person or group should be designated as the "owner" of each identified record. That owner will be responsible for ensuring that records are filed and maintained properly and that retention times are followed. To ensure accountability, it is usually best to designate a single person rather than a group, but there may be circumstances where a group or function makes sense.

You may already be keeping many of the records identified above, and in these cases identifying the owner is just a formality. For new records or records that have been poorly maintained in the past, consider the record type, location, and frequency of use. Some organizations assign a single records coordinator for each area, and others assign maintenance of different records to various people throughout the organization.

### Establish Retention Times

Establishing retention times can be a difficult process and requires some thoughtful consideration. I have heard many speakers, consultants, and course instructors advise organizations to make these decisions based on avoiding risk during an audit. They tell their clients to set only minimum retention times so that they will always be in compliance with their system. While this strategy may get you through your third-party audits, it certainly is not adding value to your system.

In making sound business decisions regarding retention times, the first step is to identify a minimum time period to ensure that the record is available should it be needed. Consider various uses of each record. For example, particular environmental records could be used to investigate an incident, a complaint, or some other type of nonconformance. They could be used to compare current performance to past performance. There may be a need to establish a longer minimum retention time to satisfy specific regulatory requirements or for reasons of product liability (e.g., the useful life of a product), or you may desire a longer minimum retention time to facilitate periodic trend analysis.

Next, consider the maximum retention times for each record. Although these will establish limits within your EMS that you will have to meet, there are very important reasons for establishing maximum retention periods. The first and foremost is for legal protection. Most medium-sized and large corporations have established very specific policies and standards regarding records retention. The primary reason for this is to protect the company and reduce legal costs.

Although some of these corporate retention times are largely ignored, consider the consequences. Suppose you are only supposed to keep 10 years' worth of production data, but you've never thrown out a single record in the 30-year life of the facility (this is not at all unusual!). Now a minor product-liability case is brought against your company. Instead of reviewing 10 years of data, the lawyers will be reviewing three times that much! This will add up to excessive costs for your company and potentially greater liability. These types of situations occur in American businesses every day.

Another reason for establishing maximum retention times is of a more practical nature and affects your day-to-day operations. If you continue to keep records long beyond their useful life, the cost of maintaining those records will continue to grow without any useful benefit or payback. These costs will result from both storage space and the increased time required to find a record as volume increases.

 Once, I was working with a client company on its ISO 9001 implementation and asked about the company's records retention. The manager laughed and said they'd need a forklift to retrieve all the records that had been stuffed into their warehouse over the years! Another client confided to me that the production managers had hundreds of binders, filled with data going back 40 years, that they would never part with. These are very real, very common scenarios that reduce the efficiency and effectiveness of your organization.

Find out if your company has any corporate rules regarding record retention. Find out which regulatory rules apply to your organization. Based on these factors, plus a consideration of how you will use the records, decide on some reasonable retention times. Then establish processes to help you stick to them.

### Define Records Handling

Next you need to determine how records will be collected, where they will be filed, how they will be safeguarded from damage or loss, and how they will eventually be disposed of. Although these decisions could be left up to the individuals with responsibility for the records, you may want to set some guidelines or standards.

Remember that records may be in paper or electronic form. Hard copy records may be simplified by using a standard form to collect the data. Similarly, computer database input forms should be designed to make data collection simple and as error-free as possible. Decide on the appropriate format for each type of record.

In determining how to handle your records, consider the following points:

- Should environmental records be kept in a single location?
- Do potential records users have access to databases or files?
- Are electronic records protected from inadvertent changes?
- Are records "readily retrievable" and available where they are most often needed?
- What type of filing or cataloging system will be used so that records can be easily located?
- Will all records of a certain type be kept in one location or will older records be kept separately?

While some of these questions may seem simplistic, it's likely that most of your current records system was defined by default. You do things a certain way simply because that's the way they've always been done. Reviewing your current practices and asking these types of questions could lead to opportunities for improved efficiency.

Finally, be sure to consider the issue not only of when to dispose of records but also of *how*. Even if you have records retention policies in place, it's likely that they are not being strictly followed. Now is the time to define the processes that will allow you to stick to your policies. Who will be responsible for disposing of records? How often will they be disposed of? How should they be disposed of? These are important questions to consider while you are defining the system.

For instance, if you have set a maximum retention time for audit records of five years, does that mean that the records need to be reviewed every week so that there are always exactly five years' worth of records available? Or will you define an annual disposal time so that the last five full calendar years of records are available? Carefully consider the realities of complying with your own policies.

DuPont has an annual records disposal campaign called "Swing into Spring." Each spring, a particular week is set aside when every employee is supposed to review his or her records against the corporate records retention guidelines and throw out any old records that were past their retention dates or no longer needed. Although people gripe about it each year, it's actually a great opportunity to clean out individual files and get rid of old information that no longer has any value.

### Define Responsibility and Authority

Besides defining responsibility for individual records, establish responsibilities and authorities for the overall records system, just as you have done for other elements of your EMS. It should be clear who has the authority to add a new record to the system, to discontinue a record, or to make any modifications to a record. Also, consider who can make changes in ownership, retention period, or handling methods.

Another important facet of records responsibility is determining accessibility to records and the authority to disseminate information. There may be certain records that have limited access or records that are considered proprietary. This could be particularly important with respect to regulatory agencies. Clearly define responsibilities and authority for communicating with regulatory bodies (see Chapter 12, "Communications").

### Define Procedures

Now that all of these elements of the records system are defined, they need to be documented. Once again, although the standard uses the term "procedures," these may be in many different formats. As mentioned earlier in this chapter, many organizations find tables or lists a simple way to identify records. To be effective, these lists should include (as a minimum) the record title, location, person responsible, and retention time. In addition to a list or database indicating which records are kept, you may need a simple written procedure or flowchart to describe your overall records practices and responsibilities.

### Communicate/Train Employees

A critical factor in any management system is ensuring that the people who will use the system have a sufficient understanding of it. Doing this may be as simple as spending 15 minutes during a weekly meeting to describe changes to the system and then distributing a procedure or as involved as providing training on a new database computer system. You have to consider your own organization's needs, including current records practices and the extent of changes to the system.

The training component can be especially critical if major changes have been made. I've done audits of organizations with computer systems that had incredible functionality but that were virtually useless because of a lack of comprehensive training. It does not matter if the record is in the computer if the employee who needs it does not know how to get to it. I can also remember the obvious pride of a well-trained mechanic showing me how his computer system tracked calibration records. Good communication and training can make the difference between a mediocre system and one that drives business improvement.

### Implement the System

Now comes the real test. You have defined a comprehensive records management system and made some improvements. How does it work in real life? The only way to find out is to use it. Encourage feedback from people and get the system operating so you can test it out. In the first few months, be on the lookout for problems. Are there missing records? Do people know where to look to find what they need? Are records located where they're supposed to be?

 The rule of thumb for the entire management system is to use it for at least three months prior to an outside audit to find and correct any flaws.

### Audit the System

This is the "Check" part of the Plan-Do-Check-Act cycle. Besides using the system in daily work, conduct periodic audits as a part of your EMS audit system (see Chapter 20). You can often uncover problems during an audit that might not show up immediately in use. Examination of records will be a natural part of every facet of the audit, so it should give you ample opportunity to look at the records system.

During audits, you will be checking to ensure that the procedures are being followed and that the procedures accurately reflect actual practice. For the records system, look at the following:

- Do all environmental records have established responsibilities and retention times?
- Are records located as documented in the lists, databases, or procedures?
- Are retention times being followed?
- Are there any records related to the EMS that have not been included in the system?
- During the course of the audit, are all records requested found in a reasonable amount of time, based on normal use?

### Improve the System

Through normal use and audits (both internal and external), you will identify ways to correct and improve the records system. In addition, you may want to establish a review period, perhaps every two or three years, to review the system as a whole to be sure it is still meeting your needs. You may find that retention times need to be adjusted, responsibilities shifted, old records obsoleted, or new records created. You want the records system to keep up with and enhance your overall business system, not detract from it by creating excess paperwork.

### Integration with Other Management Systems

Records management is an area with ample opportunity for integration with other systems besides the EMS. ISO 9001 and QS-9000 quality systems and OSHA's 1910.119 process safety system include records requirements similar to those in ISO 14001 (the section in ISO 9001 is almost identical). Combining these systems will make your overall business simpler to manage and operate.

The extent of integration is up to your own organization to determine. You could use the same general procedures but establish separate lists of environmental records. You could use a fully integrated system with environmentally related records identified within that system. You could also choose not to differentiate between environmental, quality, safety, and other records. You may find that many records are used in multiple ways, in which case distinguishing environmental records from quality records would merely add unnecessary complexity to the system. Consider your own business's use of records and make a decision that fits your needs. Remember, there's always room for improvement!

# CHAPTER 20

# ENVIRONMENTAL MANAGEMENT SYSTEM AUDIT

## ISO 14001 REQUIREMENTS*

ISO 14001, section 4.5.4, Environmental Management System Audit, requires the following:

The organization shall establish and maintain (a) programme(s) and procedures for periodic environmental management system audits to be carried out, in order to

a) determine whether or not the environmental management system
   1) conforms to planned arrangements for environmental management including the requirements of this International Standard; and
   2) has been properly implemented and maintained; and
b) provide information on the results of audits to management.

The organization's audit programme, including any schedule, shall be based on the environmental importance of the activity concerned and the results of previous audits. In order to be comprehensive, the audit procedures shall cover the audit scope, frequency and methodologies, as well as the responsibilities and requirements for conducting and reporting results.

*© International Organization for Standardization. All rights reserved.

## INTERPRETATION

The overall requirement embodied in this section is for organizations to periodically audit the entire EMS. This type of system audit is distinct from the regulatory compliance auditing discussed in Chapter 17. An EMS audit compares the system that's been implemented against the ISO 14001 standard and against the organization's own documentation describing that system.

This section clearly lays out the purpose of EMS audits and also describes their role in informing management of the status of the EMS. Notice that ISO 14001 does not require that EMS audits look at the effectiveness of the system. This is one of several differences between this section of ISO 14001 and the parallel section in ISO 9001.

Another difference is that ISO 14001 does not require these EMS audits to be internal. If you look carefully, you will notice that the word "internal" does not appear in this section at all. By contrast, the systems audit section of ISO 9001 is entitled "Internal Quality Audits." This omission was intentional on the part of the ISO 14001 authors, to allow organizations to use external auditors to fulfill these requirements, if they wish. Audits may be conducted by auditors within the EMS, by auditors from another division or corporate headquarters, or even by auditors completely external to your organization, as long as you meet the other stated requirements of this section. The pros and cons of each approach are discussed in the "Implementation" section, below.

People familiar with ISO 9001 will notice one other very obvious omission in ISO 14001: there is no requirement for auditors to be independent of the areas they audit. To be completely honest, this is mainly due to a misunderstanding by some members of the U.S. TAG (and possibly other delegations to TC 207) of what that term "independent" implies.

The argument during the U.S. TAG meetings was that small organizations may not be able to afford to establish a separate auditing staff. ISO 9001 implementers and auditors understand that this requirement for independence does not mean that a separate staff is needed. In fact, even most large corporations cannot afford to maintain a dedicated auditing staff. ISO 9001 specifies that auditors must be "independent of those having direct responsibility for the activity being audited." To meet this requirement, most organizations develop a system of cross-auditing, where auditors from various areas of the business audit areas different from the ones they work in. Thus, even an organization of two people can conduct independent audits—you just don't audit your own job function.

Despite the explanations to this effect by myself and others in the U.S. TAG, the "independence" requirement was still voted down. The final compromise within TC 207 was to include a statement in the Annex to ISO 14001 to address the need for objectivity. This statement says

> Audits may be performed by personnel from within the organization and/or by external persons selected by the organization. In either case, the persons conducting the audit should be in a position to do so impartially and objectively.*

This essentially means the exact same thing as the statement in ISO 9001/2, except that it is in the Annex and is therefore not an absolute requirement of ISO 14001.

This section does include an unusual amount of detail as to what the procedures must include. Most sections of the standard merely state that procedures are required and leave the content up to the organization to determine. This level of detail is due in part to some very strong convictions by members of TC 207 regarding the elements of an effective audit system.

The standard also requires an audit program or programs. As with the environmental management program required in section 4.3.4, the term *programme* is being used in the British sense (and spelling!) and may not be widely understood in the United States. "Program" here refers to an audit plan for the organization, indicating how all areas of the EMS and of the organization will be audited and at what frequency.

Notice that the standard calls for "periodic" audits. The frequency is left to the organization to determine for itself, based on the relative environmental impacts and importance of various functions and on the status of the EMS. Areas that have a greater environmental impact or that have had many system nonconformances in the past may need to be audited more frequently than other areas. Although no minimum frequency is prescribed, many ISO 9000 auditors have required that the entire system should be audited at least once per year.

## IMPLEMENTATION

The purpose of internal auditing is to find out whether what is actually happening is what you had planned to happen, whether you're doing what you've said you would do, and whether the systems you've implemented are effective. Although ISO 14001 does not require you to evaluate the effectiveness of the EMS during audits, it makes sense to include this function and get the most information you can from your audits. After all, what good is a clearly documented, fully implemented EMS if it is not operating effectively?

Throughout the process of establishing an audit system and the ongoing process of conducting audits, keep in mind that audits have traditionally been perceived as confrontational. In one of our courses, we

*© International Organization for Standardization. All rights reserved.

ask people for their initial impressions when they hear the word "audit." The responses are always similar. People think of being tested, of investigations, and of trying to hide errors and problems. They are apprehensive, fearful, and nervous. Most Americans immediately think of the IRS!

You don't want these kinds of reactions to your internal audits. The whole idea behind internal auditing is to get an accurate and honest idea of the state of the system so that you can improve it. Audits will be of little value to your organization if people feel that they will be blamed or punished if any nonconformances are found. Keep this perception in mind as we take a look at how to conduct effective audits and develop a solid audit system.

In order to establish an effective EMS audit system, you need to have a good understanding of how to conduct audits. As was briefly mentioned in Chapter 17, any type of audit can be broken into four distinct stages. These audit stages, shown in Figure 20-1, are Preparation, Evaluation, Reporting, and Corrective Action. Each stage includes specific activities. Although external audits follow the same general format, I will focus on the specifics of conducting an internal audit here.

### Preparation

Thorough preparation is absolutely critical to conducting effective audits. No matter how experienced an auditor you are, the time you spend preparing before an audit will always pay off. I was once asked to help a

■ **FIGURE 20-1.** Audit Stages

small client facility get started with its internal quality system audits. I visited the site and worked with the facility's two trained internal auditors to guide them through preparation for the site's first audit against ISO 9001.

The next morning, one of the auditors was called home for a personal emergency. So that the audit could be fully performed, at the last minute the site asked me to take his place to audit those areas he had been assigned. I'm a certified Quality Systems Lead Auditor and have conducted plenty of audits, but that particular audit was the worst I've ever done. Since the auditors had done most of the document review and preparation themselves, with my guidance, I was not very familiar with the details of their system and had not developed my own checklist. Lacking adequate preparation, I felt nervous and disorganized. I overlooked aspects of the system and missed opportunities for followup questions. Although the site was actually quite pleased with the overall audit, I knew it was not as comprehensive and thorough as it could have been. That day I found out firsthand just how important preparation is.

Several key activities should occur during the preparation stage of an internal audit. Some of these will occur as a part of the general audit system, and other aspects will be accomplished by the audit team to prepare for a particular audit.

**Assemble Audit Team** Internal audits may be conducted by a single auditor or a small audit team (see "What Size Should Audit Teams Be?" in the box). In most cases, the audit plan will designate who is on the audit team for each audit. That team needs to get together well in advance of the scheduled audit to begin preparing.

**Define Audit Plan** Next the team needs to understand the scope of the audit and define a specific plan for conducting it. This is sometimes done by the audit team leader and sometimes by the entire team. In most cases, the internal audit system will define the general scope for each audit. This is usually an area or functional group (such as design or purchasing), a portion of the EMS (such as document control or corrective action), or a particular project or process (e.g., a certain plant or a specific development project) although it could also be the entire EMS.

Within that general description of the scope, the audit team needs to decide exactly what should be included. If the team will be auditing an area or function, they may want to use or create a cross-reference matrix to indicate which areas of the standard are applicable and to ensure a comprehensive audit (see Table 20-1). Once they have a good understanding of the scope, they should divide it among the auditors to determine

> **What Size Should Audit Teams Be?**
>
> Internal audits are often conducted using a small team, although individual auditors can also be used. Many businesses prefer to use teams of two auditors. Inexperienced auditors are often somewhat self-conscious and nervous, and it helps to have another auditor along. It works well to pair an experienced auditor with a newly trained auditor so that the trainee has a chance to take a gradually greater role in the audits.
>
> One large pigments plant that I consulted with used three-person audit teams in a system that worked quite well. Within each audit team, one person was the designated lead auditor, another the auditor, and the third was a trainee. In this rotating system, each year the trainee would become the auditor, the auditor would become the lead auditor, the lead auditor would rotate off, and a new audit trainee would be added. The team of three would then work together throughout the year. This system allowed a wide variety of site personnel to be involved as internal auditors and avoided any excessive time commitments from any one person.
>
> That particular system worked well, but audit teams should not have more than three people, and even three people might be excessive if they stay together throughout the audit. Many people perceive audits to be somewhat confrontational and when a large group of auditors questions a single person, it tends to reinforce that perception. Even in two-person audit teams, it's best if the auditors agree to a method of alternating questions so as not to overwhelm the auditee.

each one's responsibilities. Consider both expertise and independence (or objectivity).

 Even if the auditors will be working in pairs or small groups, they should still divide the preparation and auditing among themselves so that each will have a role.

**Review Documentation** With responsibilities defined, it's time to begin the detailed audit preparation. Each auditor needs to become familiar with the documentation which is pertinent to the area(s) he or she will be auditing. At a minimum, this should include the EMS manual or equivalent and relevant procedures. The audit system should define who is responsible for gathering the documentation—the audit coordinator, audit team leader, or individual auditors. The time spent reviewing documentation is valuable because the manuals and procedures form the basis for

■ **TABLE 20-1** Sample Cross-Reference Matrix of ISO 14001 versus Plant Departments

| ISO 14001 | Administration | Purchasing | Manufacturing | Packaging | Environment | Laboratory | Shipping |
|---|---|---|---|---|---|---|---|
| Policy | X | X | X | X | X | X | X |
| Environmental Aspects | X | | | | X | | |
| Legal Requirements | | | | | X | | |
| Objectives/Targets | X | | | | X | | |
| EM Program | X | | | | X | | |
| Responsibility | X | X | X | X | X | X | X |
| Training | X | X | X | X | X | X | X |
| Communication | X | X | X | X | X | X | X |
| Documentation | X | X | X | X | X | X | X |
| Document Control | X | X | X | X | X | X | X |
| Operational Control | | X | X | X | | X | X |
| Emergency Response | X | | X | | X | | |
| Monitoring/Measurement | X | X | X | X | X | X | X |
| Corrective Action | X | X | X | X | X | X | X |
| Records | X | X | X | X | X | X | X |
| EMS Audit | X | X | X | X | X | X | X |
| Management Review | X | | | | X | | |

most of the audit. Audits attempted without the benefit of this review are much less efficient and effective because the auditor is forced to try to review and understand the procedures during the audit itself.

In addition to acting as a preparation step, the document review serves another purpose. It is actually a part of the audit known as an adequacy audit. This means that the auditors are assessing the adequacy of the documentation against the requirements of the standard. Later, the auditors will verify that what is documented is actually implemented.

**Prepare Checklists**  Once each auditor has a basic understanding of the documented system, he or she needs to develop an audit checklist. A well-prepared checklist makes the difference between a confident and effective auditor and a mediocre auditor.

An audit checklist is not a script of questions to be asked but rather a guide to help the auditor remember the key points to cover. A bulleted list usually works well, although many different formats can be used. If the checklist is too specific, listing exact questions to be asked, it will limit the audit by not allowing the auditor the freedom to pursue audit trails or different lines of inquiry which may occur.

Some businesses (and unfortunately, most registrars) use generic, pre-made checklists based on the standard. The problem with these is that they do not take into account the specific defined system which is being audited. In addition, because the checklist is already prepared, many auditors who use them end up spending little time on preparation. The result is often a limited, superficial audit.

A few clients of mine have insisted on using pre-made checklists. I encouraged them to create their own standard checklists, based on their own defined systems, rather than using a generic one. In addition, auditors should still spend some preparation time reviewing documentation and customizing the printed checklist to account for any system changes as well as their own auditing preferences and needs.

**Conduct Opening Meeting**  The final step in the preparation phase is to conduct some form of an opening meeting. In external or third-party audits, the opening meeting is a formal meeting with top management. In an internal audit, it could be similar or it could simply be a one-on-one discussion between the audit team and the manager of the area about to be audited.

The purpose of the opening meeting is to introduce the team, describe the purpose of the audit, and ensure that the area knows what to expect. Surprise audits are not a good idea, as they reinforce the confrontational perception of an audit. During the opening meeting, the audit team leader should discuss the following points:

- Introduce the audit team, if necessary (for instance in a large organization)
- Reaffirm the audit scope
- Review the specific audit plan and schedule

- Ensure that the documents reviewed prior to the audit are still current (or obtain updated copies)
- Answer any questions

When the opening meeting is finished, it's time to conduct the actual audit.

### Evaluation

During the evaluation phase, the auditors focus on interviewing various personnel and observing actual practices. Using their checklists as a guide, the auditors evaluate whether the EMS is implemented and is effective. Earlier, during the documentation review, the audit team assessed whether the documented system was adequate to meet the requirements of the standard. Now they will check to verify that the documented system is operating as described.

The attitude of the auditors is critical in ensuring open, positive, improvement-focused audits. The auditors are not looking for nonconformances. Rather, they are assuming that the system is in conformance and are auditing to verify it. This may seem a trivial point, but it is actually an important distinction. I've seen plenty of auditors who go out hunting for nonconformances and express outright glee when they find one! Imagine the impact this has on the person being audited.

Even with the right attitude, the auditors are likely to find nonconformances—examples where the documented system is not being followed or where the requirements of the standard are not being met. Although ISO 14001 uses the term "nonconformance," you can use whatever terminology makes sense for your own organization. "Discrepancy," "nonconformity," and "audit finding" are all commonly used terms. Some organizations emphasize the positive purpose of audits by using terms such as "improvement opportunity."

When an auditor finds a nonconformance, he or she needs to record it very specifically so that the area being audited can followup and correct it later. This skill takes some practice. If the write-up is not detailed enough, the area may have a hard time recalling exactly what the nonconformance was. Most businesses use some sort of form to record each nonconformance that is found during an audit.

The checklist is a handy tool during the audit. It serves as a guide to the auditor on where to go, whom to talk to, what records or documents to look at, and what details to look for. It also aids in time management, since it indicates the full scope that the auditor needs to cover in the allotted time. There never seems to be enough time during an audit! Finally, most auditors also use their checklist to take notes, both for followup points and for writing nonconformances later (if they are not written down while auditing).

Mostly, the auditor needs to ask thoughtful questions, listen carefully to the responses, and observe what's happening in the area. Asking the kinds of questions that gain valuable information while also putting the auditee at ease requires a great deal of skill. In addition, auditors need to listen carefully and ask followup questions where appropriate. It's been said that an auditor has two eyes, two ears, and one mouth and that they should be used in those proportions.

Finally, the auditor must rely on objective evidence at all times. Hearsay is not an acceptable basis for a nonconformance. Auditors must rely on written documents, records, and verified, firsthand statements. This requires careful followup on audit trails until objective evidence is found to support a suspected nonconformance. I can well remember my first ISO 9000 audits: when I'd come back to the conference room at the end of the day to write up the nonconformances, I often found that I hadn't gone far enough in my questioning and auditing to get to the evidence I needed and therefore could not write the nonconformance. This is very common with beginning auditors.

## Reporting

***Nonconformance Reports*** First, each auditor needs to write his or her individual nonconformances, using the form or format defined by the system. Each of these should be precise, factual, and based on objective evidence. Some organizations use the same form to record and track corrective actions pertaining to each nonconformance.

***Summary Report*** The individual nonconformance reports record the detailed audit findings but may not adequately describe the overall results of the audit. It's very helpful for the audit team to summarize the audit in a brief report. This report can serve several functions. It can provide management with a broad view of the results of the audit, provide the area audited with additional direction for corrective actions and improvements, and serve as a detailed record of the scope of the audit.

Many of my clients have been surprised to find that their registrars rarely provide any kind of summary report but merely record the nonconformances. This is usually because the auditors have such a heavy workload. Even so, it's still an excellent practice to write brief summary reports after internal audits.

A typical summary report includes the following elements:

- Heading, including date, area audited, audit number (if applicable), and names of audit team members
- Scope of audit, including all the areas covered

- Number of total nonconformances found (with reference to attached nonconformance reports)
- Any outstanding or excellent practices observed
- Major problem areas
- Goal date for identifying corrective actions (this may be built into the audit system)

The report is usually compiled by the audit team leader, based on input from the entire team. Some businesses use a standard form or required format to ensure that summary reports include certain minimum elements.

*Closing Meeting* When the audit team has summarized its findings, the auditors usually hold some type of closing meeting. As with the opening meeting, a closing meeting for an internal audit is much less formal than for a third-party audit. It can range from an actual meeting where personnel from the area(s) audited are invited to attend to an informal one-on-one meeting with the manager(s) of the area(s).

Regardless of its format, the meeting's purpose is to present the results of the audit. The audit team should cover the basic information included in the summary report and make sure that any outstanding questions or issues are resolved. If the written report is finished, it can be handed over at this time. Otherwise, the audit team reviews the information verbally and finishes the final report afterward.

### Corrective Action

The final audit stage is to act on the results of the audit and correct any nonconformances found. This is the job of the area that has been audited, not the auditors'. Making this distinction clear can help your audits be positive and helpful. No one wants someone from another group or area telling them how to solve their own problems—this only creates animosity toward the auditors. Besides, the people who are involved with the work and activities within the area are best equipped to develop sound and effective corrective actions. If the auditee asks the auditor for advice during or after an internal audit, it's fine to offer assistance.

At this point, the internal audit system feeds directly into the defined corrective action system. The auditees will determine the root causes of the nonconformance (although the auditor may help in that regard), select appropriate solutions, determine timing and responsibilities, and take action.

 Do not set up a separate system for dealing with audit findings; they should be dealt with just as any other nonconformance and must meet the requirements of the corrective action section of the standard.

There's one more step to the process. Once corrective actions have been taken, some later followup must be performed to ensure that the actions were effective in eliminating the problem for good (see Chapter 18). This is most often done during the next round of internal audits.

### Setting Up the Internal Audit System

With the basic audit process in mind, let's take a look at how to set up an effective audit system. Figure 20-2 describes the major steps in implementing an internal audit system. This process should begin fairly early in the EMS implementation. I've seen many implementation plans that show the start of internal audits as one of the last steps in implementation. These businesses mistakenly believe that the EMS should be fully implemented before audits can be conducted.

 There's actually a lot of value to starting internal audits early. They can help you to conduct an initial gap assessment to determine the status of existing EMS elements and can provide ongoing progress checks of the implementation efforts. Even more important, internal audits are a great way to get a variety of people from all over the organization involved in the EMS. In addition, the internal auditors will gain valuable knowledge and understanding of the EMS as they audit.

*Train Internal Auditors* Begin this process by training some personnel as internal EMS auditors. At this early stage, you may want to start with just a few people and then train additional auditors as the system is further implemented. The timing is up to you, but it's critical that internal auditors get appropriate and adequate training.

Generally, EMS auditors need knowledge and skills in the following areas:

- Management systems in general and EMS in particular
- Basic auditing skills
- Details of ISO 14001 requirements
- General environmental knowledge

This understanding and knowledge can be gained through a combination of background experience, auditing experience, and classroom training.

Most organizations already have some internal auditors, either for regulatory compliance auditing or for quality systems auditing. Either

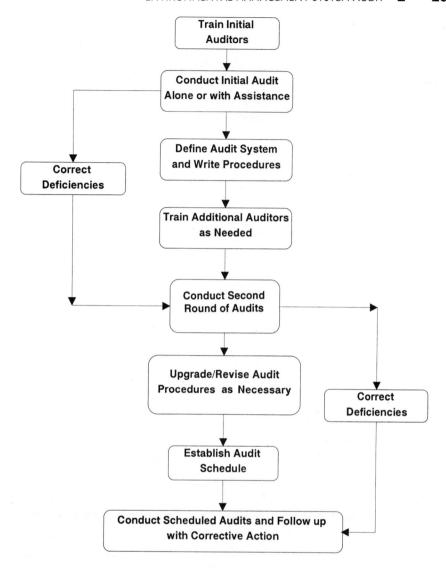

■ **FIGURE 20-2.** Establishing an Audit System

type of auditor can learn to conduct EMS audits. The regulatory auditors already have the environmental knowledge and auditing skills and will need to gain an understanding of management systems and audit practices particular to an EMS. Quality auditors have experience in auditing management systems and will need to gain a general understanding of environmental issues, as well as of those elements particular to an EMS. Both types of auditors will need to understand the requirements of ISO 14001. Internal EMS auditor training courses are typically two or three days long and may or may not include training in the requirements of ISO 14001.

Detailed knowledge of environmental regulations is not necessary to be an EMS auditor and could actually distract the auditor from focusing on management system elements. Quality systems auditors should acquire an understanding of the regulatory framework of their facility—the basic federal, state, and local regulations, permits, and requirements that must be met—but they do not need to become environmental experts.

***Conduct Initial Audit*** There are several options for conducting the initial gap assessment of the EMS. If you have skilled auditors with the appropriate expertise within your own organization, you can just go ahead and conduct your own internal audit. If you're lacking any of the basic areas of expertise listed above or simply don't feel comfortable yet with the requirements of ISO 14001, you can enlist the help of professional EMS auditors from a registrar, consulting firm, or corporate group to help you with the initial audit. You could also allow an outside audit team to conduct the audit on its own without your help, but you might as well take advantage of this opportunity to jump-start your own internal audit system and learn from the professionals you hire.

This initial audit will be quite different from your later audits because it's likely that major gaps will exist in the system and that much of the system will not yet be well documented. You may end up focusing this audit on the environmental professionals and managers, especially if few other people have traditionally been involved. In some cases, you'll ask a single question, find out that an entire system element doesn't exist, and move on.

This first audit is critical for implementation planning (see Chapter 22). It will help you to determine where your major gaps are and which areas will require the most effort. The basis for this audit will mainly be the ISO 14001 standard, especially if little facility documentation exists.

***Correct Deficiencies*** This is shown as a single step in Figure 20-2 but actually represents months of work at this stage! The audit will identify many nonconformances that need to be addressed as the EMS is developed and implemented. This stage could take six to nine months or more. One of your first steps should be to draft a corrective action system to help you keep track of all the items needing attention. The type and scope of these nonconformances will help you to define a strategic plan for implementing or upgrading the EMS (see Chapter 22).

***Define Audit System and Write Procedures*** It's very likely that one of the initial audit nonconformances you will find is that there is no system for

EMS auditing! Now is the time to define that system. Some companies prefer to define their system before the initial audit, but there are two reasons why I usually recommend waiting until this point. As I mentioned earlier, this first audit will be quite different from later ones, so a defined internal audit system may not be much help. Secondly, without experience performing an EMS audit, you may not be well enough equipped to define an audit process.

Having said that, there will be quite a few companies that already have a defined process for auditing management systems (for ISO 9000, QS-9000, or Process Safety Management). For these companies, it does make sense to use existing audit procedures for the initial EMS.

Whether you are writing a new procedure or upgrading an existing one, your EMS audit system should describe the following elements:

- Responsibilities (for managing the audit system, conducting audits, reporting, and followup)
- Training and qualification of internal auditors
- Preparation required
- Guidelines or requirements for conducting audits
- Reporting requirements, including any standard forms used
- Reference to corrective action system

These could be documented in a single procedure, multiple procedures, flowcharts, or whatever other format works for your organization. Any trained auditors should review the system and offer their input.

**Train Additional Auditors** During the period when you are correcting nonconformances from the initial audit, you should begin preparing for subsequent audits. At this point, you should consider how you want your audit system to work in the longer term.

✓ I've seen many businesses take very different approaches to choosing internal auditors. The most effective by far is to involve a large and diverse number of people. By doing so, you'll get more people involved in the EMS, and the variety of perspectives will make your audits better. For most facilities, I recommend training roughly 5 to 10 percent of the organization as internal auditors. Very large organizations may consider a smaller percentage.

The internal auditors should come from a broad cross-section of the organization, representing most or all functions and levels. This will also make it easier to plan independent audits. If you train this many people as auditors, each one will only have to spend a small amount of time auditing. Making 5 percent of many people's time available is usually much more feasible than is making 50 to 100 percent of one or two people's time available.

✓ These auditors will have the same basic training and experience requirements discussed earlier. The reason you should not train 20 or 30 people as auditors from the beginning is that they'll forget most of what they've learned if they don't have an opportunity to apply it immediately. Although just-in-time training is always most effective, it is critical in the case of auditing. Very specific skills are needed that require a lot of practice to master. In addition, many new auditors are apprehensive and nervous and will do best if they can begin auditing immediately after the training. Some training organizations offer combined classroom and on-the-job auditor training programs, in which the auditors learn skills one day and practice them in a real audit the next.

**Conduct Second Round of Audits** When you feel that you have made significant progress on corrective actions from the first audit, it's time to conduct the second round of internal audits. You can still expect to find a lot of nonconformances, but the major systems should be defined by this point. This audit will be especially helpful if many of the EMS elements have been recently implemented. It will give you a chance to find out how well they're working.

Use your audit procedures for this audit, and you'll be testing the newly defined or upgraded audit system as well. You do not need to conduct this audit all at once, but you do need to cover all areas of the organization and all elements of ISO 14001 within a fairly short time period. This is a good opportunity for your newly trained auditors to practice their skills, with more experienced auditors along to provide guidance.

**Correct Deficiencies** Once again, these audits will identify nonconformances that need corrective action. By now, your corrective action system should be defined, documented, and in use. This second round of audits may uncover even more nonconformances than the first, since there's more in place to audit now. However, there should be very few *major* nonconformances, where whole EMS elements are missing.

**Upgrade Audit Procedures** With some additional auditing experience, your internal auditors will likely have some ideas for upgrading and improving the audit procedures. It's a good idea to make an effort to solicit their feedback in order to make your audit system as effective as possible. Try to schedule a meeting of the internal auditors shortly after the second round of audits to debrief and discuss the entire audit system.

***Establish Audit Schedule*** Prior to this point, a regular audit schedule would not have been of much use. ISO 14001 does require periodic audits and defined frequencies. This is a good time to develop an ongoing audit schedule.

It's best to define an annual schedule. This will show outside auditors that you have a defined audit program and will ensure that audits cover the entire system. The frequency of individual audits is left completely up to you. Some organizations set their schedules so that every area is audited at least once a year; others audit more frequently.

The standard allows you the flexibility to schedule audits on the basis of environmental importance and previous audit results, so you may audit some areas more frequently than others. The audit coordinator (often the EMS management representative) should develop a schedule that covers all areas of the organization and all sections of the standard and that uses all auditors so that no one is auditing his or her own job functions. You may also want to plan the audits so that newer auditors work with more experienced auditors. Overall, the audit plan or schedule needs to show that the internal audit system is comprehensive.

***Conduct Scheduled Audits and Follow Up with Corrective Action*** Now the audit system is implemented. Scheduled audits occur periodically, according to a defined schedule and procedures. Audit findings are followed by corrective actions to prevent those nonconformances from recurring. Records of these audits and corrective actions are kept. The internal audit system, in conjunction with corrective action, can be a powerful tool for improvement.

# MANAGEMENT REVIEW

> ### ISO 14001 REQUIREMENTS*
>
> ISO 14001, section 4.6, Management Review, requires the following:
>
> The organization's top management shall, at intervals that it determines, review the environmental management system, to ensure its continuing suitability, adequacy and effectiveness. The management review process shall ensure that the necessary information is collected to allow management to carry out this evaluation. This review shall be documented.
>
> The management review shall address the possible need for changes to policy, objectives and other elements of the environmental management system, in the light of environmental management system audit results, changing circumstances and the commitment to continual improvement.

## INTERPRETATION

Management review is the last section of the standard and is a critical component for ensuring continual improvement of the system. While the purpose of a management review is spelled out fairly clearly in this section, many people are still not sure exactly what a management review is. One plant that I worked with interpreted it as a detailed review by management of every single document in the system. Management review is intended to be much broader than that.

*© International Organization for Standardization. All rights reserved.

The document control, measurement, and internal audit systems provide very detailed, ongoing assessments of the EMS. The role of the management review is to take a broader look at the system as a whole to determine whether it is meeting the organization's needs and whether the EMS is suitable, adequate, and effective. The management review process must include steps to collect and analyze the necessary data for the actual review.

The Annex to ISO 14001 provides further interpretation, by suggesting that the reviews include the following elements*:

a) results from audits;
b) the extent to which objectives and targets have been met;
c) the continuing suitability of the environmental management system in relation to changing conditions and information;
d) concerns amongst relevant interested parties.

The "Implementation" section, below, provides further guidance on specific topics that might be a part of the review.

ISO 14001 requires that this review be conducted by the organization's *top management,* meaning the highest levels of management within the defined scope of the EMS. If a single facility within a large corporation has established an EMS, the management review would be conducted by the highest level of management at the facility, not by corporate management. The Annex defines this further by stating that the review should be carried out by the level of management that defined the policy, objectives, and procedures.

As with many other ISO 14001 requirements, the frequency of these reviews is left for you to determine. You just need to define particular intervals for conducting the reviews. The Annex also notes that the entire EMS does not have to be reviewed all at once. The review could be split into parts as long as the entire review is comprehensive over a period of time.

The standard requires that records be kept of the reviews. The Annex adds that these records will likely include observations, conclusions, and recommendations for action. As with other records requirements, the format is left for you to decide.

The whole purpose of the review process is to determine whether the EMS is effective, so the review may highlight necessary changes to improve the system. As the standard states, these may include changes to policy, objectives, and other EMS elements. The followup and corrective action steps are a critical component of the review process.

*© International Organization for Standardization. All rights reserved.

## IMPLEMENTATION

### Participants

When defining a management review system, a primary consideration is who should participate. The standard says the review must be conducted by top management, but you must determine exactly who are the appropriate managers in your own organization.

The most common mistake made in choosing participants is to restrict the list too narrowly. Obviously, the environmental manager and the highest-level manager will be two critical participants, but there should also be broad representation from all major functional groups in the organization. These could include laboratory, purchasing, shipping, engineering, design, manufacturing, and administration departments or functions.

Look at your own organization and your own EMS to determine which areas need to be represented. The review will be most useful with broad participation from all of these groups.

Ideally, each department or function should be represented by the top manager of that function. You will need to consider how you will handle the inevitable problems of getting all of these top-level managers together. Some organizations hold infrequent management reviews, with mandatory attendance from all participants. Others allow substitutes if particular managers are unavailable.

If this is your policy, you may want to set some limits and guidelines, however. I once audited a plant whose last management review minutes showed that more than 75 percent of the participants were substitutes! It was no longer a real management review, since so few of the reviewers were members of top management.

Some organizations allow managers to be absent but will only hold the review meeting with a quorum present. Whatever your rules are, set minimum requirements for the meetings so that the integrity of the review is upheld. Also consider the message you'll be sending. If absenteeism and substitution are freely allowed, the management reviews will not be perceived as the significant events they should be.

### Topics

Now that you have figured out who will take part, what actually happens in a management review? You need to define a basic agenda and process that will be followed for each review to ensure that all reviews are comprehensive. The standard and Annex provide some general guidelines, but your own reviews need to be designed for your own business.

 During audits, the most common management review nonconformance I've seen involves reviews that simply do not meet the intention of the standard. Many companies' quality management reviews consist of detailed examinations of internal audits and corrective actions. There are two problems with this limited approach: managers are evaluating the audits and corrective actions in far greater detail than is necessary, and they're missing the big picture. You need to be reviewing a wide variety of information to help you to assess the overall performance of the EMS.

To evaluate the suitability and effectiveness of the EMS thoroughly, you must look at certain indicators to determine whether the system is achieving what it should be. Your environmental policy, business policy, and environmental objectives and targets define your overall goals. Consider what information you need to determine whether you're meeting those goals.

A critical review item will be the progress toward objectives and targets and the status of environmental programs or plans. The measurement section of the standard requires that you track this progress, so you should already have some data to evaluate. During the review, you will look at that data in a broader sense. In reviewing the policy, objectives, and targets, consider these questions:

- Is the policy appropriate for our business? Does it help us to meet our overall business mission and goals?
- Are we on track to meet stated objectives and targets in the time frame specified?
- What is the status of programs and plans?
- Will achievement of our objectives and targets help us to move toward our ultimate goal or mission?
- Do our objectives and targets support the environmental policy and overall business mission?
- Are any adjustments needed in plans to allow us to meet objectives and targets?
- Are adjustments needed in targets because of changing circumstances or business factors?

The measurement and monitoring system will provide other useful information for evaluating the overall EMS. Results of regulatory compliance audits and monitoring can provide an indication of the status of compliance efforts. Trends in environmental performance data can indicate whether the system is helping to improve the environment. Remember, though, that this is a high-level review. The detailed data collection and analysis should take place prior to the review meetings, as a part of the measurement system (see Chapter 17). Then the managers can concentrate on overall trends and data summaries during the review.

The same is true of internal EMS audit results. These are clearly a part of the management review, according to the standard and Annex, but you do not need to review every minute detail of every audit conducted. Keep in mind the relative purposes of an audit and a management review. The audit represents a detailed snapshot of a particular area or function. The management review needs to look at overall trends and conclusions, based on the whole audit program.

Information from audits that might be useful during a management review includes

- Summary of audits conducted since the last review
- Trends in number of nonconformances found
- Summary of EMS elements with the most nonconformances
- Specific nature of any major nonconformances

This data should be compiled by the audit manager or coordinator for the management review.

Similarly, a review of the corrective action system can also provide insight into the overall performance of the EMS. Consider including a review of trends in

- Number of corrective actions initiated
- Number of corrective actions completed and closed
- Number of corrective actions past their due date
- Any outstanding corrective actions that may require management intervention

As with internal audits, there's little value in management listening to a detailed presentation of every corrective action item. Rather, managers should evaluate the overall system as an indicator of EMS effectiveness.

The Annex to the standard specifically mentions the inclusion of views of interested parties. As described in Chapter 8, "Objectives and Targets," interested parties are broadly defined by the standard to include anyone who is either affected by or concerned with your environmental performance. These parties will likely include regulators, employees, customers, suppliers, the local community, shareholders, and environmental groups.

Although you are required to consider the views of interested parties when establishing objectives and targets, management review is an appropriate time to evaluate how well your EMS takes these views into account. You may want to include this as a separate agenda item in your reviews. Review any input or feedback, both solicited and unsolicited, from interested parties and consider whether the EMS addresses these adequately.

 Do not forget to include more traditional business metrics. Environmental management is an integral part of the overall business management. Financial indicators can help management assess whether the EMS is effective. Although advanced "green accounting" techniques can be very helpful, merely including the financial data you already collect will make your review more valuable.

Review key business and financial data to assess whether the business as a whole is improving or declining. Are costs up? Are sales up? This information is critical to reviewing the EMS in its proper context. A review of environmental performance data may show that energy consumption has increased, but this information is meaningless without knowing whether production has also increased. Perhaps energy use per unit of production has actually decreased because of some of the environmental programs. It is essential to review the EMS in the context of the business as a whole.

### Frequency

The standard leaves it up to you to determine an appropriate frequency for your management reviews. Although there is no minimum requirement in the standard, some registrars expect reviews to be held at least annually. Most organizations seem to conduct their reviews annually or semiannually, although there are some businesses that prefer quarterly reviews.

 I audited one company that was conducting monthly management reviews. I found, as is likely with such frequent reviews, that they were not really fulfilling the intended purpose of a review but were focused on details and ongoing progress reports. You could have these kinds of monthly management meetings if you need them, but you still need a broad-based, comprehensive review on a less frequent basis.

You may find that you need more frequent reviews during the early stages of EMS implementation or during certain periods when your organization is undergoing many changes. It makes sense to define a minimum review frequency so that you can hold additional reviews as needed. Certainly, any major organizational change should trigger a review.

### Records and Followup

Management review records are often simply the minutes of the meeting. The following items should be included as a minimum:

- Participants present
- Date
- Review of followup items from the last review
- Agenda/list of topics reviewed
- Conclusions and recommendations
- Items for followup or corrective action

This will provide objective evidence that the review was comprehensive and will also provide valuable information on the basis for decisions made.

Determining followup actions is the most critical component of the management review. This will complete the continual improvement cycle by acting on the results of the review. A comprehensive review will naturally point to areas where changes are needed. Management must decide what actions are necessary, based on the information reviewed, to improve the EMS so that it better meets the needs of the business and the intent of the environmental policy.

These actions may include changes to objectives and targets, environmental programs, procedures, or even the policy itself. This is why it's so important to review the EMS in the context of the entire business. Management review records should indicate the decisions made and changes required. These can then be fed into the corrective action system to ensure that they are completed and are effective.

### Procedures

As with all elements of the EMS, it's important that your management review system is documented so that it will be followed consistently. A single procedure is usually all that's required for management review. This procedure should include the elements discussed in this chapter: participants involved, topics covered, frequency, records, and followup.

You should also consider whether you want to conduct separate EMS management reviews or integrated reviews. ISO 9001 has very similar management review requirements, so it would be a simple process to integrate the quality and environmental system reviews. Consider the complexity and structure of your own business. For some, it makes sense to get everyone together and cover both at once. Other companies prefer to separate the reviews to ensure that each gets an adequate amount of attention.

✓ You may also consider a single, overall business review. Since traditional business measures are important to both quality and environmental reviews, it makes sense to review this information all at once. This practice would also send an important message about viewing the business as a whole rather than as a collection of different systems.

A good compromise solution is to conduct the reviews at the same frequency but to designate certain portions of the review to focus on single areas, such as quality, safety, and environmental. In this way, you can simplify scheduling, review common information once at the start of the review, and still maintain a balanced focus on each set of individual issues. Ultimately, as with the rest of the EMS, do what makes sense for your own business.

# PART 5

## GETTING STARTED

With an understanding of the requirements of ISO 14001 and the basic principles of implementing an effective EMS, it is time to consider what you need to do to actually get started on your own company's EMS. Effective planning is the key to success—whether you have an existing system that needs to be compared against ISO 14001 and improved or you need to implement an EMS from the start. Chapter 22 provides guidance on how to develop your own strategic plan, including resources, critical steps, and timing.

Besides these important decisions, the choice of a registrar can have a great impact on the value of your ISO 14001 registration. Chapter 23 describes the detailed criteria you should consider when choosing this long-term supplier. Finally, Chapter 24 summarizes the key principles of integrated management systems and the critical factors for achieving business success from your EMS efforts.

# STRATEGIC PLANNING

## INITIAL AUDIT

The first step is to determine the current status of any existing EMS elements in your organization. Even if you do not have an EMS per se, it's likely that you do have certain components that you can build on. You want to avoid creating a whole new system without integrating your current practices.

The best way to find out where you are starting from is to conduct a thorough initial audit or gap assessment against the requirements of ISO 14001. Use the standard as a model and compare your current practices against it. The purpose of this audit is to find out what systems or elements are in place. You will also be looking for any existing documentation that describes the system and any records being kept to support the system. You may be surprised to find out how much you already have in place, even without an explicitly defined EMS.

If you have the necessary expertise and auditing skills, you may decide to conduct this initial audit on your own. You can also use external auditors from registrars, consultants, or a corporate group to conduct the audit. Chapter 20, "EMS Audits" describes the process of this first audit in detail.

## STRATEGIC PLANNING SESSION

Once you know where you're starting from, it's a good idea to develop a strategic plan for moving forward. This plan will likely change and evolve during the implementation process, but drafting one early will help to guide your efforts. A lot of businesses just dive in and begin working, but a small amount of time spent planning can pay off by preventing problems from arising later. In fact, one of the main reasons for failing registration audits is the lack of adequate project planning.

Top management of the organization should be involved in defining the strategic plan, along with any expert resources available to you. These might be people from other businesses in your company who have worked with ISO 14001 or outside consultants who understand your business. Generally, you will want to set aside one to two days to discuss the results of the initial audit and begin to develop a strategic plan for implementing and/or improving the EMS.

This session has other purposes besides defining a draft implementation plan. It can serve as a forum to ensure that all members of the management group have a consistent understanding of the purpose of an EMS, the use of ISO 14001, and any registration issues. You should also use this meeting to make some critical decisions that will affect the details of the strategic plan. Some suggested steps for this planning session are described below. Use the checklist to gather the necessary information in preparation for the planning session.

 As you go through each step during the session, keep a "bucket list" of items that will need followup action.

### Understand the Issues

One of the most common problems with management system implementation is a lack of management commitment, and this usually stems from a lack of understanding. I've seen many cases where management

---

**CHECKLIST: Information needed prior to strategic planning session**

- ✓ Feedback from interested parties regarding registration
- ✓ Status of existing management systems
- ✓ Results of initial EMS audit
- ✓ List of possible candidates for management representative
- ✓ Informative overview of ISO 14001 and registration
- ✓ Scope guidelines from registration criteria
- ✓ Basic understanding of major environmental aspects and impacts of business

had little understanding of the effort involved in establishing a management system and was unprepared to provide adequate resources. Those organizations that do not have solid management support and commitment face a long struggle in implementing an effective system.

It's a good idea to begin the planning session with an overview of the pertinent information and issues that management needs to understand to lead this effort. These issues may include

- Brief background/history of ISO 14000 series of standards
- Data reflecting use of ISO 14001 worldwide, especially in key markets and regions for your particular business
- Status of ISO 14001 and registration systems
- Pros and cons of registration
- Potential for integration of ISO 14001 and ISO 9001
- Costs and benefits of an EMS
- Resources needed to implement an EMS

Your list of topics may be a bit different to meet your own needs, but these are the topics that must usually be covered to provide managers with the information they need to make informed business decisions. If questions come up during the overview that can not be answered by the people present, put them on your bucket list for further investigation.

### Define EMS Scope

Defining the scope of the EMS is one of the most critical decisions to be made at this early stage. It will affect all other EMS implementation work. For some organizations, the ideal scope is obvious and there's no real decision to be made. Other organizations may have several options to choose from, with various pros and cons to be weighed.

As described in Chapter 4, "Introduction to ISO 14001," the standard allows plenty of flexibility in its use. It is applicable to a wide variety of organizations, including single facilities, divisions, whole companies, and even nonindustrial or service organizations. You need to decide how to define the boundaries of your own organization.

This decision must be made in the context of your environmental impacts, so you may find that you need to revisit this issue after conducting a thorough evaluation of significant environmental aspects and impacts. However, you will need at least a preliminary scope definition to determine the breadth of that evaluation.

When discussing scope options, consider the following choices:

- Entire company
- Division or business unit
- Part of a division or business unit

- Single facility
- Partial facility

Ultimately, the scope of your EMS must make sense for your business and be acceptable to your chosen registrar.

Usually, your scope will be defined partly in geographic terms, simply because it is virtually impossible to separate the environmental impacts of two organizations operating on a single physical site. This becomes quite tricky when two different companies are operating on a single plant site. Situations of this type are actually becoming quite common with large corporations buying, selling, and trading particular businesses. Even within a single corporation, it is fairly common to find large facilities that include multiple divisions or businesses that operate completely independently.

Either of these situations presents some unique challenges. It's likely that facility services such as electricity, water, and steam are shared among the businesses residing at a given site. The environmental impacts of air emissions, soil contamination, water discharges, noise, and visual impacts will affect the entire location. What happens if one of these businesses is enthusiastically implementing an EMS and pursuing third-party registration and the other has no interest in doing so?

Unfortunately, there are no easy answers to these questions. Registration criteria provide some guidelines, but you will have to take a close look at the particular details of your own organization to decide how to proceed. In particular, consider management structure and authority, the scope of any permits, independence of financial resources, and control over various portions of the operation.

Conversely, your challenge may not lie in narrowing the EMS scope but in deciding how broad it should be. It is acceptable and sometimes preferable to include a larger organization in the EMS scope. For instance, in a small company, it may make sense to include the entire company, even if there are multiple locations. Similarly, a division or business unit with several plants that produce the same products and have many of the same environmental aspects may benefit from a larger scope.

The main benefit of a larger scope is the unity that can be gained from operating under a single management system. One DuPont business, consisting of two plant sites in different locations, decided to register as a business with a single ISO 9002 registration to cover both sites. To do this successfully, the sites had to agree on a single quality management system and compare all of their critical operating practices. The end result of this effort was that their products could be manufactured by either site and customers could not tell the difference because of the high level of consistency in operation.

Although environmental systems have a different focus than quality systems, a broadly defined scope carries similar potential benefits. By working together, different facilities can eliminate a lot of duplicate effort, especially if their environmental aspects are similar. Best practices developed at one location can be used in another. In the case of a multi-level EMS, including facilities as well as divisional or corporate headquarters, there is an added benefit. Some system elements are likely to be shared between levels (e.g., policies, high-level objectives, planning processes, communication) and a single EMS scope will help to clarify these interfaces.

 While you may be interested in the benefits to be gained from a larger scope, you should also be aware of some potential pitfalls. You will have to ensure that the different facilities or entities work together to create a system that is flexible enough for each to do what's best for its own unique situation. For instance, having the division headquarters create a single, detailed set of procedures for multiple facilities would create problems and reduce the potential for business improvement. There needs to be a balance between a mostly unified system and the freedom for each part of that system to customize its practices to its own culture and business needs.

Another potential problem is the additional time and effort involved. That DuPont business that registered as a single entity spent longer preparing for registration than any other single unit within DuPont. In its case, management felt that the benefits achieved more than made up for the extra time and effort necessary, but other businesses may be under more restrictive time pressures. This is an individual decision you need to make by weighing your own costs and benefits.

In addition, consider the complexity of the EMS. If your company is very large with diverse business segments, there will probably be little benefit in defining the entire company under a single EMS. If the environmental issues are similar for all groups within the company and the systems fairly straightforward, it may make sense to use a larger scope.

Because of all of these complexities, you may not be able to make a solid scope decision in this planning session. You should strive to come to agreement on a preferred scope or at least to define pros and cons of various approaches. Additional information, input, or decisions needed should be listed for later follow-up.

### To Register or Not To Register?

This can also be a difficult decision for an organization. Although it is not necessary to decide whether to register your EMS at this early point, you should give this decision some thought and discussion because it could impact your implementation plans. At the very least, decide whether registration is a possibility.

Chapter 3, "Third-Party Registration," provides a detailed discussion of potential drivers for registration. This information can serve as a guideline, but each organization needs to look at its own circumstances and business to determine if registration is either necessary or desired. It will be helpful to gather this information before the planning meeting so that an informed and useful discussion can take place.

In determining your own drivers for registration, solicit feedback from

- Regulatory bodies
- Customers
- Local communities
- Interested environmental groups
- Shareholders

You may want to consider some additional factors, such as recognition of ISO 14001 registration by financial and insurance companies. Strive to get an overall impression of the potential benefits of registration for your own business.

 In addition, try to find out what your competitors are doing with respect to ISO 14001. This can be a powerful driver in some industries.

The main disadvantage of registration is, of course, the cost. Depending on the size of your organization and its resources, this cost may or may not be significant to you. Registration costs make up only 5 to 10 percent of the overall cost of implementing an EMS, since most of the resources needed are internal. Detailed information on registration costs is included in Chapter 23, "Choosing a Registrar."

In considering registration, management should understand that this is a separate decision from implementation. You can implement or improve your EMS, using ISO 14001 as a tool, without ever seeking registration of the system. In fact, too much focus on registration as the ultimate goal can result in a bureaucratic system with little internal value or payback.

This happened to many, many businesses that sought registration to one of the ISO 9000 standards. The fortunate ones realized their mistake and spent the next several years working to improve and simplify their system so that it would add value rather than burdening the organization. The less fortunate companies never realized their systems could be any better and are still struggling with cumbersome systems that they mistakenly believe are required to maintain registration. You can avoid this plight by carefully considering registration and maintaining a focus on effective systems and improved performance as the overall goals for your EMS. Registration is merely a milestone along the way.

### Determine Resources Needed

With the EMS scope defined (or at least discussed) and registration considered, you can now begin to estimate the resources you will need to implement or improve your EMS and possibly to get registered. Before making decisions about your own business, management needs to understand what resources are generally needed and what options are available.

***Total Costs Vary Widely*** Many people are surprised to find that few of these resource costs are out-of-pocket expenses. In fact, experience with ISO 9000 standards indicates that only 10 to 20 percent of the total cost of implementing a management system consists of external costs, including training, consulting, and registration fees. Eighty to ninety percent of the cost of implementing an EMS is in the internal resources that must be reallocated in order to define, document, and implement the system.

The total cost of implementation, with or without registration, is virtually impossible to predict because it is different for every organization. I'm always amazed when I see articles that quote someone saying that ISO 9001 or ISO 14001 implementation will cost some particular dollar amount. There have certainly been a few organizations that have accurately tracked their internal and external costs, but their experiences will likely be entirely different than your own.

Overall cost of management system implementation depends on several factors. I have already mentioned that a larger or more complex scope could take longer to implement. In addition, if there are multiple locations involved, additional effort may be required just to coordinate and work together.

The most significant determinant of cost is the status of existing management systems. If your organization already has a set of well-defined environmental systems and an involved and educated workforce, meeting ISO 14001 may require little effort. If, however, the business has never considered its environmental aspects or has major regulatory compliance problems that have prevented further environmental efforts, you can count on a much longer implementation effort. Similarly, if the organization has an effective, well-established quality system that meets

ISO 9001 or 9002, many of those elements can be expanded to include environmental aspects. This could save a large amount of implementation effort. An organization with solid safety and/or process safety management systems in place and documented could be at a similar advantage.

***Determine Internal Resource Needs*** With these variations in mind, there are some average internal resource needs that can be used as the basis for your own plans. One way to organize your EMS efforts is to define various roles for the EMS implementation (and possibly beyond), including a management representative, steering group, area coordinators, and internal auditors.

The management representative is required by ISO 14001. Chapter 10 describes detailed criteria for choosing the right person for this important role of organizing and leading the EMS process. The management representative is typically one person who will need to spend 50 to 100 percent of his or her time on the EMS during the implementation phase. If your selected management representative cannot spend this amount of time, you will need a second person, acting as a deputy management representative or coordinator, who *can* spend that much time. It's a big effort to coordinate.

It's helpful to name a steering group, which is typically made up of the top management of the organization. The steering group will provide strategic planning, leadership, and support to the EMS efforts. The group will also need to follow the progress of the EMS implementation closely and ensure that adequate resources are available. Each member of this team will probably spend 10 to 20 percent of his or her time on the EMS during implementation.

An effective implementation strategy is to select area coordinators to represent each functional area, department, or group within the EMS scope. Each of these coordinators can organize and lead the efforts required of his or her own group. They will need to work closely with the management representative to ensure that their work is coordinated across the entire organization.

It's usually best to ask for volunteers to act as area coordinators, although the ultimate selection should be made by the steering group. The selection criteria listed in Chapter 10 for the management representative are also applicable to area coordinators, since they are essentially acting as management representatives for their own departments or functions. Each coordinator can expect to spend between 20 to 40 percent of his or her time on the EMS. The amount may vary, based on the relative environmental importance of each area and the status of existing systems.

Finally, you will need to train and prepare internal auditors to conduct EMS audits. You may already have a pool of skilled auditors to draw on, based on quality system or environmental compliance auditing programs. As was discussed in Chapter 20, if you train 5 to 10 percent of your organization's employees as internal auditors, each will need to spend only 5 to 10 percent of his or her time auditing. If you want to use a smaller group of auditors, each will need to spend a larger share of his or her time on this task.

Besides these defined roles, the EMS implementation effort must involve every employee whose work has a potential impact on the environment. Each person should be involved in defining his or her job qualifications, responsibilities, training needs, and any aspects of his or her job that affect the environment. In addition, the coordination and management teams should make an effort to solicit input and feedback on policies, environmental aspects, objectives, programs, and procedures. This will help to ensure that the system is a part of the whole business and that it is effective. Broad employee involvement will also help the organization to realize the full value of the EMS.

If you do some simple math with the estimates and averages stated above, you will find that a 500-person facility would probably need about 9 person-years of effort to implement an EMS fully. When I worked for DuPont, I conducted a survey of ISO 9001 and 9002 registered businesses that supports these calculations. Nineteen businesses responded to the survey. The average size of these organizations was 300 people, but they ranged from a 60-person business to an 800-person business.

The survey showed that it took these organizations an average of 18 months to implement a quality system and prepare for registration. The time for implementation ranged from 9 to 30 months (the longest time was taken by the multiple-site business discussed earlier). The actual effort needed ranged from 2 to 26 person-years, with an average of 9 person-years required. These businesses had an average of 25 people involved for at least 5 percent of their time.

Although these data were based on quality systems, they can be used to estimate resources needed for environmental systems, with a few additional considerations. An environmental system will require additional effort in the early planning stages to identify and evaluate environmental aspects and impacts, identify applicable regulations, and establish objectives, targets, and programs. If, however, you have already done a great deal of implementation work for ISO 9001, this may offset the effort needed to implement an EMS, leaving you with the main tasks of simplifying, improving, and expanding existing systems.

With all of these factors in mind, consider your own resource needs. What systems do you already have in place? What areas are likely to require the most effort? Your initial EMS audit can help to answer these questions. Also consider the amount of resources you will be able to afford since this may affect your timing (see the section "Develop a Draft Plan," below).

**Determine Training Needs** As with other resources, each business will have a unique set of training needs, based on the current level of knowledge and skills among their employees. Training can be conducted internally or by an external party, depending on the particular competencies of your organization.

Although every business will be slightly different, there are some almost universal training needs. Various groups within the organization will likely need the following types of training:

*All Employees:*
- Environmental policy*
- Environmental objectives, targets, and programs*
- Environmental aspects and significant impacts*
- Environmental impacts of each person's job function*
- General understanding of ISO 14001 and registration, especially if the organization is pursuing registration

*Management Representative:*
- Requirements of ISO 14001
- EMS implementation course
- Advanced or lead EMS auditor training course

*Steering Group:*
- Overview of ISO 14001, registration, and the worldwide impact of these

*Area Coordinators:*
- EMS implementation course

*Internal Auditors:*
- Requirements of ISO 14001
- Internal auditor training course
- General understanding of regulatory framework

*Internal Audit Coordinator* or *Manager* (if different from Management Representative):
- Advanced or lead EMS auditor training course
- General understanding of regulatory framework

*Note: Awareness training in these areas is required for employees whose jobs affect the environment, per ISO 14001, Section 4.3.2, Training, Awareness and Competence.

The general training courses mentioned above are widely available commercially but may vary significantly from one training provider to another. It's best to request detailed descriptions of courses and ask plenty of questions to ensure that the course will meet the particular needs of your business. In addition, many training providers will conduct on-site sessions that can be focused on your own organization's issues.

For planning purposes, the following list shows the number of days typically associated with each of the above training courses. Keep in mind that these may vary from one training provider to another.

- Management overview: ½ to 1 day
- EMS implementation: 2 to 3 days
- Requirements of ISO 14001: 1 day (or maybe incorporated into implementation course)
- Internal auditor training: 2 to 3 days
- Advanced or lead EMS auditor: 5 days
- Regulatory overview: 1 to 3 days (more for greater detail on the regulations)

For this initial planning session, just try to estimate the training courses or number of training days that will be required based on the existing knowledge and skills of the key people involved (if they have already been selected). Actual costs of training can vary considerably, so do some research to find out which providers can meet your overall needs before setting a more detailed training budget.

***Consider Whether Consulting Will Be Needed*** There is certainly no requirement to use a consultant to implement an EMS for ISO 14001. Whether you use consulting assistance and how much you use should be based on your organization's expertise and approach.

 Do not make the mistake of thinking that you can hire a consultant to come into your organization and implement the EMS for you. I've heard horror stories of managers who said, "OK, so we need to get registered? Go out and hire someone to do it for us." On the other hand, there are consultants who will tell you that they can implement your system for you (for an enormous fee!) and guarantee registration. It must be obvious by now that this is not an approach I would advocate!

If you do decide you need some assistance, the consultant should play the role of facilitator. He or she should be able to provide expertise and information where needed and help your own management group to guide the implementation efforts. Much of the necessary work in defining your EMS has to come from your own organization for the resulting system to be of value to you. You would not want someone to implement a "generic" management system for you because it is very unlikely that such a system would fit your own culture and ways of operating.

So, what can a consultant do for you? There are a variety of ways that a well-qualified consultant can provide guidance and add value to your efforts. You may find that you need assistance in the following areas:

- EMS auditing
- Developing a strategic plan
- Identifying and evaluating environmental aspects and impacts
- Identifying regulatory requirements
- Defining/improving management system elements
- Documenting systems

In any of these cases, the consultant should be in a supporting role. For instance, it is unwise to hire someone to write your documents for you, but a consultant may be able to lead your own employees through an effective method of documenting their processes and activities.

Ultimately, as with training, the decision is yours to make, based on your own business needs. Some companies with their own experience and expertise find that they can implement effective systems with little or no outside assistance. If you do decide to use consulting assistance, remember to shop around carefully. Look for a consulting organization with a philosophy that closely matches your own and for individual consultants who are well qualified and knowledgeable.

### Develop a Draft Plan

Finally, with all of this preliminary work accomplished, you have the information necessary to outline an initial strategic plan. This plan should include major steps, timing, estimated resources, and responsibilities. Your initial audit will provide important information concerning the areas where the most effort will be needed.

***Define Critical Actions*** Generally, most EMS implementation efforts will follow the same basic steps:

1. Conduct initial gap assessment.
2. Define strategic plan.
3. Identify environmental aspects and evaluate significant impacts.
4. Identify regulatory requirements.
5. Define environmental policy.
6. Develop objectives, targets, and plans/programs.

7. Establish baseline environmental measurements.
8. Define and implement critical management system elements, including
    - Document control
    - Corrective action
    - Record management
    - Internal system audits
    - Monitoring and measurement
9. Analyze processes and activities to identify effective practices.
10. Define and document standard procedures.
11. Train employees in new or revised practices.
12. Work on environmental programs/plans.
13. Use measurement systems.
14. Conduct internal systems audits.
15. Take corrective action based on audits.
16. Conduct periodic management reviews.
17. Maintain and improve systems.

Note that steps 8, 9, 10, and 11 will encompass a large part of your implementation effort, often requiring six to nine months or more to complete. Steps 12 through 17 are a part of the ongoing continual improvement process for your EMS.

With these basic steps in mind, draft your own implementation plan. Consider the results of your initial audit, the management system elements you already have that can be improved or enhanced, and the size and complexity of your own organization.

**Define Timing** This entire implementation process will take an average of 18 months for most organizations to complete. Consider your own status and the resources available to estimate a reasonable timeline for your own plan. Also consider any external drivers that may pressure you to implement your EMS sooner. If you are considering registration, you will have to add some additional time to your plan to ensure that the system is well established prior to the registration audit. Most registrars require the system to be in place at least three months before the audit can be conducted.

Recognize that there is no shortcut through this process. If management sets a deadline of 12 months for implementing the EMS and getting registered, the process will take the same amount of resources, as detailed earlier, but the effort will be much more concentrated. Your management representative may need to be full-time and certain coordinators may need to spend 50 percent of their time (instead of, say, 25 percent) to meet the shortened time frame.

Establishing a reasonable timetable is critical to realizing the potential benefits of an EMS. If a hasty, registration-focused deadline is established, the likely result will be a generic, overly bureaucratic system because there is too little time to analyze processes, get input from employees, and make informed business-oriented decisions. On the other hand, if no goals are set for timing, the organization will be unmotivated and may never fully establish the system. This decision requires careful deliberation to find a balance between motivation and pressure.

***Define Responsibilities*** Throughout the ISO 14001 standard, you are reminded to define responsibilities and authorities to ensure that the system works effectively. The same is true of your implementation plan. It will work only if responsibilities are clearly defined and communicated.

You can start with the general guidelines described earlier for the management representative, steering group, and coordinators. Fit these guidelines to your own individual organization. Consider existing job responsibilities, individual personalities, and the unique culture of your business. Determine what types of training or experience individuals will need to implement the EMS effectively.

With an average of 9 person-years required to fully implement an EMS, it is obvious that you will need to set some priorities and to redefine certain jobs, at least temporarily. No business today has this much extra capacity in its staff. Decide what projects will be postponed, which responsibilities will be shifted to other people, and exactly how you will find the resources to do this right. These are not easy decisions, but you must take a realistic view of the required resources if you want to improve your business through the EMS effort.

The checklist outlines the products of a successful strategic planning session. With these decisions made and a draft plan defined, you are now ready to get to work. Choose the key people who will coordinate the EMS efforts, provide essential training, and start working on the steps of your plan. Treat this as a draft plan and review it periodically throughout the implementation to make sure it is still accurate and realistic.

---

**CHECKLIST: Products of planning session**

- ✓ Understanding of EMS and ISO 14001 issues
- ✓ Scope definition
- ✓ Foundation for registration decision
- ✓ Definition of resources needed
- ✓ Potential candidates for management representative, coordinators
- ✓ Draft plan, indicating critical steps and responsibilities
- ✓ Estimated timing

# CHAPTER 23

# CHOOSING A REGISTRAR

If you plan to register your EMS, the choice of a registrar is a critical decision. Registrar organizations can operate quite differently from one another and it is crucially important to find one that meets your needs in terms of qualifications, philosophy, global acceptance, and cost. Since the U.S. accreditation systems (see Chapter 3) are still under development as of this writing, there are still some unknowns in this process, but we can use ISO 9000 experience and emerging ISO 14001 registration systems to define the critical components of this decision.

The choice of a registrar should be approached as you would approach the choice of any critical, long-term supplier to your company. Since the registration must be maintained through surveillance audits and periodic re-audits, this will definitely be a long-term partnership. Although it's not impossible to switch registrars after being registered, it can be costly, so it's best to consider all factors at the beginning.

Use whatever supplier evaluation system you have in place as a framework. Begin with a list of options and gradually narrow down your choice, using interviews, meetings, and questionnaires to assess how well each registrar meets your own individual needs. There are currently about 50 accredited ISO 9000 registrars operating in the United States and even more available in other countries. There are likely to be even more EMS choices available within the next few years. There are some particular factors you should consider when making your decision.

## QUALIFICATIONS

It's important to find a registrar with the appropriate qualifications and credentials for your own particular organization. The qualifications of both the registrar organization as a whole and its individual auditors should be considered when making your choice.

### Accreditation

Typical accreditation systems and the current status of the U.S. systems have been described in Chapter 3. The details of these systems and the array of choices within them can be quite confusing. Accreditation systems are in place to assure companies that registrars have a quality system in place, follow established registration guidelines, and are evaluated against standard criteria.

Because accreditation provides these assurances, it is usually best to choose an accredited registrar. There may be cases, however, where it makes sense to choose a registrar that is pursuing accreditation but has not yet been accredited. In order to become accredited, registrars must conduct a certain number of audits and registrations. Since most organizations look for accredited registrars, it can be difficult for a registrar pursuing accreditation to meet this requirement. If you have found a registrar that meets all other selection criteria you have, you may choose to be one of that registrar's earlier registrations. Once the registrar achieves accreditation, your registration will be recognized as an accredited one.

 If you choose this option, check with the accreditation body directly to verify that the registrar's application is in process.

Even if you definitely want to use an accredited registrar, there are still some choices to be made. Many countries have set up national accreditation systems, and the United States will soon have its own accreditation program. You could choose a U.S.-based registrar accredited by the ANSI/RAB joint American accrediting body or by another country's accrediting body. You could also choose any number of registrars operating out of other countries and accredited by their own or another accrediting body. From a qualifications perspective, most of the accreditation systems have similar or identical requirements, so other qualifications factors should be more important to you. Registration acceptance issues are discussed later in this chapter, under "Global Acceptance."

### Industry Experience

Although management systems and EMSs in particular all have the same basic elements, it's best to choose a registrar that can understand the specific environmental and operating issues of your own industry. Most accreditation systems accredit registrars to conduct audits within certain industries for which they are qualified. In the United States, Standard Industrial Classification (SIC) codes are used to designate each registrar's areas of expertise. Work is progressing on an international system to facilitate mutual recognition among various nations.

Ask each of the registrars you are evaluating which industries it is accredited for. You can also ask more detailed questions about each registrar's experience in your own industry. It's a good idea to request references within your own industry sector. These contacts can provide valuable information about the registrar's understanding of the industry as well as about other qualification criteria that are important to you.

### Auditor Qualifications

The qualifications and experience of individual auditors are even more important than a registrar's overall experience within your industry. If possible, ask the registrar about the particular auditors who could be involved in your registration. In larger registrar organizations, different auditors might visit your facility each time. Even so, it is reasonable to ask for information regarding the pool of auditors who might be involved.

Specifically, you will want to ensure that the auditors have experience in your industry or a related industry and that they are skilled and experienced auditors. Most accreditation programs require that the individual auditors within a registrar be certified through a recognized national or international auditor certification program. Auditor certification typically requires a combination of training, background experience and education, and actual audit experience.

In addition to requiring auditor certification, most EMS accreditation programs require that each team conducting an audit have skills and experience in the following areas

- Environmental science and technology
- Technical and environmental aspects of facility operations
- Relevant requirements of environmental laws, regulations, and related documents
- Environmental management systems and standards
- Audit procedures and techniques

This list of required competencies comes directly from ISO 14012, which describes qualification criteria for environmental auditors.

Ask the registrar how it ensures that all of these skills are represented on the audit team. If a registrar typically uses three or four auditors to meet the accreditation requirements, it will probably cost you more (see the discussion of costs later in this chapter). Also ask the registrar how it trains its auditors. A comprehensive, ongoing training system provides you with more assurance than does a poorly defined system. Find out how auditor trainees gain experience. I've seen cases where very busy registrars send fairly inexperienced auditors out on their own for surveillance audits. Be sure you feel comfortable with the training and qualification systems the registrar uses.

 As you narrow down your registrar choices, arrange if possible to interview or meet the auditor(s) who may be assigned to your company. This will give you a chance to ask about qualifications and experience firsthand, and it also provides a good opportunity to discuss EMS approaches and philosophy (see next section).

## APPROACH

Different registrars, and even different auditors within a single registrar organization, can have varying philosophies and approaches to an EMS and to registration. It's important to find a registrar whose approach is similar to your own and whose registration process fits your needs.

### EMS Approach

> **KEY TO SUCCESS**
>
> Overall EMS philosophy and approach is perhaps one of the most important criteria to consider—and also the one most companies overlook. You want to ensure that the registrar has a similar approach to your own to help avoid misunderstandings, misinterpretations, and lengthy debates about the implementation choices you have made. This is a difficult area to measure but can be critically important. Although you must define the particular aspects of your own philosophy and approach, there are some general factors to consider.

**What to Avoid** It is sometimes easier to define what you do *not* want in a registrar. Beware of auditors who are overly prescriptive, requiring certain implementation methods that are not a part of the standard's requirements. This is actually quite common. I've heard of auditors who declare that documents must be numbered, records must be retrieved within five minutes, internal audits must be done at least every six months, and other specifications in addition to the standard's requirements. These types of auditor requirements are especially prevalent in document control systems and can force you to add elements to your system that do not add value to your business.

Similarly, some auditors have a narrow interpretation of the requirements of ISO 14001 and are not willing to consider variations that may be necessary for an effective system in a particular business. For instance, some auditors require formal procedures in a written text format wherever the standard uses the term "procedure." These auditors may be unwilling to recognize your flowcharts, checklists, or written plans as meeting the procedure requirement as intended by the standard's authors. Additionally, auditors with limited management system experience may expect every system they audit to be like the one or two they've seen before.

***What to Look For*** To avoid these common auditor difficulties, look for a registrar organization and individual auditors who are willing to take your own business needs into account as they audit against the requirements of ISO 14001. Some extra work is necessary to determine this without actually hiring the registrar and observing its auditors in action, but the additional time spent will pay off over the long term.

Before interviewing any registrars, make a list of critical interpretation issues for your business. These may include an unusual scope definition, particular practices you've opted to use in your EMS, or specific documentation methods you've chosen. You may also want to include some specific parts of the ISO 14001 standard that are often misinterpreted or interpreted in various ways (see individual Chapters 5 through 21 for interpretation examples).

Ask each registrar you're considering how it would interpret or approach the items on your list. You will not necessarily find absolute agreement on every single item, but listen for a willingness to consider other points of view. If the registrar's representative responds to each item with a quick, no-room-for-negotiation answer, the registrar may have a narrow view of the standard's interpretation. If, on the other hand, he or she responds thoughtfully to each question, asking for additional information and considering all possibilities, the registrar is likely to be one that will take your own business into consideration.

### Registration Approach

Although accreditation criteria typically specify certain administrative and system requirements for registrars, the details of one registrar's operating procedures may differ greatly from another's. Registrars are required to have their own documented management system to define and control their operation, so you can inquire about various aspects of that system. Some accreditations require that registrars have a quality manual to describe their overall policies and systems; this could provide additional information for your organization.

Generally, you may want to inquire about the registrar's policies and processes for the following activities:

- Training and qualifying auditors
- Handling complaints and taking corrective action
- Billing and invoicing
- Handling disputes over interpretation of the standard or audit findings, including a process for escalation
- Criteria for decision to register (pass/fail criteria)
- Conditions for granting, expanding, and withdrawing or losing registration
- Combining audits (e.g., ISO 9001, QS-9000, Responsible Care®)
- Handling regulatory noncompliances and notification to EPA

This last item is of great concern to many companies. Most accreditation systems require EMS registrars to define their policies and procedures for dealing with regulatory noncompliances. Although EMS auditors are not auditing compliance directly, they are auditing your systems for achieving, monitoring, and maintaining compliance, so EMS registrars will occasionally come across a regulatory noncompliance. Most registrars' policies state that the registrar will notify the client (you) of the noncompliance and that it is then your own responsibility to notify the appropriate regulatory bodies and correct the noncompliance. Be sure that you fully understand the registrar's policies and feel comfortable with them so that there are no surprises later.

Some of the items identified above may seem insignificant to you now, compared to cost and qualification issues, but they may be extremely important to you later. Poorly defined and implemented management systems can create real problems in dealing with the registrar. I remember one ISO 9000 registrar that had no defined process for handling complaints. It became very frustrating for one company working with that registrar because the company never got timely or satisfactory responses or effective corrective actions to problems with invoicing, auditors, or other issues that arose.

In another case, a registrar's poor administrative systems resulted in long delays for manual reviews, scheduling mix-ups, and even the loss of a quality manual that had been submitted by a client months before!

During the selection of the registrar and after you have established a business relationship, remember that you are the customer. It is your right to ask for information you need and to obtain good quality service. If repeated attempts to work directly with the registrar on these issues fail, you can always contact the accrediting body to report on the problems. This is another important reason to choose an accredited registrar.

### Potential Conflicts of Interest

Concern over potential conflicts of interest has grown over the last few years. Mainly, this concern is focused on organizations that provide both consulting and registration services. Most accrediting bodies prohibit EMS registrars from also offering consulting assistance to develop, implement, or maintain an EMS. In other words, a registration would not be credible if the same organization helped you to establish your system and then came back to audit it.

However, related organizations are allowed to provide consulting if they prove to the accrediting body that the registration and consulting services and organizations are completely independent of one another. Registrars are also allowed to provide general training, as long as it is not customized to assist a particular client in obtaining registration.

These issues may or may not be important to you. Potential conflicts of interest could impact the credibility of the registration in certain sectors. You need to decide what your own position is with respect to these issues and make sure that you feel comfortable with the status and systems of your chosen registrar.

## GLOBAL ACCEPTANCE

Most organizations pursue registration mostly because of external drivers (see Chapter 3). Therefore, you want to be sure that the stakeholders for whom you are registering will accept your EMS registration. Although there are many factors to consider theoretically, in reality most accredited registrations will be widely accepted around the world. To be sure yours is among them, consider a few potential issues as you select your registrar.

### Stakeholder Preference

You may be registering your EMS at the request of a customer or to achieve some particular recognition by a regulatory body, financial institution, insurance provider, environmental group, or the local community. You want to be sure that the stakeholder(s) will accept and recognize your registration. The best way to find out is to ask them.

Some stakeholders may prefer a particular registrar or a registrar accredited by a certain accrediting body. Although these types of preferences were fairly rare with ISO 9001 registrations, they could be more prevalent within certain sectors for ISO 14001. Also be aware if certain registrars are "approved" by a particular stakeholder group. QS-9000 provides an example of this type of approval: the Big Three automakers in the United States (GM, Chrysler, and Ford) defined criteria and approved certain accredited registrars to conduct QS-9000 audits. Similar programs could be put into place for Responsible Care® verification in conjunction with ISO 14001 or for other specialized registrations.

### Accreditation and Mutual Recognition

The reason most issues around registration acceptance are merely theoretical is because most national accrediting bodies use very similar or identical criteria when accrediting registrars. ISO Guides for accreditation and registration form the foundation for most accreditation systems, meaning that registrars accredited under different systems have to meet the same general criteria. Despite these underlying similarities, there are some differences in the way each accrediting body operates.

In the last few years much progress has been made in defining international systems for mutual recognition between registrars and/or accrediting bodies. Many registrars have established memorandums of understanding (MOUs) between one another, defining how they will recognize each other's registrations. The problem with this approach is that you may have to seek out a registrar with multiple MOUs with particular registrars in other countries.

The QSAR system for establishing mutual recognition among ISO 9000 accreditation bodies (described in Chapter 3) is a more effective approach, which may be expanded to include ISO 14001 in the future. The goal of this program is to equalize all ISO 9001/2/3 registrations that are conducted by registrars accredited by recognized accrediting bodies. When selecting a registrar, ask about the status of this program and its relation to that registrar.

## COST

I have left this factor for last because, despite the fact that it is the first thing most companies look at, it is not the most important. Costs can vary a great deal from one registrar to another, so this is definitely a factor you should consider; however, qualifications and approach are much more important in the long run.

## Cost Breakdown

Although registrars all have their own fee structures, there are some aspects that are more or less universal. The registration audit itself is almost always charged on a per diem basis, so it will be directly proportional to the size and complexity of your organization. Travel and living expenses for auditors are usually charged separately (though they are occasionally included in a per diem charge), so geographic location of the registrar's auditors may be a consideration. Finally, there are always additional fees besides the actual cost of the audit, although these vary greatly from one registrar to the next.

Components of the total cost of your registration may include some or all of the following:

- Application fee
- Preparation fees
- Initial visit
- Manual or documentation review
- Preassessment audit (optional)
- Registration assessment
- Partial or full reassessment, if you fail the initial registration audit
- Surveillance audits
- Reassessment audits

Some registrars include some of these fees in the audit fees, and others charge them as separate items. Most accreditation systems require surveillance audits no less than once per year, and most registrars conduct these every six months. In addition, most accreditation systems require a full reassessment audit every three years.

There are few data available on EMS registration costs, since most registration systems are still in their infancy. We can, however, look at the limited data available, along with the extensive information on ISO 9000 registrations to get an estimate of the costs involved.

In April 1992, *Quality Systems Update* published a survey of registration costs that was conducted by UNC Manufacturing Technology. The survey included 11 different registrars and compared their cost estimates for ISO 9001 registration of a 50-person design and manufacturing facility. The results were reported as a three-year total estimated cost, including everything except travel and living expenses for the auditors, and they showed a wide variation.

The average three-year total estimate for the 50-person facility was $14,700, but the estimates ranged from $11,000 to $18,900. You could expect an even greater range of prices for larger or more complex organizations. Current per diem rates for ISO 9000 registrars vary between about $800 and $1,800. Most experts believe these will be higher for EMS registrars because of the greater breadth of knowledge required.

An article in *Quality* magazine in November 1995, entitled "Are You Ready for ISO 14000?" stated that more than 115 organizations had been registered to BS 7750 as of September 1995. Estimates of registration costs for these companies ranged from $12,000 to $100,000. Although these are EMS registrations, the costs may be a bit higher than what we should expect for ISO 14001 registrations because of the slightly more extensive requirements of BS 7750 and the U.K. registration system.

While these estimates may give you a general idea of what to expect, you will need to check with each registrar you're considering to determine what the EMS registration costs will be for your own organization. Ask for a full breakdown of costs over a three-year period so that you can be sure to take all components of the cost into account. Finally, weigh the varying costs against all of the other factors discussed here to ensure that your registrar can offer you a reasonable, credible, and cost-effective registration. A cheap registration will not be worth much to you if the auditors make you add unnecessary complexities to your system or if it is not recognized by your stakeholders.

# IMPLEMENTING INTEGRATED MANAGEMENT SYSTEMS

**PUTTING IT ALL TOGETHER**

Each of the essential elements of an EMS is reviewed in detail in Chapters 5 through 21, but an effective management system is more than just a collection of separate components. All of these elements work together to form a comprehensive system for managing the environment within your business. Chapter 1 introduced the concept of the business improvement, or Plan-Do-Check-Act (PDCA), cycle. Figure 24-1 shows how all of the elements of an EMS fit together into the PDCA framework to create a cohesive whole.

The process begins with a set of planning activities, based on an evaluation of the unique environmental aspects of your own business and an identification of all applicable regulatory requirements. With this information as a starting point, an environmental policy is defined, objectives and targets are established, and programs are developed to help achieve those goals. These elements work together to form the foundation for the EMS.

Based on the planning activities, the EMS is implemented according to your own operational controls to ensure that significant environmental aspects of your business are controlled according to your own policy and objectives. Emergency response plans serve to mitigate environmental impacts in case incidents or accidents occur.

**250** ■ GETTING STARTED

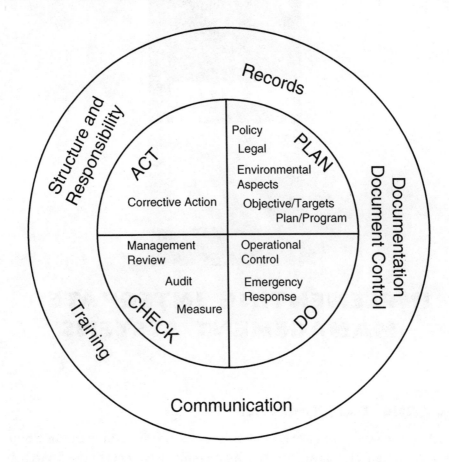

■ **FIGURE 24-1.** Elements of an Environmental Management System

The EMS is continuously monitored and checked, using audits, measurement systems, and management reviews. These elements help to track progress toward objectives, monitor operational controls, and ensure that the EMS is implemented and effective. In this way, you know whether your system is working as planned.

Any potential or actual problems detected by the checking systems are resolved through the use of corrective and preventive action. This system ensures that any problems are prevented from recurring, thus eliminating many of the urgencies and difficulties that routinely occur in every business.

Finally, all of these aspects in the improvement cycle are supported by some basic management system elements. Standard practices are documented, and document control ensures that these are kept up to date and available where needed. Responsibilities and authorities for all critical functions are clearly defined. All employees are qualified and adequately trained, and communication systems ensure that they receive the information they need to do their jobs effectively. Records of the EMS are maintained in an efficient way and are well organized so that they can be found when needed.

It's easy to see how, theoretically, all of these pieces fit together, but it's a bit harder to visualize this neat, orderly system when you are looking at your own business. This is especially true if you have a lot of existing components of an EMS that are not connected in any organized way. Although every business has its own unique systems (or lack of systems), the same general approach can be used to implement or to improve the elements of an EMS.

If you look through the chapters of this book and the flowcharts that accompany many of them, you will see a pattern repeated in slightly different variations for every single element. Once again, it all comes back to a variation of the Plan-Do-Check-Act cycle.

Begin by identifying necessary system elements and deciding what your own practices should include. Document those plans in a draft form or revise existing documents. Implement the system according to your documents in order to test it out in practice. Measure its effectiveness through feedback, monitoring systems, and audits. Act on those measurements to make improvements, revise your documented system, and try it again. The cycle continues in this way as you refine your practices, learn from your mistakes, and improve each part of the system. The end result should be an effective and efficient EMS that works for your own unique culture and changes to meet the changing needs of your business.

## INTEGRATING EMS WITH EXISTING SYSTEMS

Most organizations implementing an EMS already have some type of management system in place. Ignoring those existing systems will result in parallel or duplicative systems that will create inefficiencies and place an excessive burden on your organization. Employees will have to deal with multiple or even contradictory systems. There will be an enormous amount of excess paperwork that adds little value.

### The Fear Factor

While the value of integrating these management systems may seem clear from this argument, many organizations specifically avoid integrating their systems. Typically, these organizations are afraid that an integrated systems approach will stand in the way of their registration efforts. I've heard this fear voiced by quite a few organizations, and even those who support integrated systems still worry about this. The fear is that having a single system will open up all parts of their organization to auditors during an EMS registration audit.

While this is theoretically true, in reality there is little to fear, and the benefits of integrating management systems far outweigh any potential risks. If your focus has been on developing an effective system that works well for your business, then there's no reason to be afraid of the registration audit. I encourage my clients to focus on implementing a comprehensive and effective system. If you do so, the audit will take care of itself.

Still, I know that the fears of being audited persist, regardless of the reassurances given. A couple of additional points may help to ease your fears. First, during a registration audit, the auditors usually have barely enough time to cover all parts of the EMS completely, let alone to delve into the depths of your safety or quality systems. Registrars will tell you that they *can* audit these elements in an integrated system, but the realities of the on-site audit rarely permit an auditor the luxury of looking much beyond the environmental system itself.

Secondly, consider the worst consequences if an auditor does go into your other systems. What would happen if the auditor is looking at the corrective action system and reviews a few safety nonconformances along with all of the environmental ones? If he or she happens to find an example where corrective action of a safety problem was not taken or was ineffective, what impact would that have on your EMS registration? Most likely, it would have little impact. At worst, you will have another minor nonconformance to correct. Would an auditor actually fail your environmental system based on findings related to quality or safety? It's highly unlikely. If you're still worried, ask the registrar these questions yourself.

### Common System Elements

So, if you have decided that it makes sense to have a single management system for your business, how do you actually implement the EMS so that it fits with existing systems? It depends partly on what systems are already in place in your organization, but there are a few basic tenets that are the same regardless of the particular systems.

All management systems, by definition, include many of the same foundational elements. These are

- Policy
- Defined organization and responsibilities
- Control of critical operations, including standard practices
- Document control (ensuring that up-to-date documents are available where needed)

- Training
- Records system
- Internal audits
- Corrective action system
- Management review for continual improvement

These elements are present regardless of the topic concerned—quality, safety, process safety, environmental.

With these same elements present in all systems, you can build on existing systems rather than having to create new ones. Any of these elements can be expanded to apply to the environmental aspects of your business. Some of them may be used as they are and simply expanded to include environmental aspects, and others may require some additions or revisions so that they are appropriate for the EMS. In either case, it's a lot easier and more efficient to expand existing systems than to create a whole new system.

Varying degrees of integration are possible within any of these elements, so you will need to decide what's best for your own business. Detailed examples are described in Chapters 5 through 21, but a few basic choices are available. You can use the same general procedures for an element of the management system while carrying out the activities separately. This may be the best approach for elements such as internal auditing or management reviews, where a focus on the topic at hand is desirable.

For example, it makes sense for any organization to define a single internal auditing process. This might consist of a single procedure or set of procedures that define how audits are conducted internally, what reporting formats are to be used, and how the audit schedule will be maintained. In actually conducting the audits, a given company may choose to conduct one set of completely integrated audits, covering all aspects of quality, safety, and environmental systems. Another organization may find it more effective to conduct audits separately, using different auditors trained in each specialty field. Still other organizations could choose an in-between approach, where some system elements are audited all at once while elements particular to certain systems are audited separately. All of these approaches are based on a common set of underlying systems and procedures for continuity and simplicity.

For other system elements, a more fully integrated approach may be preferable. Document control, records management, and corrective action can all be handled using the exact same procedures and practices. Besides reducing paperwork, this approach provides a single system for employees to use, without having to figure out whether a document, record, or nonconformance is related to quality, safety, or the environment. If you prefer to keep some separation in these systems, you could develop separate document or records lists or categorize nonconformances while still using a single system. Each organization must decide for itself what degree of integration works best for its own culture and its business goals.

With these basic integration concepts in mind, take a look at how some common management systems fit together with the ISO 14001 standard. Tables 24-1, 24-2, and 24-3 show how the elements of ISO 9001, OSHA 1910.119, and Responsible Care® compare to the elements of ISO 14001. In each table, elements with similar requirements are noted by a bold **X**, while elements with a minor cross-over are noted by a lower case x. Use these tables to gain a better understanding of how your own systems might fit together.

## CRITICAL SUCCESS FACTORS

The main theme of this book can be summed up quite simply: do what's best for your own business. While it sounds overly simplistic, this approach is not often taken with management systems and ISO standards. There are some critical factors that can help you to achieve the goal of business success while also registering your EMS.

### Management Commitment and Involvement

No business system can be successful without management's commitment and involvement. I've seen many quality and environmental professionals struggle to implement a system without the necessary support from their management. The root cause of this problem is typically a lack of understanding of what a management system really is, what it can contribute, and what will be necessary to achieve it. Real commitment can only come from a solid understanding of what is involved.

With that understanding, management should strive to be actively involved in the system. Management must be involved in establishing the policy and conducting management reviews and should be involved in evaluating environmental impacts and setting objectives. In addition, management can take part in training, communication, and auditing activities. The active involvement of top management sends a much more powerful message of support than does an occasional memo or speech.

### Employee Involvement

While management's involvement is critical to leading the management system efforts, the involvement of every employee within the business is also necessary. Too often, the management system is seen as one person's project. People think that quality is the job of the quality manager, and the environment is the job of the environmental manager.

The result is that employees have little value for a system created and imposed by someone else. It is regarded as a passing fad and is either ignored or used only temporarily. Perhaps even more importantly, a system created by a small group will not be as effective as a system where everyone has input and a chance to be involved.

Obviously, the EMS awareness training requirements will begin to get people involved, but you should go much further. Seek employees' input when defining job responsibilities, qualifications, and training needs. Use the collective experience and knowledge of the organization when defining or revising procedures. Involve a broad spectrum of people in the internal audits. Document control, records, and corrective action systems will only work if everyone understands and uses them.

### Focus on Business Goals

Decide why you are implementing an EMS or other management system. Is it merely to obtain a certificate to hang on the wall, or do you really want to improve the business? If registration is your only goal, then that's all you'll get from your efforts (and your costs). A focus on business goals and improvement can yield much more.

It's easy to become focused on the registration itself, especially as the audit nears. Keep reminding the organization of your long-term goals and objectives, and treat the registration as a milestone along the way. Don't refer to your EMS as "the ISO system" but as your own environmental system.

Make every decision carefully while implementing your EMS to be sure that it supports your business goals. Do not do things that add no value just "for ISO." Examine the requirements of ISO 14001 closely so that you are aware of the flexibility you have in developing your systems. Choose a registrar that supports your views and allows you the freedom to do what's right for your business.

Finally, measure your progress and celebrate your successes. Every facility celebrates its registration, but very few recognize their own achievements in reaching targets and objectives or improving the business. Use the required measurement process in the EMS to recognize and reward accomplishments. If you can follow these guidelines and remain focused on your business, there should be many successes to celebrate.

**TABLE 24-1** Cross-Reference Matrix of ISO 14001 and ISO 9001

| ISO 14001 \ ISO 9001 | Management Responsibility | Quality System | Contract Review | Design Control | Document Control | Purchasing | Customer-Supplied Product | Product Identification | Process Control | Inspection and Testing | Control of Inspection, Measuring, and Test Equipment | Inspection and Test Status | Control of Nonconforming Product | Corrective and Preventive Action | Handling, Storage, Packaging, Preservation, Delivery | Quality Records | Internal Quality Audits | Training | Servicing | Statistical Techniques |
|---|---|---|---|---|---|---|---|---|---|---|---|---|---|---|---|---|---|---|---|---|
| Policy | X | | | | | | | | | | | | | | | | | | | |
| Environmental Aspects | | | | | | | | | | | | | | | | | | | | |
| Legal Requirements | | | | | | | | | | | | | | | | | | | | |
| Objectives and Targets | X | | | | | | | | | | | | | | | | | | | |
| Environmental Management Program | | X | | | | | | | | | | | | | | | | | | |
| Structure and Responsibility | X | | | | | | | | | | | | | | | | | | | |
| Training, Awareness | | | | | | | | | | | | | | | | | | X | | |
| Communication | | | | | | | | | | | | | | | | | | | | |

| ISO 9001 | EMS Documentation | Document Control | Operational Control | Emergency Response | Monitoring and Measurement | Corrective and Preventive Action | Records | EMS Audit | Management Review |
|---|---|---|---|---|---|---|---|---|---|
| Management Responsibility | | | | | | | | | X |
| Quality System | X | | | | | | | | |
| Contract Review | | | | | | | | | |
| Design Control | | | | | | | | | |
| Document Control | | X | | | | | | | |
| Purchasing | | | x | | | | | | |
| Customer-Supplied Product | | | | | | | | | |
| Product Identification | | | | | | | | | |
| Process Control | | | X | | | | | | |
| Inspection and Testing | | | x | | | | | | |
| Control of Inspection, Measuring, and Test Equipment | | | | | X | | | | |
| Inspection and Test Status | | | | | | | | | |
| Control of Nonconforming Product | | | | | | X | | | |
| Corrective and Preventive Action | | | | | x | X | | | |
| Handling, Storage, Packaging, Preservation, Delivery | | | x | | | | | | |
| Quality Records | | | | | | | X | | |
| Internal Quality Audits | | | | | | | | X | |
| Training | | | | | | | | | |
| Servicing | | | x | | | | | | |
| Statistical Techniques | | | | | x | | | | |

**TABLE 24-2** Cross-Reference Matrix of ISO 14001 and OSHA 1910.119 Process Safety Management

| ISO 14001 / OSHA 1910.119 | Employee Participation | Process Safety Information | Process Hazard Analysis | Operating Procedures | Training | Contractors | Pre-Startup Safety Review | Mechanical Integrity | Hot Work Permit | Management of Change | Incident Investigation | Emergency Planning and Response | Compliance Audits | Trade Secrets |
|---|---|---|---|---|---|---|---|---|---|---|---|---|---|---|
| Policy | | | | | | | | | | | | | | |
| Environmental Aspects | | X | X | | | | x | | | | | | | |
| Legal Requirements | | x | | | | | | | | | | | | |
| Objectives and Targets | | | | | | | | | | | | | | |
| Environmental Management, Program | | | | | | | X | | | X | | | | |
| Structure and Responsibility | X | | | | | x | | | | | | | | |
| Training, Awareness | | | | | X | x | | | | | | | | |
| Communication | | | | | | x | | | | | | | | x |
| EMS Documentation | | X | | X | | | | | | | | | | |

258

| ISO 14001 \ OSHA 1910.119 | Employee Participation | Process Safety Information | Process Hazard Analysis | Operating Procedures | Training | Contractors | Pre-Startup Safety Review | Mechanical Integrity | Hot Work Permit | Management of Change | Incident Investigation | Emergency Planning and Response | Compliance Audits | Trade Secrets |
|---|---|---|---|---|---|---|---|---|---|---|---|---|---|---|
| Document Control | | | X | | | | | | | | | | | |
| Operational Control | | | | X | | x | | X | x | | | | | |
| Emergency Response | | | X | | | x | | | | | x | X | | |
| Monitoring and Measurement | | | | | | | | x | | | | | | |
| Corrective and Preventive Action | | | | | | | | | | | X | | | |
| Records | | | | | | | | | | | | | | x |
| EMS Audit | | | | | | | | | | | | | X | |
| Management Review | | | | | | | | | | | | | | |

**TABLE 24-3** Cross-Reference Matrix of ISO 14001 and Responsible Care®

| | Responsible Care® Codes of Management Practice | | | | | |
|---|---|---|---|---|---|---|
| ISO 14001 | CAER | Pollution Prevention | Distribution | Process Safety | Employee Health/Safety | Product Stewardship |
| Policy | | **X** | | x | | x |
| Environmental Aspects | | **X** | x | x | | x |
| Legal Requirements | | **X** | x | | | |
| Objectives/Targets | **X** | | x | | x | |
| EM Program | | **X** | x | x | | x |
| Responsibility | | | | x | | x |
| Training | **X** | x | x | x | | x |
| Communication | **X** | x | x | | | |
| Documentation | | | | x | | |
| Document Control | | | | | | |
| Operational Control | | **X** | x | x | | x |
| Emergency Response | **X** | | | x | | |
| Monitoring/Measurement | | **X** | x | x | | |
| Corrective Action | | x | x | x | | |
| Records | | | | | | |
| EMS Audit | | x | | | | |
| Management Review | x | x | | | | x |

Note: A bold **X** indicates complete overlap; a lowercase x indicates that there is some degree of overlap.

# ADDITIONAL INFORMATION

**U.S. TAG TO TC 207**

To get involved with the U.S. Technical Advisory Group (TAG) to TC 207 or for information regarding any of the ISO 14000 standards under development, contact the TAG Administrator at ASTM (American Society for Testing and Materials) or the TAG chairs:

TAG Administrator
Kathie Morgan
ASTM
100 Barr Harbor Drive
West Conshohocken, PA 19428-2959
Phone: 610-832-9721
Fax: 610-832-9666

Chairman: Joe Cascio
Global Environment & Technology Foundation
7010 Little River Turnpike
Suite 300
Annandale, VA 22003-9998
Phone: 703-750-6401
Fax: 703-750-6506

Vice-Chairman:  Mary McKiel
 EPA
 Office of Pollution Prevention and Toxics 7409
 Room 423 ET
 401 M Street, SW
 Washington, DC 20460
 Phone: 202-260-3584
 Fax: 202-260-0178

## STANDARDS

To obtain any ISO standards, including Draft International Standards (DIS), contact

> American National Standards Institute (ANSI)
> 11 West 42nd Street, 13th Floor
> New York, NY 10036
> Phone: (212) 642-4900
> Fax: (212) 398-0023

> ISO
> ISO Central Secretariat
> Case Postale 56
> CH-1211 Geneve 20
> Switzerland
> Phone: 41 22 749 01 11
> Fax: 41 22 733 34 30

In addition, most ISO 9000 and ISO 14000 series standards can be obtained from

> American Society for Quality Control (ASQC)
> P.O. Box 3066

or

> 611 East Wisconsin Avenue
> Milwaukee, WI 53201-3066
> Phone: 800-248-1946, 414-272-8575
> Fax: 414-272-1734
> E-mail: asqc@asqc.org

## REGISTRATION/ACCREDITATION

The following organizations are involved in establishing accreditation systems for the United States for ISO 14001 registration, including auditor certification and training course accreditation:

American National Standards Institute (ANSI)
11 West 42nd Street, 13th Floor
New York, NY 10036
Phone: (212) 642-4900
Fax: (212) 398-0023

Registrar Accreditation Board (RAB)
P.O. Box 3005
Milwaukee, WI 53201-3005
Phone: 800-248-1946 or 414-272-8575
Fax: 414-765-8661

# REFERENCES

## STANDARDS

ISO 9001: "Quality Systems—Model for Quality Assurance in Design, Development, Production, Installation, and Servicing." Geneva, Switzerland: International Organization for Standardization, 1994.

ISO 14001: "Environmental Management Systems—Specification with Guidance for Use." Geneva, Switzerland: International Organization for Standardization, 1996.

ISO 14004: "Environmental Management Systems—General Guidelines on Principles, Systems and Supporting Techniques." Geneva, Switzerland: International Organization for Standardization, 1996.

## WORKS CITED

Business Charter for Sustainable Development, 1991. "Principles for Environmental Management" (April). International Chamber of Commerce, Paris, France.

Business Charter for Sustainable Development, 1993. "Supporting Companies and Business Organizations" (May). International Chamber of Commerce, Paris, France.

Clifford, Hal, 1995. "Pay Dirt." *Profiles* (October 1995), 47–51.

Covey, Stephen R., 1989. *The Seven Habits of Highly Effective People*. New York: Simon & Schuster.

Hemenway, Caroline G. 1995. "Are You Ready for ISO 14000?" *Quality* (November), 26–28.

*International Environmental Systems Update*, 1995. "Companies in Hong Kong Value Implementation" (August), 20.

*International Environmental Systems Update*, 1996. "Seif testifies to Penn Senate That ISO 14001 Offers Alternative" (April), 5.

*International Environmental Systems Update*, 1966a. "French Industry Pilot Leads to 14001 Certification" (April), 17.

*International Environmental Systems Update*, 1966b. "Japanese Firms Certify to ISO 14001 Despite Absence of National Program" (June), 7.

*International Environmental Systems Update*, 1966c. "EPA Launches 'Star Track' Assurance Test" (June), 20.

ISO 14012, 1996. "Guidelines for Environmental Auditing—Qualification Criteria for Environmental Auditors." International Organization for Standardization. Geneva, Switzerland.

ISO/WD 14031, 1996. "Environmental Performance Evaluation, Working Draft no. 4" (April). ISO Technical Committee 207, Subcomittee 4.

NACCB, 1995. "NACCB Environmental Accreditation Criteria (AU/2/23)." United Kingdom Accreditation Service, London, United Kingdom.

NPDES Program, 1995. "Performance-Based Reporting and Monitoring" (Draft, June 14). U.S. Environmental Protection Agency, Office of Wastewater Management, Washington, D.C.

*Quality Systems Update*, 1992. "Register Study, Part 2" (April), 6.

*Quality Systems Update*, 1995a. "Global System Clears Final Administrative Hurdle: Operational Details Pending" (July), 1, 15.

*Quality Systems Update*, 1995b. "Purchasers Eye ISO 14001 Registration But Are Reluctant to Commit Suppliers" (August), 14, 20.

*Quality Systems Update*, 1995c. "Worldwide Registrations Near 100,000 (September), 1, 7.

RAB, 1996. "Criteria for Accreditation of Registrars for Environmental Management Systems: (draft, February 16). Registrar Accreditation Board, Milwaukee, WI.

Rice, Faye, 1993. "Who Scores Best on the Environment?" *Fortune* (July 26), 114–117.

SAGE, 1992. "ISO/IEC Strategic Advisory Group for the Environment SGI: Document 46, Position Paper, September 1992."

SCRAG, 1995. "Recommendation to the U.S. Technical Advisory Group on Accreditation of Registrars, Certifications of Auditors, and Accreditation of Course Providers for the ISO 14000 Series of Standards" (March 5).

Walley, Noah, and Bradley Whitehead, 1994. "It's Not Easy Being Green." *Harvard Business Review* (May-June): 46–52.

# SAMPLE ENVIRONMENTAL POLICIES

The policies reprinted in this appendix represent many different approaches in terms of style, format, and content. Many of them include safety and health, as well as the environment. Most were written prior to the development of ISO 14001 and may not completely address all policy requirements of the standard. However, all are perfectly acceptable environmental policies and could meet the requirements of ISO 14001, possibly with some minor changes. Each reflects the unique culture and perspective of its company. They are reprinted to provide an understanding of the range of possibilities, not to serve as models or "perfect" examples. Your own organization's environmental policy needs to be specific to the needs of your own business.

From AT&T's 1994 Environment & Safety Annual Report:

## AT&T

### Environmental Vision

AT&T's vision is to be recognized by customers, employees, shareholders and communities worldwide as a responsible company which fully integrates life cycle environmental consequences into each of our business decisions and activities. Designing for Environment is a key in distinguishing our processes, products and services.

## AT&T

### Environmental Policy

AT&T is committed to protection of human health and the environment in all operations, services and products. AT&T will integrate life cycle environmental quality into design, development, manufacturing, marketing and sales activities worldwide. Implementation of this policy is a primary management objective and the responsibility of every AT&T employee.

From DuPont's Safety, Health, and the Environment 1995 Progress Report:

## DUPONT

### Commitment to Safety, Health and the Environment

We affirm to all our stakeholders, including employees, customers, shareholders and the public, that we will conduct our business with respect and care for the environment. We will implement those strategies that build successful businesses and achieve the greatest benefit for all our stakeholders without compromising the ability of future generations to meet their needs.

We will continuously improve practices in light of advances in technology and new understandings in safety, health and environmental science. We will make consistent, measurable progress in implementing this Commitment throughout our worldwide operations. DuPont supports the chemical industry's Responsible Care® and the oil industry's Strategies for Today's Environmental Partnership as key programs to achieve this commitment.

***Highest Standards of Performance, Business Excellence*** We will adhere to highest standards for the safe operation of facilities and the protection of our environment, our employees, our customers and the people of the communities in which we do business. We will strengthen our businesses by making safety, health and environmental issues an integral part of all business activities and by continuously striving to align our businesses with public expectations.

***Goal of Zero Injuries, Illnesses, Incidents*** We believe that all injuries and occupational illnesses, as well as safety and environmental incidents, are preventable, and our goal for all of them is zero. We will promote off-the-job safety for our employees.

We will assess the environmental impact of each facility we propose to construct and will design, build, operate and maintain all our facilities and transportation equipment so they are safe and acceptable to local communities and protect the environment.

We will be prepared for emergencies and will provide leadership to assist our local communities to improve their emergency preparedness.

***Goal of Zero Waste and Emissions*** We will drive toward zero waste generation at the source. Materials will be reused and recycled to minimize the need for treatment or disposal and to conserve resources. Where waste is generated, it will be handled and disposed of safely and responsibly.

We will drive toward zero emissions, giving priority to those that may present the greatest potential risk to health or the environment.

Where past practices have created conditions that require correction, we will responsibly correct them.

***Conservation of Energy, Natural Resources, Habitat Enhancement*** We will excel in the efficient use of coal, oil, natural gas, water, minerals and other natural resources.

We will manage our land to enhance habitats for wildlife.

***Continuously Improving Process, Practices and Products*** We will extract, make, use, handle, package, transport and dispose of our materials safely and in an environmentally responsible manner.

We will continuously analyze and improve our practices, processes and products to reduce their risk and impact throughout the product life cycle. We will develop new products and processes that have increasing margins of safety for both human health and the environment.

We will work with our suppliers, carriers, distributors and customers to achieve similar product stewardship, and we will provide information and assistance to support their efforts to do so.

*Open and Public Discussion, Influence on Public Policy*  We will promote open discussion with our stakeholders about the materials we make, use and transport and the impacts of our activities on their safety, health and environments.

We will build alliances with governments, policy makers, businesses and advocacy groups to develop sound policies, laws, regulations and practices that improve safety, health and the environment.

*Management and Employee Commitment, Accountability*  The Board of Directors, including the Chief Executive Officer, will be informed about pertinent safety, health and environmental issues and will ensure that policies are in place and actions taken to achieve this Commitment.

Compliance with this Commitment and applicable laws is the responsibility of every employee and contractor acting on our behalf and a condition of their employment or contract.  Management in each business is responsible to educate, train and motivate employees to understand and comply with this Commitment and applicable laws.

We will deploy our resources, including research, development and capital, to meet this Commitment and will do so in a manner that strengthens our businesses.

We will measure and regularly report to the public our global progress in meeting this Commitment.

From Eastman Kodak Company Health, Safety and Environment 1995 Report:

## EASTMAN KODAK COMPANY
### Health, Safety, and Environment Vision

Eastman Kodak Company is a world-class company and the leading imaging company in protecting the quality of the environment, and the health and safety of its employees, customers, and the communities in which it operates.

## EASTMAN KODAK COMPANY
### Health, Safety, and Environment: Guiding Principles

*Kodak Guiding Principle No. 1—Research Support*  To extend knowledge by conducting or supporting research on the health, safety, and environmental effects of our products, processes, and waste materials.

*Kodak Guiding Principle No. 2—Plant Operation* To operate our plants and facilities in a manner that protects the environment and the health and safety of our employees and the public, and is efficient in the use of natural resources and energy.

*Kodak Guiding Principle No. 3—Management Planning* To make health, safety, and environmental considerations a priority in our planning for all existing and new products and processes.

*Kodak Guiding Principle No. 4—Product Process Modification* To develop, produce, and market products and materials that can be manufactured, transported, used, and disposed of safely and in a way that poses no undue environmental impact, and to provide services in a safe and environmentally sensitive manner.

*Kodak Guiding Principle No. 5—Customer Information* To counsel customers on the safe use, transportation, storage, and disposal of our products, and for those services we provide, to provide them safely.

*Kodak Guiding Principle No. 6—Public Policy* To participate with governments and others in creating responsible laws, regulations, and standards to safeguard the community, workplace, and environment and in applying environmentally sound management practices and technologies.

*Kodak Guiding Principle No. 7—Performance Measurement* To measure our environmental performance on a regular basis and provide— to officials, employees, customers, shareholders, and the public—appropriate and timely information on health, safety, and environmental hazards, initiatives, and recommended protective and preventive measures.

*Kodak Guiding Principle No. 8—Response to Community Concerns* To recognize and respond to community concerns about our operations and to work with others to resolve problems created by handling and disposal of hazardous substances.

*Kodak Guiding Principle No. 9—Employee Involvement* To encourage employees to apply off the job the same principles for health, safety, and environment that are applied at work.

From Duke Power's Environmental Leadership Policy, 1996:

## DUKE POWER COMPANY

### Environmental Leadership Policy

1. *Core Value*: I care for the environment and realize that its protection is an important part of my job.
2. *Waste Reduction*: I plan my work to avoid or reduce waste, recycle as much as possible, and safely dispose of that which cannot be re-used.
3. *Energy Efficiency*: I look for ways to produce and use energy more efficiently.
4. *Quality of Life*: I perform my work in a way that seeks to protect the environment and improve the quality of life now and in the future.
5. *Environmental Compliance*: I comply with all applicable environmental laws, regulations, and company environmental policy.
6. *Effective Communications*: I maintain open, two-way communications on environmental matters.
7. *Continuous Improvement*: I look for ways to continuously improve performance and better protect the environment.

# INDEX

Accreditation. *See also* Quality System Assessment Recognition (QSAR) program; Registration
   of auditor training courses, 30, 32
   certification of auditors, 30, 32
   global recognition of, 30, 245–246
   of registrars, 28–32, 240
   systems:
      British, 30–31
      U.S., 29, 31–32
American National Standards Institute (ANSI), 13, 29–30, 31–32
Annex to ISO 14001, 39–40, 54, 59, 112, 174–175, 199, 216
ANSI, *see* American National Standards Institute
Area coordinators, 130, 232
Asia-Pacific region, ISO 14001 activity in, 34–35. *See also* Japan; Korea
Aspects and impacts, environmental, 53–64
   definition of, 41, 53
   determining significance of, 54, 59–63
   identifying and evaluating, 54–63
   ISO 14001 requirements for, 53
   and operational control, 146, 148
   records of, 63
Audit:
   checklists, 201, 204
   difference between EMS and regulatory compliance, 168–169, 198
   EMS, 197–213
      ISO 14001 requirements for, 197
   planning, 201–205, 213
   of records system, 195
   regulatory compliance, 168–170
   reports, 206–207
   stages of, 169, 200
Auditors:
   internal, 233
      independence of, 198–199
      training of, 234
   qualification of, 31, 241
   third-party, *see* Registrars
   training for, 208–210, 211–212
   working in teams, 201–202
Authority, *see* Responsibilities and authority

BS 7750 standard, 22–23, 30–31, 33, 54, 57

Calibration of equipment, 160, 164–167
Certification to ISO 14001, *see* Registration
Communication:
  of emergency response plans, 155
  external, 51–52, 106, 108, 155, 171
  internal, 105–108
    of document changes, 134–136
  ISO 14001 requirements for, 105
  procedures for, 107–108, 109
  records of, 108–109
  with regulatory agencies, 106, 155, 194
Communities, *see* Interested parties
Competitive pressure to register to ISO 14001, 1, 34
Consultants, use of, 57–58, 93, 115, 235
Continual improvement, 70, 176
  commitment to, 48
  definition of, 40–41
Corrective and preventive action, 173–185. *See also* Procedures; Records
  of audit findings, 89, 207–208, 212
  based on measurement data, 170–171
  of calibration problems, 167
  ISO 14001 requirements for, 173
  review of, 102, 219
  root cause identification, 89, 179
  tracking of, 181–183, 210
Costs:
  of EMS implementation, 8, 231–236
  reduction of, 8–10, 170–171
  of registration, 8, 246–248
Customers, *see also* Interested parties
  requiring ISO 14001, 33

Department of Defense, U.S., 6
Department of Energy, U.S., 33
Design, product and process, 78, 144
Discrepancies, *see* Nonconformances
Documentation, 111–124. *See also* Procedures
  balance with training, 118–119, 148
  of emergency response plans, 152
  EMS manual, 113, 115, 120–122
  excess, 5, 7, 112–113
  formatting, 136–138
  ISO 14001 requirements for, 111
  of job qualifications, 99
  review of, 129–130
  tips for effective, 122–124
  of training needs, 100
Document control, 125–141
  distribution of documents, 133–134
  documents needing control, 128
  of emergency response plans, 152
  ISO 14001 requirements for, 125
  of job descriptions, 99
  records of, 132, 139–140
  responsibility for, 130

EAR, *see* Environmental Auditing Roundtable
Eastern Europe, 34
Eco-Management and Audit Scheme (EMAS), 21–22, 31, 39, 54
Emergency planning and response, 151–156
  defining procedures for, 153–156
  identifying potential emergencies, 152–153, 177
  ISO 14001 requirements for, 151
Employee involvement, 86–88, 115–117, 119–120, 123, 177, 233, 254
EMS Audit, *see* Audit, EMS
Environmental activists groups, *see* Interested parties
Environmental aspects, *see* Aspects and impacts, environmental
Environmental Auditing Roundtable (EAR), 31–32
Environmental Auditing standards, 16–17, 19, 241
Environmental impacts, *see* Aspects and impacts, environmental
Environmental Labeling standards, 16–17, 19
Environmental management program, 77–81
  definition of, 77
  ISO 14001 requirements for, 77
  link with objectives and targets, 78–79
Environmental Management System (EMS):
  definition of, 3–6
  standards, 16–18

Environmental performance evaluation (EPE), 160–164, 167–171
  standard for, 16–17, 20, 160–163
Environmental Protection Agency (EPA), 35–37, 43, 48, 160. *See also* Regulatory agencies
  Common Sense Initiative, 35
  Environmental Leadership Program, 35
  Project XL, 35–36
  StarTrack—Region 1, 36
Environmental regulations, *see* Regulations, environmental
EPA, *see* Environmental Protection Agency
Europe, 39. *See also* Eco-Management and Audit Scheme (EMAS); France; United Kingdom

Failure Modes Effect Analysis (FMEA), 60, 153
Flowcharting and process mapping, 58, 115–117, 179
France, 34

Gap assessment, initial, 6, 115, 210, 225

ICC, *see* International Chamber of Commerce Business Charter for Sustainable Development
Impacts, *see* Aspects and impacts, environmental
Implementation of EMS:
  steps, 236
  time required, 232–233, 237
Initial gap assessment, *see* Gap assessment, initial
Integration:
  benefits of, 6–9
  with ISO 9000, 12, 103, 147, 149, 164, 165–166, 185, 196, 211, 256–257
  of management systems, 6–7, 12, 109, 147, 222, 251–254
  of policies, 50
  with process safety management, 6, 164, 185, 196, 211, 258–259
  with QS-9000, 185, 196, 211

  with Responsible Care®, 6
  with safety and health systems, *see* Integration, of management systems
Interested parties, 34, 106, 219, 226, 230
  considering the views of, 70, 72–73
  definition of, 70
International Chamber of Commerce Business Charter for Sustainable Development, 25, 49
International Standards Organization, *see* ISO
ISO, 11
  nations participating in, 14
  standards development process, 12–16
  Technical Committees, 12
ISO 14000 series of standards, 16–20
ISO 14004 standard, 17–18, 163, 174
ISO 9000 standards, 4–5, 7, 232. *See also* Integration, with ISO 9000
  audit requirements in, 198
  calibration requirements in, 165
  differences from ISO 14001 standard, 89, 112, 126, 160, 173–175, 188, 198
  management review requirements in, 221
  preventive action requirements in, 175
  records requirements in, 188

Japan, 34, 39
Job descriptions, 87–88

Korea, 34

Legal requirements, *see* Regulations, environmental
Life cycle assessment, 58
  standards for, 16–17, 20

Management commitment, 226, 254
Management representative, 86, 232
  choice of, 89–93
Management responsibility, *see* Responsibilities and authority, of management

Management review, 215–222
    follow-up from, 221
    ISO 14001 requirements for, 215
    topics, 217–220
    using audit results in, 219
Management system:
    components of, 4, 252–253
    definition of, 3–4
Measurements, *see* Monitoring and measurement
Memorandums of understanding, 30
Monitoring and measurement, 159–171. *See also* Calibration of equipment; Regulations, environmental, compliance with, evaluating
    environmental performance indicators, 160–163
    use of in management review, 218
    ISO 14001 requirements for, 159
    using performance data, 170–171

Nonconformances:
    audit, 205–206
    identification of, 177

Objectives and targets, 69–75
    corporate, 73–75
    corrective actions when not met, 81. *See also* Corrective and preventive action
    definition of, 69–70, 71
    examples of, 74–75
    ISO 14001 requirements for, 69
    link to environmental management program, 78–79
    link to policy, 49, 70
    measuring progress toward, 162
    prioritization of, 71–72, 89
    records of, 63
    resources for achieving, 89
    setting of, 71–74, 116
Operational control, 143–150
    ISO 14001 requirements for, 143
Organization, definition of, 41–42
OSHA 1910.119, *see* Process safety management

Plan-Do-Check-Act model, 18, 45, 102, 140, 157, 195, 249, 251

Planning, 45. *See also* Aspects and impacts, environmental; Environmental management program; Objectives and targets; Policy, environmental
    Strategic, 225–238
Policy, environmental, 47–52
    defining, 49–51
    examples of, 269–273
    ISO 14001 requirements for, 47
    making available to the public, 49, 51–52. *See also* Communication, external
Pollution, prevention of, 48, 60
Preventive action, *see* Corrective and preventive action
Procedures:
    for aspects/impacts evaluation, 55, 63–64
    for auditing, 211
    changes to, 175. *See also* Document control
    for communication, 107–108, 109
    for corrective and preventive action, 185
    developing, 117–120
    for document control, 140–141
    for emergency response, 152, 154
    for environmental management programs, 80–81
    for management review, 221
    for monitoring and measurement, 163–164
    for operational control, 144–145
    for records management, 194
    for regulatory requirement identification and tracking, 67
    for training, 103
Process control, *see* Operational control
Process hazards analysis, 60, 153
Process mapping, *see* Flowcharting and process mapping
Process safety management, 6. *See also* Integration, with process safety management
Purchasing, *see* Suppliers, working with

Qualifications, job:
    defining, 98–99
    documenting, 99

of management representative, 91–93
Quality System Assessment Recognition (QSAR) program, 30, 246
Quality tools, use of, 58, 60, 179
QS-9000, *see* Integration, with QS-9000

RAB, *see* Registrar Accreditation Board
Records, 187–196
    of aspects and impact evaluation, 63
    of audits, 206
    of calibration, 165, 167
    of communication, 108–109
    of corrective and preventive action, 180–181, 184
    difference between documents and, 126
    of document changes, 127, 132, 139–140
    establishing retention times for, 191–192
    ISO 14001 requirements for, 187
    of management review, 216, 221
    of objectives and targets, 73
    of training, 101–102
Registrar Accreditation Board (RAB), 29–30, 31–32, 240. *See also* Accreditation
Registrars, *see* Accreditation, of registrars; Auditors; Registration
    choosing, 239–248
    conflicts of interest and, 245
    qualifications, 240–242
Registration, 27–32. *See also* Accreditation; Registrars
    audit, what to expect in, 28–29, 251–252
    benefits of, 33–38
    costs of, 230, 247–248
    decision to pursue, 229–231
    ISO 9000, 27–30
    surveillance audits, 239, 242, 247
Regulations, environmental:
    auditors' knowledge of, 209–210
    compliance with, 48
        evaluating, 160, 162, 168–169
        managing, 57, 59, 65, 218
    EPCRA, 151–152, 155
    identifying and tracking requirements of, 66–67
    SARA Title III, 57, 109
    training on, 234
Regulatory agencies, *see also* Environmental Protection Agency
    communication with, 106, 108, 155, 194
    state, 36–37
Resources needed, 231–236. *See also* Costs
Responsibilities and authority:
    for corrective action, 180–183
    defining and documenting, 86–89
    for evaluating environmental impacts, 57–58
    for implementing the EMS, 238
    ISO 14001 requirements for defining, 85
    of management, 50, 57, 89, 98–99, 216–217
    of management representative, 89–91, 232
    for monitoring and measurement, 163
    for records management, 191, 194
Responsible Care®, 6, 23–25, 49, 67, 152, 260

Safety and health management systems, *see* Integration, of management systems
SAGE (Strategic Advisory Group for the Environment), 11–13
Savings, cost, *see* Costs, reduction of
Scope, of EMS, 41–42, 55, 96–98, 227–229. *See also* Organization
Site, *see* Organization
Stakeholders, *see* Interested parties
Steering group, 232
STEP program, 6
Suppliers, working with 145, 149–150

TAG, *see* U.S. TAG
TC 207, 12, 39–43
Technical Advisory Group, *see* U.S. TAG
Technical Committee 207, *see* TC 207
Third-party registration, *see* Registration

Time required for implementation, 232–233, 237
Training, 95–103
  of all employees, 99–100, 234
  for area coordinators, 234
  auditor, 208, 212, 234
  awareness, 88, 96, 101–102, 105, 234
  balance with documentation, 118, 148
  ISO 14001 requirements for, 95–96
  on the job, 96, 101
  for management, 99, 227, 234
  for management representative, 234
  methods, 100–102,
  records of, 102
  on records system, 194

United Kingdom, 35. *See also* Accreditation systems, British; BS 7750 standard
U.S. TAG, 13–16
  to TC 207, 31, 42–43